MAUREEN DONALDSON began her career as an assistant in the Beatles' office, before moving to America where she eventually became editor of *TEEN* Magazine. In the mid-seventies, at Cary Grant's suggestion, she switched to photography. Today, Maureen flies all over the world shooting pictures for such publications as *Cosmopolitan*, *TV Guide*, *US* magazine and *People*. She currently lives in Hancock Park, California.

WILLIAM ROYCE is an entertainment writer and producer based in Los Angeles. His professional tours of duty include such programmes as the *Today* show, *Entertainment Tonight* and, currently, *The Arsenio Hall Show*. A graduate of the University of California, he lives in Beverly Hills.

AN AFFAIR TO REMEMBER

My Life with Cary Grant

Maureen Donaldson
and
William Royce

Futura

A Futura Book

First published in Great Britain in 1989
by Macdonald & Co (Publishers) Ltd
London & Sydney

This edition published by Futura Publications in 1990

ISBN 0 7088 4470 7

Typeset by Leaper and Gard Ltd, Bristol
Reproduced, printed and bound in Great Britain by
BPCC Hazell Books Ltd
Member of BPCC Ltd
Aylesbury, Bucks, England

Futura Publications
A Division of
Macdonald & Co (Publishers) Ltd
Orbit House
1 New Fetter Lane
London EC4A 1AR
A member of Maxwell Macmillan Pergamon Publishing Corporation

ACKNOWLEDGEMENTS

I'd like to express my heartfelt gratitude to the following people:

My mother and father, for blessing my early years with the joy of laughter and continuing to enhance my life with their wit, encouragement and unconditional love.

My brother, David, for teaching me as a child that your dreams can never be too grand.

My co-author, William Royce, for his invaluable insights as both a writer and a friend, and especially for reassuring me that the truth can be told with compassion.

My agent, ICM's Jed Mattes, for his unwavering faith and for always promptly returning my phone calls.

Chris Schillig and Phyllis Grann of Putnam's, for their perception and wisdom as well as their total commitment to this book.

My British agents, Elaine Greene and Ilsa Yardley, for their much appreciated advice and support whenever needed.

Peter Lavery and Alan Samson of Macdonald for believing in this book from the beginning.

My attorney, William Krasilovsky, for his brilliant mind and his willingness to help at all times.

Everyone who tirelessly helped with the editorial and photographic research, including Janette Dimond, Gail Harvey, Suzanne McDonnell Long, George Rodriguez, Rob Salem, Paul Smith, Kas Schlots-Wilson and Rita Zekas.

My dear friends, for sharing their memories so willingly with me: Bobby Birkenfeld, Cindy Crowe, Bonnie and Chris Holland, Dee Joseph, Countess Christina

Wachtmeister and Willie Watson.

Last but hardly least, I'm indebted to the many wonderful friends who gave me their emotional support during the writing of this book: Michael Aldred, Jane Badler, Hunt Block, David Crane, Susie Curtois, Annie Hallam, Richard Jordan, Jaan Kaufman, Juanita and Nicholas Kerman, Rosemary Lord, Ruth McShane, Roger and Jennifer Smith, Judith Steier, Pamela Townley, Reet Von Schummer, Jackie Zeman and Linda Zimmerman.

Finally, to Michael Ivey, who passed away last year. He will always be in my heart.

MAUREEN DONALDSON

This book would not have been possible without the generous assistance of many people on both sides of the Atlantic.

In Bristol, the staffs of the Bristol Reference Library, the Bristol Civic Society, the Register's Office at Quakers Friars, and the Hippodrome Theatre were particularly helpful. Paula Crook of *The Bristol Evening Post* deserves special thanks for her enthusiastic help.

In London, the staff of the British Film Institute Library extended itself beyond the call of duty. In New York, the staffs of Actors Equity and the Theater Collection at the Library of the Performing Arts at Lincoln Center were equally accommodating.

In Los Angeles, the staffs of the American Film Institute Library and the Margaret Herrick Library at the Academy of Motion Picture Arts and Sciences provided immense guidance and assistance.

For professional support and insight, I'd like to thank Rona Barrett, David Black, Bonnie Rogers Fuson, Peter Hammond and Suzanne Munshower, with a special debt of gratitude to Madelon Dribble, M.F.C.C., L.C.S.W., for her psychological insights. Where research was concerned, P.J. Steier often accomplished the impossible on impossibly short notice.

For their unflagging interest and understanding, I am personally beholden to Karen Dola, Woody Fraser, Tom Gray, Arsenio Hall, Marla Kell-Brown, Vail Kobbe, Shelley Ross and J. Saul.

Finally, I'm indebted beyond words to my wife, Kathy, not only for typing the manuscript and providing invaluable editorial suggestions every step of the way, but also for an infinite amount of . . . patience.

WILLIAM ROYCE

In loving memory of Cary Grant

CONTENTS

PROLOGUE

ᑼ᙭᙭ᑐ

PEOPLE WILL TALK

IT was a photo opportunity that brought Cary Grant into my life in 1973 and changed it forever.

It was another photo opportunity fourteen years later that brought his ex-wife Dyan Cannon into my life one night and helped me decide finally to write about the man I had loved and lived with for four turbulent, unforgettable years.

As a former entertainment journalist and now an international photographer, I knew the term 'photo opportunity' was a Hollywood euphemism for 'cost-effective publicity.' Throw a party, invite a good mix of columnists, photographers and celebrities, and the result was usually reams of favorable copy in magazines and newspapers.

But tonight I had a feeling this party or 'opportunity' had the potential for something more. The date was December 1, 1987 — just a few days after the first anniversary of Cary's death. He had passed away from a stroke on November 29, 1986.

Hoping to put this particular anniversary out of my mind, I had decided to attend a party for best-selling author Sidney Sheldon at the Bistro Garden restaurant in Beverly Hills. He was celebrating the success of his latest page-turner, *Windmills of the Gods*.

Cary was still uppermost in my mind as I walked into the plush restaurant, because Sidney had won an Oscar for writing the screenplay for one of Cary's biggest box-office hits, *The Bachelor and the Bobby-Soxer*. I headed for the back room, where Sidney's party was in full swing, and started in the direction of the buffet table where serious grazing, media style, was now in progress. Then I heard it. It stopped me literally in my tracks.

It was the laugh that fans and interviewers had often described as joyous and earthy, but Cary had characterized it in frustration on more than one occasion to me as 'maniacal.' Almost involuntarily I was pulled toward it. No one else in the room mattered. I saw nothing of the usually impressive surroundings, including booths carved from rich dark woods and plants of every variety. The laugh seemed to come from deep in the gut and then just explode. It was full and honest and unmistakable.

It belonged to Dyan Cannon, the actress who had done the impossible (she was the only one of Cary's five wives to give him a child, Jennifer) and then topped it with the unthinkable (she walked out on him eight months after their daughter was born in February of 1966).

Now I was standing next to her. As she turned around, Dyan seemed to notice at the very same moment I did that we were both wearing basic black with pearls.

'Hello,' I said, returning Dyan's smile, 'I'm Maureen Donaldson.'

Her brilliant blue-green eyes focused intently on me. Then she tossed her mane of tawny curls to one side, a bit puzzled.

'I *know* you,' she said slowly as she extended her hand, but she hadn't placed me yet.

But I would never forget her. The last time I had seen her face to face like this was over ten years ago in Malibu, when she had a home in the exclusive beachfront retreat of the stars called The Colony. Cary had a house just a few doors away, which he had rented to be near Jennifer, who was in her mother's custody for most of the time except on weekends, when Cary had her. Often I would escort Jennifer, then a schoolgirl, from Cary's door to Dyan's because the former husband and wife were not, at that time, on very good terms.

During these years, all I would see of Dyan was a face behind some curtains as I brought Jennifer to her doorstep. She rarely emerged from the shadows. The most I would hear from her was a quick 'Thank you.' It was an awkward situation then for both of us, but sometimes I had wanted to grab her by the arm and say, 'I understand, Dyan, more than you know.'

Our lives had intersected then, but had never really connected until now, in the back room of this packed restaurant. The contrast between that woman and this lady was startling. The 1987 version of Dyan radiated an inner peace and glow that seemed to connect her to everyone in the room rather than distance her from them.

Now staring at my blonde hair, Dyan had finally put my face together with those days in Malibu so many years before. 'You had brown hair then,' she exclaimed. 'You lived with Cary. I'd see you at the door, wouldn't I? When was that?'

'In 1973 and 1974, when he still had the house at the beach.'

'Ummm,' Dyan murmured. 'Tough times. Cary and I actually became friends later, but it wasn't easy getting there. You got him during some very difficult times, I'm afraid.'

'It was a challenge,' I said.

Then, seemingly out of left field, she asked me: 'Why did you leave him?'

It was such a direct question from such a direct person, it deserved an honest answer, not a flip, cocktail-party evasion.

First, I mentioned all the contradictions. And each step of the way, Dyan nodded her head in agreement. Cary was the idol to so many millions of women for so many years, yet his childhood relationship with his mother had left him deathly frightened of women. His sharp business mind had helped him amass many millions, yet he had largely refused to give himself permission to enjoy his wealth. And he had such a fierce desire for privacy, yet sometimes was consumed with the idea that he would be forgotten by the public.

There were many more contradictions and complexities, but in the end what it came down to was this:

'I loved the man,' I told Dyan, 'but I couldn't live with him. With one hand he was always pulling me toward him, but with the other he always seemed to be pushing me away. Am I making any sense?'

'*Exactly!*' Dyan concurred. 'And the funny thing is, everybody else thinks you are the luckiest girl on earth. After all, you've got Cary Grant. The man of every girl's dreams. But they don't understand the baggage that comes along with that — and neither do you, at least at the top of the relationship.'

Now I was the one laughing in recognition. God, it was good to discuss Cary with someone who really knew him and loved him. It was also very rare.

So many memories began to flood through my mind. There had been the incredibly frustrating times — Cary was such an enigma, there had to be — but there were so many good times too.

'Are you happy?' Dyan asked me. It was a familiar question. Cary had asked me that at the very beginning of our relationship, and then again many years after we had parted — just a few weeks before he died. I think he had finally achieved a kind of inner peace with his fifth wife, Barbara — the woman who moved into his home after I left — and this was now his way of wishing the same for me.

'I am happy, Dyan,' I told her, 'but it took a long time for me to say that.'

'Me too,' she said, nodding her head again. Then she told me about the man she called her 'prince' — real estate investor Stan Fimberg. Dyan said, 'I was ready for him, do you know what I mean? I had to go through all of that with Cary and to put it all behind me — along with some other things — before I could really go on and find real happiness. We were both so young when we came into his life. My God, Maureen, we were *children!*'

Dyan was right. Cary was everything to me — lover, father, teacher and much more. I walked into his life at age twenty-seven as an insecure movie-magazine writer, unsure of my looks and talent and most everything else.

Four years later, when I walked out, I was a different person, who had embarked on a whole new career in photography.

'He still wanted the child I was when I first met,' I explained to Dyan, 'but it took a woman to leave him. And because of everything I learned from him and everything I went through with him, I became a woman.'

'He was the Master,' Dyan offered. 'That's what I called him. And I meant it in every sense of that word.'

I felt a real kinship with Dyan, as if we were graduates of a very exclusive (and very tough) school.

I looked at my watch; we had been talking for over twenty minutes. But the minutes had seemed like seconds. It was time for us to part, but I didn't feel sad. I felt great.

As I drove home, I couldn't help thinking how much Cary had really gotten under my skin. He was like an onion — you peeled off one layer of skin, and there would be another and another and yet another. I don't know if I ever reached the core, but I came damn close.

Talking with Dyan made me realize how much I had really loved the man. It also made me realize how it would take much more than twenty minutes truly to encapsulate such a man, even with someone like Dyan, who knew him so intimately. It would take a book.

If he had changed my life, perhaps now was the time to tell our story, especially since I had been approached before and after Cary's death to write about him. At first I had resisted the idea. But after mourning him and going through all the diaries I'd kept during our relationship, filled with all the memories I had of our time together, the idea just wouldn't go away.

So I talked it over with my parents. They urged me to go ahead, pointing out all the distortions about our relationship that had been printed while he was alive. Now that he was gone, the problem had been compounded by books written by people who did not know him at all. They rehashed the same old stories and the same old rumors, not even beginning to scratch the surface of this fascinating, complicated man.

Moreover, they were filled with inaccuracies about my relationship with Cary. For example, during our years together I never once talked on or off the record, with any member of the press. Yet here I was in print, gushing on about how I had supposedly left Cary for a younger man — Warren Beatty.

Nothing more than recycled rumors. I owed it to Cary and to myself to get it right. As Cary had always said: 'If you're going to do something, do it right for God's sake or don't do it at all!'

I had already begun writing a book in my head, but running into Dyan spurred me on further, making me promise myself I would finally begin the process of putting it all down on paper as soon as possible. And now was the time, especially with the publication of books that had, in my opinion, so little to do with the real Cary.

The stories they had picked up from the tabloids and had recycled were colorful, perhaps even flattering. But they weren't remotely the truth.

This is.

1

NORTH BY NORTHWEST

'**H**OW can a woman as pretty as you be destroying her life by smoking a cigarette?'

It was not my idea of the perfect opening line from Cary Grant, but there it was and there he was. It was August 1973.

I was sitting in a coffee shop having breakfast with a rising young singer, Michael Franks. He had a new album out on the Brut label and I had flown up to Sun Valley as part of a press junket to promote an upcoming slate of Brut films (including *A Touch of Class*) and recordings like Michael's album. I was working as a journalist for Rona Barrett's then flourishing stable of fan magazines.

'I really don't know,' I said, grinding the cigarette out in an ashtray and looking up into Cary's deep brown eyes. 'What are you doing here?' I stammered, wondering if he'd remember meeting me at a party in Beverly Hills eight months earlier.

At first he didn't. 'Excuse me,' he said, nodding to Michael. 'I don't mean to be rude. I'm Cary Grant and I just had to say to this young lady that smoking that thing will shorten her life. I used to be a very heavy smoker myself, so I know what I'm talking about. She has too much to live for to be ruining it with that nasty habit!'

Cary was looking at me, not Michael, as he concluded: 'If you care about this lady, you will help her stop smoking.'

And with that he was gone. Michael laughed and said,

'That's the best come-on I've *ever* heard.'

'What do you mean?' I said, trying to sound both innocent and indignant.

'That man went way out of his way to get your attention. You should take it as a compliment because it was.'

'Do you really think so?' I said. Of course, that thought occupied me for the rest of the day as I arranged and conducted interviews with stars such as Gene Hackman and Laurence Harvey, who were participating in the Brut Film Festival. George Barrie, the head of the Fabergé cosmetics company, had branched out into films and records through the Brut division, and this star-studded festival was his method of drumming up some national publicity. Cary was on Fabergé's board of directors.

Later in the afternoon, I passed him in the hall of the hotel where all the press and stars were staying.

'Mr. Grant,' I said, screwing up all my courage, 'I don't know if you remember me —'

'Of course I do,' he said. 'You're the young woman in the coffee shop I gave a very sincere warning to about cigarettes this morning, aren't you?'

'Why, yes,' I replied, 'but we've met earlier.'

'We have?' he said, cocking an eyebrow. It was a gesture I had seen in so many of his films.

'Yes, several months ago at the Henry Hathaway tribute at the Beverly Hills Hotel. I was a bit more presentable then,' I said, awkwardly indicating the simple top and jeans I was wearing. 'That evening I had a green tweed suit on.'

'You asked me to do an interview?'

'Yes, I did,' I said, a smile starting to fill my face.

'Of course, I remember you. It's just so hectic up here, I haven't been able to think straight for days. How are you doing? Are you still working for Rona Barrett?'

'Well, yes, in a manner of speaking. I don't actually work for her personally. I do interviews for her magazines.'

'Yes, yes. I remember.'

'And I'd still like you to think about giving us an interview. Everybody complains about fan magazines, saying they make things up, but then they won't give real interviews to them in the first place.'

'That's a very persuasive argument,' he said, now resting one of his arms against a doorway and scratching his head. 'But only for people who are still making films. I'm done with all that. But I tell you what. I'll talk to Mr. Barrie this evening and tell him to give you carte blanche with all the stars who are here.'

'Oh, you don't have to do that,' I offered.

'It's the least I can do. And I'll make this deal with you — if you'll seriously consider giving up smoking, I'll seriously consider giving you an interview when and if I decide I have something interesting or valuable to say. Is it a deal?'

'You got it!' I practically shouted.

This man could charm fleas off a cat, I told myself. But how in the world was I going to stop smoking? I decided I would smoke my brains out the rest of the day and then begin a no-smoking program tomorrow.

I ran up to my room, ordered room service and placed a call to my best friend, Dee Joseph, in Los Angeles. 'You'll never believe what just happened,' I said, puffing away madly.

'What?' she asked.

'I'm going to the Cary Grant Schick Center for the Control of Smoking!'

'Excuse me?' she laughed.

'Cary's here!' I told her about the exchange in the coffee shop and our deal.

'Do you really think you can give it up?' Dee asked me, knowing I had indulged the habit for the past few years.

'For Cary Grant I can!' I said in my most assured voice.

The junket went on for two more days and Cary and I played a variation on tag with each other. I would spot him across a room smiling at me, I'd smile back, and then he'd be gone. Or he'd pass me in the hall, wave hello and stare at my hands, making sure there was no cigarette in them. It got to the point that I would pop up my hand when we'd see each other, so he could see I wasn't lighting up.

On the last night of the junket, a lavish buffet had been prepared in the hotel dining room. I was working my way through at one end of the table when I came right up against Cary.

'Doesn't it taste better?' he said.

'What?' I said, confused.

'Food. The food. Doesn't it taste better now you've given up smoking?'

'Well, it's been only two days,' I said, 'but you may be right.'

'Oh, trust me. I'm right because —'

'Smile!' a photographer said, rushing up to us. As we turned around, the flash went off and we were temporarily blinded.

'Now I can't even see what I'm eating, much less taste it!' I giggled.

'I hope you don't mind that,' Cary said casually.

'You mean the photographer?' I said.

'Uh, yes,' he said, sounding truly embarrassed.

'Well, I shouldn't. After all, it was my magazines' photographer. He has a habit of doing that. Charming, isn't it? Would you like me to get the negative? It really wasn't fair. Kamikaze Camera, we call him.'

'No, no. I'm used to having my picture taken,' he assured me. 'I was thinking about you. You'll ruin your reputation having your picture taken with me!'

'I should be so lucky,' I said, looking him straight in the eye. 'I'll be the envy of the office ...'

'Well, if you think it's okay,' he said, genuinely concerned. 'People print all kinds of things about me, you know. It might not be to your best advantage.'

'It's a privilege,' I said, still staring into his bottomless brown eyes. 'Now I expect you to keep your word about our deal. Here's my card.' I slipped it into his hand. 'I want you to call me when you have something to say.'

'I always keep my word,' he smiled, 'especially with a lady.'

'Good, I'm going to hold you to it!'

Then George Barrie led him to another part of the room. After the dinner I went to my room to pack for the trip back to Los Angeles and turned the TV on. And I couldn't believe what I saw.

It was Cary in a scene with Deborah Kerr from *An Affair to Remember*, my great-aunt's favorite film.

I swept my clothes off the bed. The packing would have to wait. I sat enraptured through the entire film.

Then I called Dee in Los Angeles.

I told her what had just happened.

'I don't think it's a coincidence,' I told her. 'Do you?'

'Nothing's a coincidence with you, Maureen.'

'I hate to sound silly, but it's a sign. I know it's a sign,' I blurted out.

2

ONCE UPON A TIME

CALL it coincidence or call it fate, but the fact was Cary and I shared more than a few things in common before we ever met. We had both been born in England. He came from the bone-cold seaport city of Bristol. I was born and raised in somewhat less frosty Muswell Hill, a suburb in north London.

Our mothers even had the same first name — Elsie — and our fathers preferred to be called by their middle name, James.

We were both known as pranksters around school, often getting into trouble with the teachers. I once almost successfully blew up a chemistry lab. Cary was expelled from his school for peeking into a girls' bathroom, he said.

We both left England for America at early ages — he sailed for New York when he was sixteen. I was eighteen when I flew to the same city.

And we both ended up making our living in Los Angeles.

But for all these similarities, there was one important difference: I had a blissfully happy childhood and Cary did not.

I was born September 27, 1946, and unlike many children who grew up during the fifties and sixies, I never really had any problems with my parents. There was never any 'generation gap.' I loved them and they loved me. Fortunately that has always been the case.

We did not have a lot of money, but there was an abundance of the things that mattered most to me as a child — laughter and guidance and care. My mother worked as a switchboard operator for BBC-TV news, while my father, Jim Payne, was a fireman.

My home was within spitting distance of the fire station with its gleaming fire engines always kept ready to wheel. Ours was a modest two-story affair at the end of the firemen's yard, sandwiched between four other homes. The bedrooms were upstairs, while the kitchen and living room were downstairs. There was no central heating — just a fire in the living room — while a larder had to serve as our refrigerator.

The only real problem was that there was no inside bathroom. If we wanted to wash, the kitchen sink had to do. And if there was anything more complicated, then the outside toilet was it. How I hated that damn shed. Getting up in the middle of those cold English nights and having to traipse outside to the toilet was not my idea of fun.

Everybody in post-World War II England had inconveniences to put up with, but as a child I could only nod my head when my father pointed out how lucky we really were compared to all the people who had lost their homes and loved ones during the war. What really compensated for everything was the fact that those blazing red fire engines made me very popular with the boys.

They didn't follow me home because they found me so attractive. In fact, I was a rather chunky child and more than a bit of a tomboy as I grew older. But those fire engines — and the chance that my father or one of his mates might let one of my friends up on the machine for a full inspection — made me a hit with the lads at school.

As for the girls in school, I was pretty popular with them too. Not only did I have good grades and a sense of humor, but I was ten or fifteen pounds overweight. That meant I was no serious competition. It also meant I didn't have my first date until I was sixteen years old.

But I really didn't mind. My eye was not on any boy at grammar school — I aimed much higher. Like millions of girls around the world, I had discovered the Beatles in 1963. I liked them all, but Paul McCartney was my favorite. His long lashes and sexy chestnut eyes stirred something within me that no real-life boy could hope to ignite.

The more I saw Paul on television and the more I saw his picture in the magazines, the more determined I was to meet him. I was convinced that once he met me, he would see I was unlike all the other girls who adored him. And he would marry me.

But turning that fantasy into reality was going to take some work. It took one bus and two train rides just to get me to the North End Music Stores (NEMS) offices in London. That was the company owned and operated by Brian Epstein, manager of the Beatles. Every day after school I'd embark on this long trip and arrive on the NEMS doorstep. I asked anyone there for any kind of job. I wasn't proud. Just so I could be close to Paul.

The girls in the front office took pity on me and let me stuff envelopes and do other assorted tasks. There was no pay, but I felt useful and somehow connected to Paul. I just *knew* I would meet him if I kept pushing in this direction.

My determination finally caught Brian's eye. He gave me a job for about eighteen dollars a week at the Beatles Fan Club offices. I would answer the telephones and also help out sorting through the mail, which contained thousands of jelly beans, supposedly the boys' favorite.

When I went home to share the good news with my parents, I didn't quite get the reaction I had anticipated. I informed them (as well as a visiting neighbor, Elsie Grunsell) that I was leaving school at age sixteen to begin work the following Monday for the Beatles. The three of them had been sitting there enjoying their tea when I unleashed this particular bombshell. Rising slowly, my father stood ramrod straight and said firmly:

'You're not going to work — I repeat *not* — for those ... those *yobos*!'

I started crying. I had to take that job because that was my only route to Paul. When my parents saw how determined I was and what it meant to me, they relented. Years later they told me they hoped I would come to my senses and get bored with life with the Beatles. Actually, it was the beginning of an odyssey that would take me all the way to America.

I began work at the fan-club office on a Monday. Four days later I met Paul in the flesh. He had dropped by to take us hard-working girls to a Chinese lunch. I was so awestruck being in the same room with Paul I simply couldn't eat. I just picked at my plate. Besides, I didn't know how to eat with chopsticks.

Instead I feasted on the sight of Paul, who actually had a bit of a shy streak. But when he kept talking about Jane this and Jane that, I poked one of my coworkers in the arm and said: 'Who is this Jane?'

I was told all about Jane Asher, a pretty red-haired actress who was Paul's steady. I was crestfallen at first. But I was too busy for disappointment. London in the early sixties seemed to be the center of the universe, and I was now part of it. Mary Quant was revolutionizing fashion on Carnaby Street; the Beatles and the scruffier Rolling Stones were changing the sound of rock music; and a stick-thin fashion model named Twiggy was making thin 'in.' Fortunately I had begun to lose all my baby fat and got swept up in the excitement and intensity of all the changes London was going through.

I had been at my new post in the fan-club offices for about three months when I answered the phone one day. It was Brian. 'Who's this?' he asked.

'This is Maureen Payne,' I said shyly.

'Well, I'd very much like to see you in my office tomorrow at ten o'clock.'

'Me?' I said, simply astounded.

'Yes, *you!*' he barked from the receiver. 'I've got a job for you.'

It turned out Brian liked the sound of my voice and wanted me back at the NEMS offices, where there was an opening for a receptionist. There was not only a raise of approximately fifteen dollars a week but also the opportunity of assisting Brian in the press office with its blizzard of press releases and bulletins released almost daily to the media.

Brian was a mercurial man — one minute up, the next down. But he was always buzzing about the place like a hornet, trying to find some new way to keep the press and the fans interested in 'the boys.' Then one day I helped to oil the publicity machine in my unique way.

Sometimes the girls and I in the NEMS offices would get restless, so we conducted elevator races. There was a rickety old elevator in dire need of repair; we would cram into it and push the buttons like crazy. It would take forever for the contraption to reach the next floor, but we didn't care — we'd be laughing and screaming so hysterically we would hardly notice. Of course, this all happened when Brian was out of the office.

But one day some of Brian's other clients — including Billy J. Kramer and the Dakotas, and another group called the Fourmost — dropped by, and we were especially bored. It was raining outside, one of those dark days that needed a little juicing up. So we girls invited the boys to get into the elevator with us. We wanted to see how many of us the silly thing could hold without expiring.

The answer: not many. About eight of us had gotten in when the elevator crashed. It fell down only a few feet, but a fire truck had to be called and firemen sent in to retrieve us. Since this occurred at the Beatles offices, it showed up on the evening news.

So there we were, being pulled out of the lift by the firemen and escorted in the pouring rain into a truck waiting to take us to the hospital to be checked for any possible injuries. Only our pride had been hurt. We were horribly embarrassed later, when the boys took special delight in telling us that the firemen had huge grins on their faces as they 'rescued' us, because they could see up our mini-skirts!

The next day Brian called us into his office and threatened to dock our pay because of the incident. He was just bluffing, though; we heard him laughing the minute we left his office.

But these carefree days were destined to come to an end soon. In the press office, I had met Derek Taylor, the darkly handsome Svengali who managed all the Beatles' media appearances, statements and so on. One day he asked me to take a crack at revising a press release. I think

I may have told him how much practice I'd got as a 'writer' in detention during my school days, when I was told to write an essay on my misbehavior at least two or three times a week.

After a few weeks of detention, either you become very clever with words or you die of boredom. I began concocting the most elaborate explanations for my offenses as well as outlandish programs for my possible reform.

Luckily, my sense of humor surfaced in what I wrote for Derek and he began shoving more things under my nose for a quick rewrite or touch-up. Then, as 1964 drew to a close, he had an even bigger surprise for me. He wanted me to go to America with his wife, four children and him.

In his mid-thirties he was tired of all the frenzy surrounding the Beatles. He had been offered a well-paying job in the States, managing a music newspaper. He also wanted to get into managing some American groups. The family nanny had gotten cold feet when the time came to apply for a visa, so Derek asked me if I wanted to accompany the family to New York and then Los Angeles.

Being Mary Poppins to four young children was hardly my life's ambition. The time I had spent in the press office convinced me I wanted to be an entertainment writer. But Derek explained this would be a way to get me into the country. Once safely settled in the States, he and his wife would hire a new nanny and I could rejoin him in the office.

I knew my parents would have apoplexy. The only city I knew was London. Now, at the ripe old age of eighteen, I would be flying thousands of miles to the United States with someone I had known only a year or so. My father opposed the plan from day one. But just as he had acquiesced about my going to work for the Beatles in the first place, he gave in this time when he saw how serious I was.

'Dad,' I said, looking into his eyes as he tried to avoid mine while we battled in our living room. 'I don't want to live a life of "If only I had ..." An opportunity like this comes how many times to a girl like me? I don't want to spend the rest of my life regretting the fact I didn't do this. You *must* let me go!'

He ultimately relented when he was persuaded that Derek's intentions were strictly honorable. He was convinced they were when Derek not only agreed to become my guardian but also promised my father he would pay my way back to England if things didn't work out in the States.

With my father's objections out of the way, now there was only one hurdle: It was January 1965 and Derek was due in Los Angeles in February. There wasn't enough time for me to get a green card through conventional channels. It usually took months. But thanks to the Beatles name and other connections, I got a card within three weeks.

Soon I was crying and waving to my parents at the airport as we boarded a plane for New York. After a brief stayover there, we went on to Los Angeles, where Derek quickly found a lovely house in Nichols Canyon in the Hollywood Hills. But my life in the United States was not all I had pictured it would be.

Caring for four young children is not fun, no matter where you live. Washing the floor, cleaning up messes, laundering diapers — this was hardly glamorous. In fact, within four weeks I just about had my fill. I was desperately homesick and wanted to work with Derek in his new offices. Where was the nanny he said he would hire the minute we landed?

Derek said he would take care of it but he had a new job occupying all his time. I promised to be patient and keep my end of the bargain if he would keep his. But the weeks kept passing, and the most I was seeing of Los Angeles was a mountain of diapers inside one home in a lonely canyon.

One day, after another confrontation with Derek, I got so frustrated I just packed my bags and left the nursery in Nichols Canyon. I had the address of one English couple, friends of a mutual acquaintance. When I got to their house, someone staying there said they were off visiting other friends. I began sobbing, feeling stranded, when this friend-of-a-friend told me of another couple who were looking for a tenant for a house in a nearby canyon. Not only did I move in that day, but those people helped me get a job in Hollywood at Petersen Publications which published *Teen* magazine and a wide range of automotive magazines.

By day I worked there as a file clerk, and by night I began making contacts in the rock clubs along Sunset Strip. America was still in the grip of the so-called British invasion of groups like the Beatles, Herman's Hermits and the Dave Clark Five. Not only were there more than a few people I knew from London hanging out at Gazzari's and the other clubs, but virtually anyone with a British accent was hired to write an article or do an interview as an authentic 'Beatle boy' or 'Beatle girl'.

Since I had really worked in the Beatles offices, I suddenly found myself a hot property. Once I was invited to appear on a show taped in Bakersfield called *Shebang*, a typical teen dance program. Outfitted in my Beatle boots and miniskirt, I rode up in a bus with Dick Clark to be quizzed intensely about the various intricacies of being 'a real Beatles girl.'

On the ride back to Los Angeles, Dick and I began talking and I could tell he was impressed by my background with the Beatles. He also was interested in my writing ambitions. 'If you ever need a job, I think I could find something for you,' he offered.

And that's how I became Dick Clark's radio producer. He had a syndicated radio show called *Hollywood Hotline* and my job was to interview all the hottest rock groups. Naturally, I loved it. I'd get some good bites and then write an introduction for Dick. He'd come into the studio and tape it and that was it. He was a joy to work for — he gave me free rein as far as who was or was not invited to be interviewed. I think he thought I was the audience, so my instincts should be trusted.

But Dick did something else for me — he introduced me to my future husband. In the mid-sixties Dick produced a fairy popular daytime teen program called *Where the Action Is*. The Robbs, a group who were reportedly gigantic in the Midwest, had been quickly signed to be the show's house band. Dick thought it might be a good idea for me to meet some of the boys and possibly work in a radio interview.

The show was taped on the beach, so one day I got a ride out to Santa Monica to meet these up-and-coming performers. No sooner had I arrived on the set when I spotted a young man with blue eyes and sandy hair staring right in my direction. He had an undeniable kind of midwestern wholesomeness, but I thought I detected a cool arrogance as well.

As for me, I must have been a sight in my miniskirt and thigh-high boots. He seemed to be saying to himself, 'You must think you're really something, don't you, girl?' With a swift toss of his mane of hair, he turned his head.

It was not love at first sight, but hate. We both detested the sight of each other because we *assumed* the other was conceited and self-absorbed. But there was just as undeniably a very definite attraction. It was hate mixed with lust, and there's nothing more powerful or intoxicating.

We spent most of the taping alternately eyeing each other and then pretending not to notice one another. After the last shot one of the producers grabbed me and brought me over to the man who had been repelling and fascinating me for the past thirty minutes.

'Maureen, I'd like you to meet Dee Robb Donaldson, the leader of the group.'

I extended my hand limply and he touched it just as unenthusiastically. But his eyes, like mine, betrayed his attraction. I was introduced to the rest of the members of the Robbs — Dee's two brothers and a cousin. But I couldn't take my eyes off him.

'Well,' I said, trying to gather my wits, 'we have an interview to do. Should we get on with it?'

We retired to a trailer, but my mind was not on my

questions or his answers. I had never felt such a combination of repulsion and lust in my entire life. What the hell was going on?

After the interview was over, that was precisely Dee's question to me.

I didn't know what to tell him. Perhaps, I offered weakly, we got off on the wrong foot.

'Shall we drop our first impressions and begin again?'

He laughed and I was hooked. We spent the rest of the afternoon on the beach just talking and getting acquainted. As the sun set, I knew this man was going to be my husband. I didn't dare say it — it would scare him off — but I didn't doubt it for a second.

Dee felt the same way. After that initial stumble we somehow felt magically linked to each other and began dating. Soon after, we started talking about marriage.

I had been in the States only a few months. If I dropped this on my parents now, they would surely collapse. It was a huge step and I wanted to be sure everyone involved felt good about it. I needed time to break it gently to my parents in my letters. And then there was Dee's career to consider. In the Midwest he was a big heart-throb and the thinking in those days was that a teen idol had to be single. In the swinging sixties a single image was promotable. Marriage and rock-and-roll didn't mix, with the possible exception of Sonny and Cher.

Six months after I joined Dick Clark's organization, I left to become a rock-and-roll wife. Dee and the group were leaving *Where the Action Is* to return to the Midwest, where they were big fish in a little pond, so to speak. In Los Angeles they were just one more backup group. It made much more sense financially to go back to Wisconsin, where they had first risen to stardom, and tour.

It would also give me a chance to meet Dee's parents. They lived in a beautiful house on the outskirts of Milwaukee and were very wealthy. But my welcome was not what I expected. I was barely in the door of their home when Dee's mother said to me, 'You do know, don't you that my son is going with you for the sex?'

It was like a kick in the stomach. What had I ever done to make this woman treat me so unkindly?

Fortunately, Dee's father was a lovely man who took matters firmly in hand. He suggested Dee and I live in the boathouse on the estate until Dee's mother got a little bit more used to the idea of having a daughter-in-law.

I later tried to construct some kind of relationship with the woman, but she wouldn't have it. I didn't have too much time to dwell on this because the Robbs were booked all over the Midwest. They were so successful, we eventually bought a Greyhound bus for touring. The money rolled in and we held off getting married for a few years. We knew that the minute it was out Dee was married, his viability as a heartthrob would be gone forever.

Finally, on March 18, 1969, we could wait no longer. That was our wedding day. Dee rented a tuxedo and I had a beautiful white lace wedding gown made for me. We took the Greyhound bus to church, got married and then had the reception at a local McDonald's. It might sound a bit whimsical or even sarilegious now, but you have to remember what the late sixties were like. Hippies and the summer of love had freed millions of kids from convention. And that's what we were — kids who wanted to have a good time, even at our own wedding.

After wedding toasts at McDonald's, we headed back into the Greyhound and had our wedding pictures taken at a local hospital. A good friend had just had a baby, so we decided to visit her in the maternity ward. My friend gathered her child in her arms, and Dee and I and the rest of the wedding party surrounded her. And that's where our wedding pictures were taken — in a hospital maternity ward.

After our honeymoon we were back on the road again, but Dee ultimately found life as a rock-and-roll idol unfulfilling. He was more interested in going behind the scenes producing music than he was in getting up on stage and singing. He wanted his own studio.

And that meant moving back to Los Angeles, where all the top groups were recording and blazing trails in the studios there. Dee's mother still hated me so much, she stayed in Milwaukee, refusing to go with the rest of the family, including Dee's dad. Their relationship was essentially over anyway. We found a ranch in Chatsworth in the San Fernando Valley, and we all put our heart and soul into it — Dee, his two brothers, a cousin, and his dad. It was like *The Egg and I* crossed with *Eight Is Enough.*

The Robbs were still performing to save up enough money to run the ranch and build a recording studio, while I had landed a job as entertainment editor at *Teen* magazine, where I had worked just a few years before.

The ranch began overflowing with a wild assortment of chickens, horses, rabbits and even some orange orchards to keep us busy. Later we moved to an even bigger spread.

But this time things were somewhat different. After so many years on the bus with the boys, I felt Dee and I needed more privacy. So we lived in the guest house, and Dee's dad, brothers and cousin moved into the main house. In addition to holding down a full-time job, I was cooking, ironing and washing for all of them. Feminism was beginning to be felt all over the United States, but it hadn't hit Chatsworth yet.

The strain was beginning to show when Dee thought the solution would be for me to give up my job and concentrate solely on the ranch and the family. I explained I couldn't do that. I had developed into a pretty good writer and was proud that I had managed to snag the likes of Robert Redford, James Caan, Ryan O'Neal and many others to sit down and talk with me.

But Dee forced the issue, giving me an ultimatum: Choose between the job and him. I had an ultimatum for him: Move out and get our own place and really live together like man and wife, or let's forget it. I wanted a real marriage; life with the boys was always an adventure, but it was not what I had considered a marriage. And no one could call me impatient — I had been functioning as a housewife for five men. Enough was enough.

We were perched on the edge of this Mexican standoff when Dee's mother came on the scene. She was visiting California and one day at our ranch she haughtily informed me, 'I'm going to take the boys — no wives — out to Laguna Beach for a holiday. I hope you don't mind.'

She knew I had to mind. After all, I was the only wife among those particular boys. There had never been any love lost between the woman and myself, but this shocked even me. It was going too far. Either I was Dee's wife or I wasn't. How long was he going to let this woman manipulate him?

We went around and around on this issue. Finally I told Dee I had had enough. If he went off with his mother for a holiday, I would not be there when he got back. It was not a threat; it was a matter of fact.

Off Dee went with his mother and the rest of the boys, so out I went. The marriage was over, but my career as a writer was in high gear. In 1973 I received an offer from the Laufer Company, which published a group of magazines under the name of entertainment reporter Rona Barrett. She was unhappy with the magazines; though they were selling well, she felt they lacked real news and interviews. Since I had managed to get Redford and some other big names for *Teen*, perhaps I could do the same for Rona's magazines to give them some credibility. I accepted the offer.

Little did I know Rona's magazines would provide me with the opportunity to meet Cary Grant, and the chance to corral him after we met in Sun Valley.

But I did. Eventually.

3

THIS IS THE NIGHT

IN early September the magazine's publicity office sent some photos to Cary from the Sun Valley junket, including the one that had been taken of us together.

Then my birthday, September 27, arrived and I got a very special surprise after some of the people in my office had taken me out for lunch. I picked up my messages at the front door and the receptionist said, 'Cary Grant called you.'

'Right,' I said, thinking it was a birthday prank. 'Along with the Queen Mother, Jimmy Stewart and Grand Funk Railroad.'

'I'm not kidding,' the girl said. 'It really was him, or a damn good imitation. Here's his number,' she said, handing me the slip of paper.

I rushed to my office and dialed the number. I got his secretary, then Cary came on the line.

'Hello?' I heard the familiar clipped tones.

'It *was* you!' I said, unable to contain my happiness.

'Of course it was me!' he said, slightly annoyed.

'Well, this is the best birthday present I could have gotten,' I said, 'a phone call from Cary Grant!'

'Is it really your birthday?' he said, softening quickly.

'Yes, it is. I'm twenty-seven years old today.'

'My goodness,' he said. 'I think that deserves a birthday drink. I'm tied up this evening and next. Could you do something on the weekend, perhaps?'

'I'd love to!' I practically squealed. There was no point in trying to mask my pleasure. I wanted to see him. Why pretend? And I could tell he was pleased that I was excited.

'I wish I had this effect on everybody I spoke to!' he said, slightly flustered. 'Could you make it Sunday afternoon?'

I told him that sounded fine. He explained he had custody of his daughter, Jennifer, on the weekends (as well as one month during the summer).

'That's my number-one priority. I have a place in Malibu near my ex-wife's, so Jennifer doesn't have to travel back and forth between my ex-wife's home and mine in Beverly Hills. So if you wouldn't mind driving out to Malibu, we could make it around five-thirty for drinks. How does that sound?'

I said that would be perfect, since I was planning to visit some friends who lived in Malibu that weekend anyway. I'd see them earlier in the afternoon and then drop in on him.

He gave me the address and the phone number in Malibu in case I got lost. Fat chance.

'So how's the smoking going?' he asked me.

'Stopped cold turkey up in Sun Valley,' I said.

'You mean you haven't gone back to it?'

'Nope, not yet.'

'Good girl!' he exclaimed. 'Good stuff!'

'When I decide to do something, Cary, I can be very determined.'

'Well, I can see that. By the way I got the photo of you and me together. I still say it will ruin your reputation!' He laughed.

'We'll see,' I said.

The days flew by and now it was Sunday afternoon. For some reason, I was a wreck. I had interviewed everyone from Robert Redford to Alice Cooper and no one had rattled me before. I was really shaking. I was sitting on the deck of my friend's house in Malibu — Cary's home was about ten minutes away by car. But it seemed like thousands of miles from us. What was I walking into? What had I talked myself into? I was on the verge of hysteria.

What could Cary Grant possibly see in me? I was an

attractive girl — five feet, five inches tall, slim, long dark hair, deep brown eyes — but I was no raving beauty. Not like Dyan Cannon. Not like most of the socialites and movie stars Cary had dated.

My friend fortunately brought me to my senses. 'Look,' she said, 'why make yourself so upset? He may not even like you. Perhaps he's just being polite. After all, it's just a drink, for Christ's sake. If you can't handle that, how could you handle a relationship with him?'

I didn't even dare think of that. All I knew was that I had to know this man better. He was totally unlike the rock-and-roll singers and songwriters who had been a large part of my life since Dee Donaldson had come into it. Cary was a man who seemed to know who he was and what he wanted. He seemed so elusive and yet so serene at the same time. I had never come across anyone like him.

I took a Valium my friend offered and let it calm me down a bit. But an hour later I was still jumping in my skin. And it was time to go to Cary's place. It was sink-or-swim time.

I drove up to the house and was pleased it was not one of the glass showplaces that dominated so much of the beachfront in The Colony. It was a simple place made of wood and stucco and slightly weatherbeaten.

I rang the bell and a black woman in a white maid's uniform came to the door. 'Are you Maureen?' she said softly.

Luckily, she had the kindest brown eyes in the world. They instantly brought me down to earth. She had a warm, full face and she smiled at me.

'Mr. Grant is expecting you. I'm Willie and I'm glad to meet you.' She escorted me into the living room and then retired to the kitchen, where she was preparing a meal.

'You have terrific taste!' Cary said as he grabbed my hand and held it for a moment or two.'

'Excuse me?' I stuttered.

'The Blassport. You have exquisite taste,' he said, pointing to the gray Blassport blazer and pants I was wearing (along with my platform shoes). 'Norman Zeiler is a friend of mine and he owns Blassport. He will be so pleased to hear that a nice young woman like you has the good taste to buy his stuff.'

Evidently, I had passed muster without even trying. I breathed a huge sigh of relief and caught someone else inspecting me with almost microscopic intensity.

It was Jennifer, Cary's seven-year-old daughter. She had Cary's strong bone structure, but it was her eyes — mirrors of her mother's — that dominated her face. She looked so much like Dyan it was intimidating.

She was pretending to have tea with a young friend from up the beach, Donna Mayotte.

While Cary got me a drink, I went over to where the girls were serving each other and glimpsed their toy tea service. They were quite proud of it and instantly offered me some 'tea'. I took the saucer and cup in my hands and pretended to swallow the whole thing in one gulp.

Jennifer loved that and laughed. She was an even more beautiful child when she smiled. 'I like her,' she said simply.

Within minutes of arriving, I had passed my second test. Then I caught Donna looking out through the sun porch to the waves beyond.

'Would you like to go outside for a minute?'

'Oh, yes!' the girls shouted together, looking quickly to Cary for approval.

'Well,' he said somberly, 'if Maureen goes with you, I suppose it'll be all right.'

As I grabbed Jennifer's hand and then Donna's, I saw Cary's eyes following Jennifer. He was like a movie camera recording her every movement. She was never out of his line of sight.

'Come on, Daddy!' Jennifer said, inviting her father to join us.

'No, I don't think so, dear. I don't have my shoes on.'

'Well, let's take our shoes off, too,' I said, reaching for mine and slipping them off.

Jennifer instantly searched her father's face for approval to remove her shoes, too, and he nodded. She smiled even wider this time.

'Let's go!' she said, pulling my hand. So off the four of us went, barefoot.

There was a lemony autumn sun, which Cary and I basked in while the girls raced along the beach. I could tell by the way he positioned his face, trying to catch the sun's rays from the best possible angle, that he loved the sun. His seemingly perpetual suntan also testified to his devotion to it.

'It's lovely out here, isn't it?' I said, struggling for something intelligent to say.

'Yes it is,' he said sweetly. 'I'm so glad you came. And I can tell Jennifer likes you, too. Children have very good instincts that way, I've discovered. You must be a very special person.'

'God knows I try to be!' I said, awkwardly trying to make light of the moment. I realized I wasn't used to men paying me such compliments, much less Cary Grant. Not that long ago, I had spent six years on and off the road with six men whose most common comment to me was: 'What time is dinner?' It would take some time to get used to the contrast.

'Look,' Cary said, as he kept his eye on Jennifer and Donna playing. 'I had dinner prepared only for the children because I have to bring Jennifer back to her mother around seven. I was planning to drive back to Beverly Hills and have something at the house there, but if you're willing to wait while the kids eat and give me a few minutes to drop off Jennifer, I could take you to dinner somewhere out in this area if you haven't made any plans.'

'That sounds wonderful,' I replied.

'Have you been to the Discovery Inn?' he asked. 'It's a lovely French restaurant at the top of Topanga Canyon' — the canyon was nearby. 'You could leave your car at the bottom of the hill and we could drive up in mine.'

A nice quiet dinner at a French restaurant couldn't have been better if I had planned the evening myself. It was perfect.

An hour and a half later, we were sitting in the dimly lit restaurant. We started with some white wine and it seemed to loosen both our tongues. After a few minutes, Cary hunched over his part of the table like a jockey at the finish line and said:

'I have something very important to ask you.'

'Yes?' I said, curious.

'Do you know where you can get some decent bangers and mash in this godforsaken city?'

I roared and almost spilled my wine. Bangers are an English sausage, very difficult to find in America, even in the big cities, especially if you want to get decent, authentic ones.

'There's only one place where you can get the real thing,' I assured him. It was a little British restaurant in Santa Monica, run by an old couple whom I had met a few times. The mashed potato wasn't bad either.

'Will you take me there?' Cary asked with all the enthusiasm of a child.

'Name the day,' I said, imagining myself walking into the tiny shop with Cary Grant. The owners would have kittens.

So we spent the next thirty minutes in a French restaurant discussing British food. A detailed survey of the kinds of fish and chips available in greater southern California was the highlight.

By this point, we were both a little high from the wine and obviously enjoying each other's company. This was the man who had invented masculine charm. Dressed simply in a blue-green sweater and gray slacks, he outclassed the other gentlemen in the room with their trendy suits without even trying. And there was a spirit he brought to everything we discussed that was eternally youthful and inquisitive. He reminded me so much of my brother, David, whom I idolized as a child. He now lived in Paris with his wife Christine and I rarely got a chance to see him.

Out of the blue — and almost as if he were reading my thoughts about my family — Cary switched the subject.

'Are you happy?' he asked. He wasn't kidding. He was perfectly serious and wanted a perfectly serious answer. The fun and frivolity of the past half-hour seemed to evaporate in an instant.

'I'm happier than I've been in a while,' I said cautiously, thinking of my breakup with Dee, 'but not as happy as I plan to be.'

'Good stuff!' he said forcefully. 'It takes work to be happy, and as long as you realize that, you'll be fine.'

I nodded, not really knowing what to say. What was he getting at? But before I had time to figure it out, he had another question for me.

'Do you love your mother and father?' he asked. Again, he wasn't kidding.

'Why,' I said, taken aback. 'Of course I do! Why would you ask a question like that?'

'Because a lot of people don't. They really don't, you know.'

'I love Jim and Elsie,' I said, relaxing.

'Elsie?' he said. 'Did you say, "Elsie"?'

'Hmmm, yes. Elsie Maud Payne. That's me mum.' I adopted a Cockney accent.

'My mother's name was Elsie. Elsie Maria Leach,' he said, trying to sound casual.

'So let me ask *you* — did you love her?' I said.

'As a matter of fact I did. But it took me many years to say that. She died just this January. She was ninety-five.'

'That means you're going to live a long, long time, too. What do you mean, it took you a long time to say you loved her?'

'You don't know?'

'No.' All I knew about Cary was that he had been married four times, Dyan Cannon being his last wife. And that she had given him Jennifer.

'Well, when I was ten years old, I came home one day and I was told my mother had gone away, to a resort. Actually, my father had put her away in a sanitarium in Bristol, where I was born. It wasn't until twenty years later, when I had become known as Cary Grant that she was released from the place. We were absolute strangers.'

'God, I'm so sorry,' I said. 'It sounds horrible, just horrible.'

'It was sad and then confusing,' he said. 'But many years after she got out, we finally did get to know each other. And let me tell you, she was some kind of character!'

We laughed and then he asked me all kinds of questions about my childhood in Muswell Hill. He seemed absolutely transfixed by even the most trivial detail. When I told him about being repeatedly sent to detention and developing a love for writing there, he told me how he had been expelled in front of his entire school as a teenager. He had run off to join a boys' acrobatic troupe called Bob Pender's Knock-About Comedians and his father had dragged him back to school. He hated his classes so much after getting a taste of show business, he deliberately misbehaved so he would be expelled. Then his father was forced to let him rejoin the Pender troupe.

Over the next year and a half, he became an accomplished tumbler and stilt-walker, and jumped at the chance to travel to America with Pender when he was only sixteen.

When I mentioned how I had left for America, too, at age eighteen, he was particularly interested in how I got my parents to go along with the idea.

'I held my breath!' I laughed before giving him a fairly decent replay of my 'I may never get another chance like this' speech.

Afterwards he said: 'You've got guts, don't you?'

I blushed a little and then tried to get him to tell me more about his childhood and his early years in America, but he always turned the subject back to me and my experiences.

Then I told him about my days as a rock-and-roll wife and my wedding pictures in a Milwaukee maternity ward. He refused to believe it at first.

'You didn't! You couldn't!' Then he told me he was sure about what he had suspected all along:

'You're a wild child! You're a hippie, aren't you?'

I was definitely a child of the sixties, but I had never considered myself part of the peace-and-love brigade, like the hippies who had hung out just a few years before on Sunset Boulevard.

'No, no,' he said. 'You are a free spirit. I saw it today on the beach with Jennifer and her friend. You're comfortable anywhere. I say that in admiration, Maureen, not in reproach, you understand.'

If Cary Grant was convinced I was some kind of flower child, so be it for now. There were worse things he could think. I hoped he would get to know me better.

Then I turned the tables on him for a bit and tried to find out how he saw or defined himself. I was not going to just sit there petrified with fear, as I had many years ago with Paul McCartney at a Chinese restaurant in London. Every instinct I had was saying, *Be yourself and go for it, Maureen.*

Oh, I'm just an old, old man,' he said. 'I'll be seventy in January, you know. My life is really devoted to Jennifer. She is going to have the kind of childhood I never had. She's going to know at all times where her mother and father are, and she will be totally secure in our love for her, even if we are divorced.'

He briefly mentioned how lonely he felt after his mother disappeared overnight from his life. He would wander the quays at Bristol, imagining one of the tall ships carrying him far away. He and his father lived with his grandmother for a time and he remembered her as 'a cold, cold woman.' After his father developed a relationship with another woman, Cary began to feel squeezed out. He never wanted Jennifer to feel as if she had nowhere to turn.

'Jennifer is the woman in my life now.' He said it with an unmistakable finality, almost as if by rote. He was making a point and I got it.

The wine was beginning to wear off and our meal was over.

'Someday you'll find a nice young man who will treat

you the way you deserve and you will be very, very happy.'

As we got up to leave the restaurant, I could distinctly hear doors closing, not opening as I had hoped.

Once we got in the car, I grabbed his hand and looked in his eyes.

'I know what you're doing, Cary. You're putting me off — and you are making a big mistake. I have a lot to offer you and if —'

'Don't,' he said, interrupting me. 'I'm not blind, Maureen. You are a beautiful young woman. And I said *young*. You just turned twenty-seven, didn't you?'

I nodded my head weakly.

'I'll be seventy soon. Do I have to do the arithmetic for you — I'm more than forty years older than you. Do you know what people will think if we started seeing each other?'

'I don't bloody well care what other people say, and neither should you.'

'You really don't care what other people say?' The way he posed the question, it was a challenge.

'Well, let me tell you what people say about me — that I'm a homosexual and that I'm a miserable old tightwad. And I care because it hurts. So you just can't wave away blithely what people say or don't say.'

He started driving the car down the mountain. I was determined not to give up without a good fight.

'Well,' I said, 'people must be wrong about you, because you just paid for dinner!'

It was just the right stroke. We both burst out laughing at the same time.

We pulled up next to my car and I could hear my inner voice saying again, *Don't you walk away without saying what you really feel, Maureen. You go for it or you'll always regret it.* Better to go too far than not to go anywhere at all.

He started to get out of the car to escort me to mine, but I signaled for him to stop.

'Now, let's make sure I've got all this straight, Cary,' I said, doing my best to make light of all the roadblocks he seemed to be trying to put in front of us. 'You are sixty-nine years old. Your life is totally devoted to your daughter and you have no room for anyone else. And you are an accused tightwad and homosexual.'

'That's right,' he said, trying not to break into a smile.

'Well,' I continued, 'all I can say is, what a shame, because I have a feeling we will make a great couple.'

'Really?'

'Really!' I said. He reached over and kissed me gently on the lips.

'I'll call you,' he said, as he got out and came over to my side of the car and opened the door. 'If you don't,' I said, getting out, 'I'll call you.' And then I kissed him, just as gently and just as sweetly.

I got in my car and started the engine. In my rearview mirror I could see him in his car. He would be following me all the way from the beach back to Beverly Hills.

What the hell have I done? I said to myself. *This man must think I'm crazy.*

As I made my way down the Pacific Coast Highway, my spirits sank. *I came on to him too strong*, I said to myself. Then a mile would pass and my spirits would soar. *Well, at least I did make a move. Better to do something than nothing. Better to be honest, than pretend I'm not interested.* And then I'd start verbally whipping myself again.

Back and forth it went, all the way to Beverly Hills.

When I pulled into the driveway to my apartment, I was convinced he would never call me again.

4

THE BACHELOR AND
THE BOBBY-SOXER

THE next day, I came home from work early, changed
into my tennis outfit and ran off to a nearby court. I
told my service I would be playing tennis for an hour and
would be back later.

When I got back home and checked with my service, I
got Nora, a very proper English lady who went through
my messages one by one, feigning disinterest, until she
came to the final one.

'And, oh, Cary Grant called you. Is that *the* Cary
Grant?'

'Yes, it is.' I replied, trying to sound casual.

'Well, we told him you were out at your tennis lesson
and he said that was jolly good. He wants you to call him
in Beverly Hills when you have a moment. He said you
have the number.'

'Thank you,' I said, starting to hang up.

'Oh, Maureen?' Nora said.

'Yes ...'

'Good for you!'

'Thank you,' I said, stifling a laugh.

He kept his word and called! Maybe there was a
chance for me with Cary after all.

I returned his call and he sounded genuinely happy to
hear from me.

'Look,' he said, 'If you're not doing anything special, I
thought you might like to come up here for a bite to eat.

Nothing fancy, just sandwiches or something. How's that sound?'

'Great! But I've just come from playing tennis so I'm not all dolled up, if you know what I mean.'

'Don't worry,' he said, 'it's strictly "come as you are." I'm just lounging around in a shirt and slacks. The house is being remodeled so everything's a mess. We couldn't be formal if we tried.'

'All right, then,' I said. 'I'll see you in fifteen minutes.'

I lived in a small apartment on Oakhurst Drive near downtown Beverly Hills. His home was ten minutes away in Benedict Canyon, a few miles past Sunset Boulevard. I wrote his address down and then rushed as fast as I could to put on some kind of face.

I drove up Benedict Canyon Road and then up a hill onto Beverly Grove, where he was converting a farmhouse he'd bought from Howard Hughes into a proper home for him and Jennifer. I pulled into the driveway and was somewhat surprised how modest the house was. This was not the typical movie star mansion. It had three bedrooms as well as quarters for a maid and butler. There was no tennis court, but there was a swimming pool.

The main attractions were the privacy — just portions of a few other homes were visible — and the view. From his hill in Beverly Hills, Cary could look down on Sunset Boulevard and on a clear day one could see the Pacific Ocean on the horizon. Directly below the property were the sixteen acres of the estate of the late Harold Lloyd, which was destined to be subdivided by developers. A large garden and a wooden gate ensured that the rustic beauty of Cary's house would never be disturbed. It was being remodeled in classic Moroccan style.

After I parked, I made my way to the front door, where Cary was waiting for me. And I swear he was positively beaming as he stood in the doorway.

'Hello and welcome,' he said, escorting me in. 'You're going to have to watch where you step.'

He was not exaggerating. There were ladders and paint pots all around. The living room was in complete disarray.

Only two bedrooms and bathrooms for Cary and Jennifer were finished.

'It's quite a project, isn't it?' he said, a bit embarrassed. 'But to do things right takes time, doesn't it, Bill?' he said, indicating a portly, balding man who walked into the living room where we were standing.

'Inch by inch!' he said cheerily. Bill Weaver was Cary's longtime secretary, and I liked him instantly. He just exuded confidence and well-being. Unlike some of Cary's male secretaries who came along later, he didn't make me feel like an intruder.

Then the other half of Cary's domestic inner circle walked into the room — his maid, Willie Watson, whom I had met just the day before in Malibu. Her eyes seemed to sparkle as she said, 'It's so nice to see you again Miss Donaldson.'

Turning to Cary, she said: 'I can serve you and Miss Donaldson in about ten minutes if you'd like.'

'That sounds just fine,' Cary said. 'It'll give me a chance to show Maureen the property.'

'I love the view,' I said as the sun started to set. 'I swear you can see all the way to the ocean.'

'It is spectacular, isn't it?' he said proudly.

He gave me a brief history of some of his more famous ex-neighbors in the area, including Charles Boyer and Rudolph Valentino. I mentioned that I was halfway familiar with this part of the canyon because Alice Cooper, the shock-rock star I had befriended in my *Teen* magazine days, lived nearby.

'My goodness!' he exclaimed. 'Jennifer will be tremendously impressed that you know him!'

I laughed as we made our way back into the house. We went into his bedroom, where Willie served us turkey sandwiches on white wicker trays. We sat on the bed and watched television. In the four years I got to know and love the man, I rarely saw him eat a meal on a dining table in his house. Dinner was always served on those trays in his bedroom. Sometimes there was breakfast out on the terrace, but that was a special occasion when a close friend like Charlie Rich, the co-owner of the Dunes Hotel in Las Vegas, or Roderick Mann, an entertainment writer for the London *Sunday Express* and then the *Los Angeles Times*, would come by.

At first I thought Cary kept most of his friends away from the house because he didn't want them to see it in the middle of remodeling. Actually, he was a very private man with very simple tastes. He liked being left alone. Jennifer, Bill, Willie, and soon, I were the only ones he allowed around the house on a regular basis. He was not as reclusive as his friend Howard Hughes, but private enough to be counted as a close cousin.

As we sat on the bed nibbling our sandwiches, he asked me if I knew Roddy Mann, his longtime friend who also happened to be in the business of writing about celebrities.

'Not really,' I said. 'I've met him a couple of times and he seems like a very nice person, though.'

'You're right,' Cary said. 'He's also one of the very few people in your business one can trust. I mean, if you tell him something, he doesn't twist it all around. And if you tell him something but tell him to wait a bit to publish it, he will honor his word. He's always played straight with me.'

I sensed I was being put through another test. This one was the 'Why do you want to do *that* for a living?' test.

'Well, you know, Cary,' I offered, 'not every reporter or columnist is unethical. That's like saying every mechanic is dishonest.'

'I'll tell you one thing,' he countered. 'Hedda Hopper was a bitch. I don't mean to speak ill of the dead, but she was. She just liked hurting people. Must have been an unhappy woman.

'And,' he continued, 'I don't understand that woman whose name is on the magazine you work for.'

'Rona?'

'Yes,' he said. 'She is fascinated with everything I do. Just loves to report the tiniest thing.'

'Surely after this many years in the business, Cary, you

must realize everybody's interested in what you do.'

'But I'm no longer in the business, darling.'

'It doesn't matter, Cary. It's like Garbo — they'll always be interested. Besides, the thing I like about Rona is that she really makes an effort to call and talk to the people she writes about. She doesn't just make it up out of whole cloth.'

After a lot of verbal seesawing on this issue, it finally slipped out what bothered Cary Grant about Rona Barrett — she was the first reporter to have broadcast the story he and Dyan were splitting up. Cary just thought it was a lousy business for someone to be in — reporting the misfortunes of others.

'That's not precisely what *I* do, Cary,' I tried to assure him. 'I interview people. I'm an interviewer. I am not a reporter or columnist.'

He could see I was getting my defenses up. 'Don't worry, dear,' he said. 'If I can trust Roddy, I can trust you. I just want you to promise me one thing.'

'What's that?'

'You will never report or tell anyone else what you see or hear in any of my homes or any place we go as long as I'm alive.'

'You got it,' I said. 'You want to shake on it?'

'No. I know your word is good. Otherwise you wouldn't be sitting here with me in the first place.'

With that out of the way, we both could relax. I had passed another test. I didn't know how many more tests there would be but I was confident I could pass them all. Cary Grant did not give his trust easily.

Over the course of the next few weeks, we settled into a routine we both found comfortable and convenient. During the week, I would visit him once or twice up at the Beverly Hills house, while on the weekends when he had Jennifer, I would drop by either Saturday or Sunday afternoon in Malibu to spend part of the day with Cary and her.

Like most English people, I have a real sensitivity about not overstepping my bounds. Up to this point, nothing more had happened between Cary and me than a simple kiss hello or good night. I wanted to make sure, after pushing Cary so strongly that night at the Discovery Inn, that it was he who set the pace for the rest of the relationship. In this way, I came into Cary's and Jennifer's lives without any of us feeling any pressure at all. More and more, I just seemed to be there. And each time I drove up to his front door, there he was, positively beaming. It was the greatest compliment a girl could get.

One night at the Beverly Grove house, I knew he was beginning to really care for me from his reaction to my doing something so simple as taking the trays off the bed after dinner and putting them in the kitchen.

I returned to the bedroom and found him just staring at me, open-mouthed in amazement.

'You are a dear, *dear* girl!' he said.

'And what did I do to deserve that?' I wondered.

'By doing what you just did. No one had to tell you. It was something natural for you. Do you know how many women I've had in my life who have expected me to wait on *them*? I think they thought if Cary Grant waited on them, then they were really something. Or it was something they could brag about to their friends. You're just a dear, dear girl.'

I blushed. And I thanked him for noticing. 'I like doing things for you,' I said.

For my part, I was also beginning to care not only for Cary but also for Jennifer, whom I saw on weekends down at the beach. Like her father, she was very intelligent and had her defenses up much of the time, at least in the beginning. But since I was so much closer in age to her than to her father, I think she felt freer around me. The fact that I loved to play rock-and-roll music when Cary wasn't in the house was also a big plus.

Like most seven-year-old girls, she wanted to enjoy herself and run free. But out of his protectiveness, Cary watched her like a hawk. Sometimes she had to feel like a tiny animal in a gilded cage. She was also in a tremendously awkward position, trying to please both her mother and her father. Even she knew their divorce had been bitter and rancorous. Cary made a policy of never saying anything cross about Dyan in Jennifer's presence, but the child was so smart and so sensitive she had to feel the tension. Cary never referred to Dyan by her first name; it was always either 'Jennifer's mother' or 'my former wife.'

I got the feeling Jennifer loved her father but was frightened of him at the same time. She was in the middle of a tug-of-war and my heart went out to her. It made me realize how lucky I had been having my parents under one roof while I grew up. One of my first times out at the beach, I saw something that almost made me cry.

Cary had made no secret that his world revolved around Jennifer, but this particular weekend he couldn't have her. Jennifer was walking by with a group of friends on the beach. Cary had been sitting all day in the glass-enclosed sun porch, just waiting for a glimpse of her. But as Jennifer walked by, all she could manage was a nervous little wave in his direction. It was as if she were afraid doing more would get her in trouble. The look on Cary's face was heartbreaking. He had waited so long to have a child, and then he had to see her leave his home when she was still an infant.

I walked up to him after Jennifer had walked by and I put my hand in his. 'God,' I whispered. 'I'm so terribly sorry.'

He didn't say a word. He just looked straight at the beach. I backed quietly out of the room and left him alone. He sat in his chair for at least another half-hour. I vowed to myself I would do my best to help him find some real joy with Jennifer in the time he was allowed with her.

And I think I really did. Most of the time he was at a total loss what to do with a growing little girl. He always made sure that one of her friends was with her. He was deathly afraid that Jennifer would be bored, alone with him. I also suspected that his own childhood had been so horrendous he had lost the ability to remember what being a child was like.

So I became a go-between for Cary and Jennifer,

helping bridge that sixty-two-year gap between them by playing with her. For a former nanny, it wasn't all that hard. Plus, she was so sharp it was a pleasure to be with her. Her mind was always in overdrive.

For example, sometimes I would drive her and Willie to the Malibu market in my little Triumph sports car and we'd play a game called The Vicar's Horse. The idea was to think of words, in alphabetical order, to describe the vicar's horse: 'The vicar's horse is an asinine horse!' 'The vicar's horse is a beastly horse!' and so on. One time we were driving back from the market when Jennifer figured out that she was going to get to *f* when it was her turn.

And she just couldn't wait. Finally her turn came and she announced ever so proudly:

'The vicar's horse is a *farting* horse!'

It wasn't long before Jennifer was asking me instead of Willie to take her back to Dyan's house down the beach. Willie usually had that assignment since Dyan and Cary avoided eye-to-eye contact at all cost in those days. And every time I walked into his house on the weekend, she'd be sure to tell him:

'Oh, thank you, Daddy, for inviting Maureen! I like her!'

So within a very short amount of time I had passed more than a few tests.

But one night up at the Beverly Grove house came a test I never expected.

After a light dinner, Cary clicked off the television and said, 'I don't mean to frighten you, dear, but we must really discuss something.'

'Yes ...' I hesitated.

'I think it's clear by now, you and I are going to become very close friends.'

'It sure is,' I said, smiling. 'Much closer.'

'Then there's something I must tell you and you must make me a promise.'

'Yes ...' I said, still mystified.

'Well, you know how I tend to drop off sometimes while we're watching television?'

He had already done it a few times.

'Well, dear, if I should die in my sleep and you are here with me, I do not — repeat not — want you to call an ambulance.'

'Oh, Cary!' I cried. 'I don't want to hear this . . .'

'If you're my friend, you *must*. If I should pass away and you're here or in Malibu with me, I want you to call Stanley Fox. He's been my friend and my attorney for many, many years. I'm going to give you this piece of paper with his name and all his numbers on it. You must promise me that you will call no one — not even an ambulance — until you find Stanley and let him take charge. I've gone over this with him many times. He knows what to do. I can trust him to follow my instructions to the letter. Do you understand?'

I nodded. I felt as if I were in a daze, but I nodded. For once I had not a word to say.

'You promise?'

'I promise,' I said, trying not to hear the words.

'I know I've shocked you, dear,' he said soothingly. 'But we all do go sometime, and I just want you to be prepared, that's all.'

The less I thought about this, the better. I had to change subjects — *fast*.

'Look,' I said. 'I will not allow you to die until you give me that interview!'

'Oh, ho!' he laughed. 'Then I know I'm going to live for a very, very long time, aren't I?'

'You better believe it!' I said unequivocally.

5

CRISIS

JUST how important Jennifer was in Cary's universe was made clear to me one afternoon.

I walked into the office after doing an interview and the Laufer receptionist told me there had been an emergency phone call from Cary. I thought the worst because of the recent 'death drill' he had put me through. He must be seriously ill, I feared.

Since it was the middle of the week I dialed the Beverly Hills number, but there was no answer, which was very odd. Usually Bill Weaver or Willie would answer if Cary wasn't there (which was rare in itself).

I called the Malibu number; there was an answer after the first ring. 'Hello! Hello!' I heard. I didn't recognize the voice.

'Who is this?' the voice demanded.

'It's Maureen Donaldson calling for Mr. Grant,' I said.

'Oh, Maureen! Thank God you've called.'

'*Cary*??' I said. He sounded so depressed and desolate. 'What's the matter?'

'There's nothing you can do. There's nothing I can do.'

The agony in his voice was startling; he didn't remotely sound like the smooth, always-in-control man I thought I had come to know the past few weeks. The man on this phone sounded positively suicidal.

'What is it?' I said, bracing for the worst.

'I'm not going to stick around here anymore to get kicked in the teeth like this. I'm going to take care of me. I will not take crumbs from her table like this. I'll move to Switzerland.'

God, his voice was so cold and bitter. I assumed he was

talking about Dyan. She obviously had committed some transgression concerning Jennifer.

'What did Dyan do?' I asked.

'*Dyan?*' he said, annoyance rising instantly in his voice. 'I'm not talking about Jennifer's mother. It's *Jennifer*. I'm going to protect myself. She won't have a father at all. Let's see how she likes that. I can tell you it's no picnic, that's for sure.'

What had caused this breach? At this point in our relationship, I couldn't imagine him even listening to someone *else* speak disparagingly of his child, much less speaking so harshly about her himself.

'I gave up a career to help raise this child,' he went on, 'but I was warned that a child becomes a pawn, and it sure does.'

'Cary?'

'What? What is it?' he said, distracted.

'I want you to do something for me,' I said, trying to sound as calm as I could.

'And what's that?'

'I want you to stop talking and just take a few breaths — long, deep breaths.

'It's not my breathing that's impaired, dear girl,' he said sarcastically. 'It's my relationship with my child.'

'I know that, and that's why I want you to calm down and just take a few breaths. You're saying things I know you don't mean. I don't know you well, but I do know you love Jennifer. I want you to stop and think what you're saying, okay?'

'Well ... okay,' he said, suspiciously, and began to return to earth. 'I'm just so upset....'

'Cary, I hate hearing you sound like this. Would you like some company? I don't know if I can help....'

'Do you think you could get away?' he asked, brightening and starting to sound a bit like himself again. 'I'd like you to come. Is there any chance you could?'

'I don't see why not; all my deadlines have been met,' I said. As long as I turned in my articles on time, I was given quite a bit of leeway at Laufer. So even though it was three in the afternoon, I could leave right away.

'Oh, good,' he said, sounding relieved. 'How long will it take you to get here?'

'About an hour. In the meantime, why don't you have a glass of wine? It sounds like you could use one.'

I knew he rarely had a drink before six, but it was definitely time for an exception.

'Is Willie or Bill there?'

'No, they both have the day off.'

'Then just hold tight, and I'll be there, okay?'

I actually got there in forty-five minutes, pushing hard to get through the traffic. Once I arrived and had a drink myself, Cary began to tell me just what had happened to make him so upset.

He had gone down to the Malibu house to find some paperwork he'd left there from the previous weekend and he decided to hang around to see Jennifer come home from school He went out to the bus stop, and when he noticed how chilly it was, he went back inside and got a sweater.

When Jennifer got off the bus, she was wearing only a simple dress; she didn't have her own jacket or sweater. So as the other kids poured off the buy, Cary went up to her to offer his sweater.

'No,' she said. And then she took off with one of Dyan's servants.

'There was no thank you or even a hug good-bye. *Nothing*,' he said, the desolation still piercing right through him. 'Why did she do that? I'm not such a bad guy, you know. She *knows* better.'

'No, she doesn't, Cary,' I said. I knew I was risking his wrath by disagreeing with him about Jennifer, but I had to tell him what I thought.

'Oh, yes, she does,' he snapped back. 'I don't know what my former wife may be teaching her, but I have been teaching her proper manners and respect, you know.'

'No, no, that's not my point, Cary. Listen, don't you remember when you were her age? She's seven, just a child. At that time, I was always wanting to show my parents and even my brother that I didn't need anybody else's help — especially in front of my friends. Remember how proud we'd get when someone thought we were even a half-year older or an inch or two taller than we were? We were in such a hurry to grow up....'

He looked at me quizzically at first, his mind chewing the idea over and over. I could see he wanted to make certain I wasn't just trying to make him feel better.

After what seemed like many minutes — it was just a few seconds, actually — his whole face seemed to light up.

'Of course, you're right, Maureen. Of *course!*' Then he grabbed me and pulled me closer to him on the couch and kissed me long and hard.

'You know, you *are* a dear, dear girl,' he said once again. For him it was the ultimate compliment. 'I *know* you're right. What a silly, silly old fool I was.'

'No,' I said. 'You care very deeply for Jennifer. But you must never forget she's just a seven-year-old girl, a *child*, Cary.'

'Oh, I know,' he said. 'But she's the girl I'm in love with obviously, and it's difficult sometimes.'

I tried not to pull away from him, but I began to. I felt pulled in two directions. On the one hand I was 'a dear, dear girl.' On the other, Jennifer was 'obviously' the only girl who mattered in his life. I told myself it was still too early in the relationship to rush to judgment about how he really felt about me. I had to believe that once he got to know me more and more, he would love me. I would be just as important in a different way soon.

Besides, his love for Jennifer was something I didn't want to compete with in any way, shape or form. She was too sensitive and too beautiful a child for me to feel any resentment. She was completely unaware of the effect she had on her father. I couldn't blame *her* for *his* insecurity.

But the incident with the sweater was just the tip of the iceberg as far as Cary's feelings toward Jennifer were concerned. In the coming months and years, there would be more crises revolving around her and the imagined slights Cary held in his heart. There would always be great, great lows followed by great, great highs.

That night we made a simple little dinner for ourselves and got tipsy on the bottle of wine we had begun earlier in the day. Later we consumed another bottle. And initially the alcohol had two effects: it loosened his tongue, and for a while I saw him become downright silly for the first time.

We walked along the beach in our bare feet and he started flirting with the idea of buying a house in Malibu. He was only renting the house he was living in now. So we walked hand in hand past the houses in the area, judging each on its merits.

'Now that one looks cozy,' he said, pointing to a two-story brick affair.

'No, too modern,' I said.

Then he spotted a New England-style cottage. 'How about that one?' he said.

'That's more like it!' I said.

'Then let's go in,' he said, starting to pull me in the direction of the house, 'and we'll ask for dessert.'

I resisted, but he kept pulling me along.

'C'mon, darling,' he said. 'We'll just stay a minute. We'll eat and run.'

'What's this?' I said. 'Malibu roulette, Cary Grant style?'

'Oooh, I like the sound of that. Now you've done it. We really must invite ourselves in, Maureen.'

We went right up to the gate but, fortunately, he did not open it.

But as the wine began to wear off, so did his good spirits.

It started innocently enough.

'Tell me more about Muswell Hill and Jim and Elsie.'

'Oh, Cary,' I protested, 'You don't want to hear that stuff anymore. My life's been so boring, especially when you compare it to yours. I mean ... my God ... you know what I mean!'

'Well, I don't know about that,' he said. 'None of my wives ever had her wedding portrait taken in a maternity ward!'

'It seemed like a good idea at the time,' I laughed.

'I think you are a true bohemian, Maureen. You really are. But you're a barefoot bohemian. No sandals for you.'

'The fifties and sixties are gone, Cary. I don't think my parents raised a beatnik or a flower child. I'm just a normal person.'

'A normal person?' He rolled the words around on his tongue as if he were tasting a new dish or something.

'Yeah,' I said, kicking up some sand as we walked.

'Sounds easier than it is.'

'What do you mean?'

'No one's normal, Maureen. There's no such thing.'

'Oh yes, there is,' I insisted. 'You're pretty normal.'

'Hah!' he said. 'That's the last thing I've been accused of.'

'There you go again, caring what the neighbors think. And you could buy the whole neighborhood!'

'You have to, if you're in the business I'm in. It's part of it.'

'Okay, so who are you? I mean, what's so bad that if people found out, it would be such a frightful disaster?'

'Okay,' he said. 'Tell me what you *think* you know about me.'

He smoothed out a place in the sand and indicated I should sit down beside him.

'Well, that's a big order, isn't it?' I said, taking a deep breath. 'Now, let's see ...'

Since our dinner at the Discovery Inn, of course, I had gone through his clip file at Laufer, filled with news clippings and past studio biographies. With small variations, the story that emerged was consistent.

So I regurgitated what I had read.

He was born Archibald Alexander Leach in Bristol in 1904. Five years before, his mother, Elsie, had given birth to his older brother, John, but about eight months after he was born, he died of tubercular meningitis. He had always been sickly from birth. Elsie, as a result, became over-protective of Cary when he came along. His father, Elias, was a tailor's presser who did his best to combat Elsie's possessiveness with the child. But then she developed mental problems and was institutionalized when Cary was just a boy of ten. After that Cary lived with his father and grandmother, but he felt lost and abandoned.

He used to haunt the local vaudeville palaces in Bristol. He eventually joined a boys' acrobatic troupe and sailed with them for an American tour when he was sixteen. After the tour he stayed in New York and worked as everything from a stilt-walker to an actor. On the stage he began carving out a niche for himself as a young, handsome British male ingenue. He modeled himself after Noël Coward and began to lose his original accent, adopting the fancier one that became world famous.

He got his first name from a character he'd portrayed in a play and his last from a phone book in an executive's office after he signed a contract with Paramount Studios in 1931. His distinctive accent and dark good looks soon helped him emerge as a leading man. From *This Is the Night* in 1932 to *Walk, Don't Run* in 1966, he made a total of seventy-two films.

Cary was not only one of the most popular stars but also one of the smartest. After Paramount, he was one of the first to free-lance among the studios, picking the best roles, without being bound to one studio. Along with his lawyer, Stanley Fox, he later made deals with the studios to take a lesser salary up front in exchange for a portion of the picture's box-office profits. Still later, he and Fox made deals by which ownership of his films reverted to him after their first seven years in release.

His personal life was not as charmed. His first marriage to a blonde beauty named Virginia Cherrill, who had been one of Charlie Chaplin's leading ladies, lasted last than a year. His second wife was Woolworth heiress Barbara Hutton. The papers dubbed the union 'Cash and Cary.' It lasted three years. His third marriage, to a young actress named Betsy Drake, was his happiest and longest-lived (thirteen years). But it was his short marriage to Dyan Cannon that gave him his first child, at the age of sixty-two.

When Dyan divorced him in 1968, allegations that he had used LSD surfaced at the trial. This seemed to be the most damaging information that had ever surfaced in the press about him, with the possible exception of rumors about his relationship with Randolph Scott, an actor with whom he lived before and after his first marriage. He was also believed to have kept the first dollar he had ever earned.

'How's that?' I asked, after my recital.

'You did your homework, didn't you?' he said. I nodded my head.

'Now would you like to hear the *truth*?' he said.

Of course I couldn't resist the challenge, but he said it more in sadness than in defiance. After the emotional fireworks earlier in the day, I didn't know how wise it would be for me to urge him to push any more psychological levers.

'Cary,' I said gently. 'I'm tired and I know you're tired. I should be getting back to my apartment. It's a long drive back, you know?'

'Why? Don't you want to hear the truth? Journalists *love* to hear the truth, don't they?'

His voice was suddenly angry.

'Let's start with how my brother supposedly died. It was quite simple, actually. He didn't die from meningitis. He died from gangrene. My mother had the baby over her shoulder and she accidently closed the door on his thumb. He developed gangrene and died. And she blamed herself for the rest of her life. She was not a happy woman. I was not a happy child because my mother tried to smother me with care. She was so scared something would happen to me.

'I was never out of her sight. I was in baby dresses and curls and all that stuff when all the other boys were already out playing. She and my father fought about me constantly. He wanted her to let go. She couldn't. I never spent a happy moment with them under the same roof. And that's a *fact*. That's the *truth*.'

'Cary, don't,' I said, pleading for him to stop. He had

been digging a hole in the sand. The more furiously he had scooped out the sand, the faster he had talked.

'So, Maureen, I know a thing or two about men and women. And especially how women like to control you and, if they can't have that control, what will happen.'

I wanted to cup my hands over my ears. I could feel the hostility toward his mother. It was frightening. The somewhat colorful, hermetically sealed past I had spent hours reading about was being peeled away in a few minutes. It was almost as if Cary were performing some kind of psychological striptease, but for whom? I was the audience, but I felt as if he were performing for so many others.

There was now a sizable hole in the sand where he had been digging. The tide was starting to come in, and I began pushing the sand back in the hole.

Without a word Cary joined me. By the time we had filled the hole, the water was starting to edge around it.

It got up and signaled for Cary to join me.

We started to walk away, when I turned around and saw the water washing over the hole Cary had dug.

'Look,' I said, taking his hand in mine. 'All gone.'

He tried to smile.

I wanted Cary Grant, but I had discovered someone else that night. His name was Archie Leach.

6

SINNERS IN THE SUN

THE next day Cary called me at the office. There was absolutely no mention of the incident with Jennifer or what he had told me at the beach.

When I started to say, 'I hope you know, Cary, I'm not like the other women in your life,' he interrupted me.

'Well, of course you're not. I know that, dear girl.'

If he remembered what he had said the night before, he certainly was not going to acknowledge it now. It had been erased. Permanently.

'You're a unique person,' he continued. 'That's why I would like you to join me and Jennifer down in Palm Springs this weekend. Charlie Rich, my very good friend from the Dunes Hotel, has a home down there and we've been invited. Jennifer and I think it would be a lovely idea if you came down too.'

'Sounds fabulous,' I said.

'But there's only one problem,' he said. 'We'd like to leave early Friday afternoon to beat the traffic. Do you think you could get away?'

'I think I can arrange that.'

'Good stuff! Well, let's plan to leave from Malibu about two o'clock. Are you sure you can manage it?'

I was certain I could do that. What I wasn't certain about was what Cary wanted from me, considering what he had said on the beach about women. Was I going to be just his friend? Or Jennifer's buddy? Or would our relationship deepen into something more? I had to find out just where this relationship was going.

The three of us took off at the appointed time, along with another of Jennifer's young friends, Hillary. We played The Vicar's Horse on the way down, but for Cary's sake, it was a much more sanitized version than the one Jennifer and I would play with Willie.

When we finally pulled up to Charlie Rich's place in Palm Springs for our three days of fun-and-sun, I could not believe the opulence of his estate. This place made Cary's look like a shack. Electric gates opened and we parked right behind them on the grounds. A fully uniformed butler was waiting for us in a golf cart for a long drive to the main house. It was a stunning Spanish mansion, surrounded by a rose garden, a putting green, a fish pond and a swimming pool with a pool house. Huge palm trees shaded the estate.

I stayed in the main house with Charlie and his lady, Marjorie, while Cary and the girls had the pool house to themselves. The pool house was completely different from the main house — it was a Grecian structure embroidered with Grecian statues. The contrast would have resulted in cultural clash anywhere else, but in Palm Springs this mixture of Grecian and Spanish motifs somehow looked completely natural.

For all the size of the estate, Charlie and Marjorie were among the most unpretentious people I had ever met. He was a short, bald man a little younger than Cary. He had been best man at Cary's wedding to Dyan in Las Vegas in 1965. Marjorie was a lovely, earthy lady. They encouraged Cary and the rest of us to treat the place as our own and they meant it. The butler and some maids provided for our every need. I couldn't have asked for a more idyllic location to spend some quiet time with Cary and that's just what I got.

During the afternoon we'd play miniature golf and do some swimming. At night Cary and Charlie would teach me backgammon, which I loved.

The girls stayed largely to themselves, often going horseback riding, which was strictly supervised. I had never seen Cary so relaxed and happy.

Or so attractive. He lounged around the pool, and it was the first time I had seen him without his shirt on.

Some men at that age have stooped or rounded shoulders, but not Cary. He had a massive chest, with a small thatch of silver hair, and beautiful strong shoulders. And his legs were thin and muscular. He even had a firm stomach.

He truly did not look his age. I couldn't help being attracted to him and he caught me giving him the eye as we sunned ourselves.

'You have a great body,' I said, meaning every word.

'You do too,' he said, returning the compliment.

I asked him what he did to keep in shape and he said, 'Nothing.' He liked to swim occasionally, but that was it for any so-called exercise program. If he ever started to develop a pot belly, he just cut back on eating, but he said it was rare he had to do that.

'Then it's just a gift from God,' I concluded.

He roared. It was good to hear him laugh because in my mind I could still hear echoes of that night on the beach.

On our second afternoon at the estate, Cary and I were lying around the pool alone again. Jennifer and Hillary were out horseback riding, while Charlie and Marjorie had gone in the main house to take a nap before dinner, which was served promptly and formally at seven.

Cary reached over and patted me on the arm and said he was going inside the pool house to read for a bit.

'If you get bored out here,' he said, trying to sound casual, 'why don't you come in for a visit?'

The directness yet the elegance of the move impressed me. I could not be imagining this. It was five o'clock at a plush estate in Palm Springs and Cary Grant was asking Maureen Payne to join him in his room. If only they could see me in Muswell Hill now, I thought.

So I waited about twenty minutes and drank a glass of wine to calm down a little. I had to admire the man's class. He had left it all up to me. If I entered his room, we both knew it would be my decision.

He wanted me there and I wanted to be there so I finally got up and walked over to the pool house. The sun was already beginning to set.

I knocked on the door of his bedroom and he said, 'Come in.'

I walked in and he was lying on the bed, reading some newspapers. He had his black glasses on; he took them off and patted the bed with them.

'Why don't you join me?'

An elegant gray paisley robe covered most of him, but I could see part of his chest. God, he was attractive.

I walked over and sat on the bed. He reached over and kissed me gently. Then he put his arms around me, and the tenderness with which he surrounded me excited and moved me.

Then it was my turn to surprise him. I was right on the verge of crying. Perhaps it was the anticipation of the moment, mixed in with the wine. I began to feel incredibly foolish, yet my body was still on the verge of exploding.

'Thank you,' he said as he saw my eyes welling up. 'You've paid me the most wonderful compliment, Maureen. I shall never, ever forget it.'

I felt too embarrassed to say anything. I looked deeply into his eyes. He kissed me again.

Then he drew me even closer and began to caress my breasts. The moment was electrifying. I had never felt anything like it before, and this certainly was not my first experience with a man.

The intensity of what I was feeling frightened me. It was as if I were going to lose all my senses. His hands began to explore the rest of my body, and I completely surrendered myself to him, the moment, the passion, everything.

Then our bodies joined together and I could not believe the joy I felt. Cary was not the most greatly endowed man I had ever made love with, but that afternoon he was undoubtedly the most tender and the most passionate.

As we made love, I remember studying his dark eyebrows, his eyelashes, his perfectly shaped nose, his thick, white hair, his long fingers. There was no part of his body I didn't find fascinating and perfect.

Then this man who had already showed me so many surprises showed me yet another.

He laughed when he came.

It was a light, gentle laugh, almost like a whisper.

Later I had to ask about it. I was terrified of offending him, yet no one I had ever been with had done such a thing at such a moment.

But he didn't seem embarrassed or annoyed in the slightest.

'Well,' he said, cupping my face in his hands, 'why wouldn't I laugh? After all, it's a happy moment, isn't it?'

Virtually every time we made love after that, I would hear his soft little laugh at that moment.

And I learned to love it, just as I learned how to love many more things about this extraordinary man.

But I was only beginning to learn what he was really like and who he really was.

7

NIGHT AND DAY

CARY Grant yielded even more surprises in the privacy of his own bedroom as the weeks passed by.

Some were innocuous, like his preference for wearing ladies' stretch nylon briefs. One night up at Beverly Grove as we prepared to go to sleep, he very casually removed his pants and showed me the briefs he was wearing underneath.

'I like them because they're cooler than men's underwear and they're so much easier to wash,' he explained. 'I don't want to make a big thing about this, but I thought you should know, since you might have read somewhere that I prefer to wear women's panties.'

I wasn't disturbed in the least, because they looked just like men's swimming trunks; they were hardly lacy or frilly. He was clearly wearing them for utilitarian reasons, not for anything remotely kinky.

What did disturb me was the growing realization that every time we made love, whether it was day or night, it was always in the shadows. If we were at the beach or up at Beverly Grove, he always dimmed the lights down quite low before making love. In my insecurity, I thought Cary might be ashamed of me. In my mind I started to compare myself to Dyan Cannon and women he had dated after their divorce. As if Dyan weren't intimidating enough, there was Raquel Welch and a stunning blonde Italian actress. But the most serious alliance he had made since Dyan had been with a delicate French beauty, Clothilde Feldman, the widow of a powerful Hollywood producer. When she grew too dependent — by his terms — the relationship unraveled.

With these 'ghosts' in my mind, I reached over one night at the beach as Cary began to turn down the lights.

'I wish I were beautiful enough so you could leave the lights on,' I whispered.

'Oh, Maureen,' he said, both startled and touched. 'You mustn't think that. It's not you. It's me. It's this chicken skin. You don't want to see that while we're making love. But in the dark you can imagine I'm one of those young men your age.'

Now it was my turn to be startled. The last thing I wanted to imagine while I was in bed with Cary Grant was someone else.

'What on earth are you talking about?' I said. 'You're in great shape — and I don't mean just for your age, either. And I would like you to know that the *only* man I'm thinking about is you.'

'But Maureen,' he protested, 'that's impossible. You can't be just with me. After all, you're a young girl and you're a very sexual creature. I know I'm not enough for you.'

This was his way of acknowledging what we both knew — we were making love on the average of once or twice a week.

My heart began to pound uncontrollably. I wished I had never said a word about the lights when the subject could turn so dark, so quickly.

'Cary,' I said quietly, 'I think you'll agree with me that where most things are concerned — and sex is certainly one of those things — it's not a matter of quantity but quality. I'm talking about passion and love. You're talking about arithmetic.'

'Well,' he said gently, 'I hope you'll always feel that way.'

I was glad to see the book close on the subject that evening, but it would be opened and reopened many more times. His insecurity was mixed with a kind of suspicion that alternately touched me and frightened me. I wanted to envelop him in my arms where he would remain young forever, but that was impossible — Cary usually did not like being touched, much less held for any length of time. I was completely the opposite and, as our relationship grew, my need for this kind of physical reassurance also grew. If I left my hand on his arm for more than a few seconds, he would begin to fidget and fuss. If I started running my hands through his hair while we were watching TV, he'd start to pull away instinctively. In short, I had to face quickly the fact there were not going to be many nights when I fell asleep in his arms.

His sleeping habits were equally troubling. He suffered from insomnia, and always took one Seconal sleeping pill before he went to bed, which was usually at nine or ten at night. Then he slept until two or three in the morning, when he would pop up, wide awake. He'd read for a half-hour or so, then fall back to sleep until six or seven in the morning.

I hadn't been seeing Cary long when one evening he fell asleep on the bed without taking his Seconal. Around midnight he awoke with a start. I put down the magazine I was reading and reached over to stroke his cheek.

'Stop it! Stop it!' he shouted. He was truly terrified. I don't think he had the slightest idea where he was. His eyes looked right through me.

'Cary, it's Maureen,' I said. 'You fell asleep while you were watching TV, don't you remember?'

He looked to the right and then to the left. Then he looked me over carefully, suspiciously.

'*Who are you?*' he demanded. The words were both angry and fearful.

'Cary, it's Maureen, and you're in your own home and your own bedroom. Please stop — you're scaring me!'

His eyes changed from hostile and glassy to their usual calm and gentle appearance as he finally realized he was home and safe. But that haunted look in his eyes, of a lost little boy, would never leave my memory.

There was no denying the strong physical attraction I felt for Cary, but there was something much more powerful keeping me attached to him as the days with him became weeks and the weeks turned into months. I had seen it one night on the beach and now I had seen it when he woke up frightened in his own bed. There was an aching force — some secret well of longing and hurt — that touched me to my very core. I wanted to dig as deep inside Cary as I possibly could so I could calm his troubled waters. But every time I started to get close, he'd push me away — sometimes gently, sometimes not so gently, but always demonstrating to me how much more digging I had to do in order to reach the essence of this man.

I first began to feel Cary distancing himself from me when he started repeating the jokes he'd made when I first met him about how dating him would 'ruin my reputation.' He was also becoming too insistent about his being 'too old for a girl like you.'

I tried, just as lightly and, I hoped, just as effortlessly, to slough off these notions of his. But he held onto them, and wouldn't let go. I realized how firmly he clasped them one night at the beach after Jennifer had gone back to Dyan's home and Willie had gone back to Beverly Grove. We took a walk along the beach, barefoot in the dark.

I found the combination of the sea and Cary extremely romantic and told him so. 'It's lovely, isn't it?' he agreed. I couldn't help noticing that every so often Cary would reach down and pick up a small, smooth stone or pebble. By the time we got back to his house, he had a rather large handful of them.

'And what are you going to do with those?' I asked as he closed the sliding doors behind him.

'We're going to do something romantic,' he said with a mischievous smile on his lips. 'We're going to get stoned.'

I laughed because I knew he couldn't possibly mean smoke some marijuana — he hated the mere idea of smoke and he had already once rejected my suggestion we smoke some grass one afternoon as a prelude to making love.

He sat down on the floor in the living room and patted the carpet next to him. When I sat down, he began to take off my sweater and then my top. Then he started to massage my neck and shoulders, gently but firmly. Next I felt one of his fingers working its way down my back.

Then I felt something cool and foreign slip down my back. It happened again. And again, but with increasing frequency. Finally I realized it was those smooth little stones Cary had collected on the beach. Now they were sliding down my back and the effect was unbelievable.

I began to moan softly when Cary turned me around to face him. With a fire blazing in the fireplace behind him, his face was framed in a soft romantic glow. Now he started to slip the stones down my neck and between my breasts. I closed my eyes and felt as if I were floating. The only thing keeping me on earth was Cary's touch.

I could not believe how something as inanimate as a stone could make me feel so alive. 'Your turn,' I said as I helped Cary off with his sweater. I gathered up some of the pebbles and started them on a journey down Cary's back.

'That's a good girl,' he whispered, filled with the moment as much as I was.

After a few minutes he took the stones from my hands and began to let them slide all over me again. As I removed the rest of my clothes, I knew there was no part of my body those precious little stones wouldn't explore.

Later in the evening, as I was still lost in my amazement over the incredibly sensual effect this had on me, I reached over to touch Cary's hand, but he pulled it away sharply. I looked over and didn't say a word but my expression betrayed my confusion.

Cary's face was suddenly harsh and cold. 'Is it ever enough?' he said.

'What do you mean, darling?' I said, not yet catching on.

'I mean that you should give some very serious thought, my girl, as to whether you're a nymphomaniac.'

'Cary!' I laughed. 'I do hope you mean that as a compliment.'

'Well,' he said, backing off somewhat, 'you really are insatiable, Maureen.'

'Well,' I said, my senses coming on the alert and trying to make light of the moment, 'you can't blame a girl for trying, now can you?'

'Oh yes, you can,' he said, as indignance took command of his voice, 'if it's going to give a man a heart attack.'

'Now, really!' I said, hurt and annoyed. 'I will never apologize to you or anyone else, for that matter, for liking and loving sex. It's perfectly natural. It's perfectly healthy. And by the way, it's something no one can ever get enough of. You must know that, Cary. I mean, after all, you're ... you're Cary Grant!'

'That I am,' he said, 'so I want you to listen to the voice of experience. You must have heard of the Chinese proverb "You take my cum, you take my strong." It means you have only a certain amount of strength and every time you make love, you lose some of that strength. And if you give too much of it away, you give your life away.'

I was absolutely bewildered. I had never heard anything so ridiculous in my life — and I had heard a lot of ridiculous things after my years in Hollywood. Surely the dashing romantic icon that Cary Grant had come to represent for so many decades on the screen couldn't believe such a pile of rubbish.

I thought the best tactic would be to make light of the idea, but it only served to inflame him.

'That's right,' I said. 'And if you play with yourself, you'll go blind!'

'I'm not joking with you,' he said, completely straight-faced. 'There is a medical basis to that proverb, and if you had any sense you'd realize that. And if you had any regard for me, you would listen to me rather than urge me on to have a heart attack!'

I thought the room was going to explode in a million pieces, and I along with it. I had seen, in Palm Springs and at Malibu earlier this evening, the most exquisite side of Cary. Now I was seeing another, much darker, side. Ugly snakes were springing forth from his mouth and I had to stop him — and them.

'Okay, Cary,' I said, trying to sound composed. 'I believe you believe that. We've had a beautiful night and I think we should drop this, don't you?'

He grumbled a bit and rolled over on his back. But on other nights this concern raised its head again and again, just as the 'jokes' about his ruining my reputation and my being better off with younger men kept resurfacing regularly. This obsession about his heart got to be so insistent I felt compelled to make my own joke about it the second he even broached the subject. I'd put my hand to my lips and yell:

'Dr. DeBakey! Calling Dr. DeBakey!'

This trick worked. It almost always got a smile out of Cary because it succeeded in making him feel so foolish. The minute I mentioned the cardiovascular pioneer and superstar surgeon, Cary would retire any mention of his heart for the day. And I was pleased, not because I didn't have any concern for his health, but because I knew just how ridiculous this obsession was. He had regular check-ups and was in excellent health.

But now I had some questions and concerns of my own. Sexually, there was no doubt we were a combustible combination. But emotionally, I had my doubts, especially because of that question which kept rolling around in the recesses of my mind: 'Is it ever enough?'

I was falling in love with the man but he seemed to be doing his damnedest to prevent that — and yet he needed love more than anyone I had ever encountered. 'He drew women to him by making them feel he needed them,' film critic Pauline Kael once wrote about Cary's on-screen identity, 'yet the last thing he'd do would be to come right out and say it.' It was just as true offscreen.

It was in this confused, insecure state that I learned something else that only increased my confusion and insecurity: I knew Cary had been seeing other women when we began dating — one was a young tour guide from Disneyland, and another was a TWA executive whom Cary saw when he visited New York. I'd hoped they would drop out of his life as our relationship deepened and ripened. Within a matter of months that's precisely what happened. But there was one lady who didn't drop out of the picture in 1973 and for the first half of 1974.

She was Victoria 'Vicki' Morgan, an aspiring actress Cary had met in the office of a mutual friend, director Mervyn LeRoy. They had known each other for about a year when I entered Cary's life. They met on the average of once a week. But Vicki was still in love with and the mistress of Alfred Bloomingdale. (She was bludgeoned to death ten years later, after Bloomingdale's death and her unsuccessful suit for 'palimony'.)

Her relationship with Cary was strictly sexual; she hoped he would help her along in her career. I learned all this when 'friends' called me to tell me about my 'competition'. But how serious could her relationship be with Cary when Bloomingdale was still in her life?

Of course I wanted to ask Cary about her, but we were still just months into our own relationship and I suspected if I made an issue of his connection to Vicki, he would only hold onto her more strongly. Yet once I knew of her presence in Cary's life, I couldn't get her out of my mind. The thought of her sharing Cary's bed gnawed and gnawed at me. I felt myself starting to hold back with Cary in our private moments together when what I really wanted to do was give over to him everything I had inside me.

I would have to wait for the relationship with Vicki to burn itself out. But I was used to waiting to get what I wanted.

8

TALK OF THE TOWN

BY December 1973 word had begun to leak within the entertainment industry about our burgeoning relationship, and Cary began to prepare me for what he called 'The Onslaught.'

He meant the onslaught of the press that would erupt once it had been confirmed we were dating. Thus far we had been very discreet, meeting only at his homes in Malibu or Beverly Hills, with an occasional trip down to Palm Springs behind the closed gates of Charlie Rich's estate.

When we started to go out to restaurants, we both knew our relationship would soon find its way into print. Cary was, of course, instantly recognizable and, as for me, my connection to Rona's magazines didn't make me exactly inconspicuous either.

'I don't mind if you don't mind,' I told Cary over dinner one evening. It was a small Italian restaurant along the Pacific Coast Highway.

'But you will. You'll see,' he said with matter-of-fact certainty in his voice. 'I'll ruin your reputation.' That was quickly becoming his favorite expression — one I dreaded hearing.

'Cary, I'm honored to be seen with you, as would any woman,' I said. 'What can the press do with the mere fact that we're seeing each other?'

'You should know that better than I!' he replied. 'After all, you work for an entertainment magazine. You'll see, Maureen, you will not like it one little bit.'

Then, unexpectedly, I got a small preview of what he was talking about. Our dinners arrived. I had ordered pasta and began to twirl it into my mouth with gusto. Suddenly, I could feel eyes following my every move. I glanced out of the corner of my eye and spotted at least two people at other tables taking a good, long look at me as I awkwardly tried to force some unwieldy spaghetti from my spoon and fork into my mouth. Since I was with Cary, they obviously wanted to see what I looked like.

I felt self-conscious and embarrassed. I cursed myself for ordering pasta. Why couldn't I have ordered something simple like salad, which I could spear daintily like a lady as I passed inspection?

Cary caught sight of my predicament but fortunately resisted the temptation to say, 'I told you so.' Going out with Cary Grant put one under a very powerful microscope. I would find out just how powerful in a matter of days. But for now I had to chew over very carefully what Cary had told me.

The reaction of some of my friends to my dating Cary was almost equally divided. Friends from my rock-and-roll days thought I had rocks in my head — what in the world was I doing with someone that old? True, it was Cary Grant, but he was old enough to be my grandfather. Still, if I was happy — and I certainly sounded happy to them — then it was all right with them. Friends from publishing and the movie end of the business were genuinely thrilled for me and perhaps even a little bit jealous. There was no denying that, at whatever age, Cary Grant was a real catch. And of course my closest friends thought it was wonderful and a bit of a giggle.

But the reaction that caused me the most concern was the one I could only hear, not see, because my parents were still thousands of miles away in England. How do you explain to your father that you are seriously involved with a man who happens to be thirteen years *older* than he is?

Luckily, my father couldn't have been more understanding and supportive. When I called, he was the first to answer the phone so he was the first I told the news to, after exchanging the usual how-are-yous and catching up.

'Daddy, I think I love him. He's a very complicated probably will be reading about, and I wanted to tell you first.'

'And what's that, darling?' he asked.

'Well, believe it or not, I'm dating Cary Grant.'

'The film star?'

'Yes,' I said.

'The one who was married to Betty Hutton?'

'No, Daddy.' I laughed. 'The one who was married to *Barbara Hutton*, the Woolworth heiress.'

'Yes, yes,' he said. 'That's the one.'

There was a long silence.

'Daddy, I think I love him. He's a very complicated man and he scares me sometimes, but I really do love him.'

'Well, Maureen,' he said finally, 'you know what I've always said — if it makes you happy, then that's my happiness.'

I could tell he meant it, but I also could tell how shocked he was, from how quickly he turned the phone over to my mother.

'If you're pulling your father's leg, I'll give you a good spanking the next time we come face to face with you,' my mother said, having overheard Daddy's end of the conversation.

'It's no joke, Mummy,' I shouted into the phone. Then I told her how I met him and how I had fallen in love with him so quickly. I also mentioned Jennifer and how this seven-year-old girl had the ability to touch my heart just like her father.

I could tell my mother was thrilled for me. She could not hide the pride in her voice, just as my father couldn't disguise his concern.

When we started to wrap up the conversation, I got my father back on the phone and told him:

'Now, Daddy, Cary and I are counting on you for one thing.'

'What's that, Maureen?'

'You know how aggressive some reporters can be,

especially the ones in London. If anyone for any reason calls you and begins asking you questions about Cary and me, you are to say "No comment" and ring off. Got that?'

'Understood,' he said.

'Those orders come straight from Cary,' I added.

'Good as done. Tell him not to worry. And I don't want you to worry either, dear.'

Cary's warning did not come a moment too soon. On December 23 the first mention in print of our relationship broke in Army Archerd's column in the show business trade paper *Variety*:

'The audience at the Mayfair Music Hall in Santa Monica flipped when one of the hecklers was — Cary Grant. He promised to show up one night and perform "Albert and the Lion" onstage — or at the bar. Grant was accompanied by Maureen Donaldson.'

Obviously someone in the Mayfair management or its publicity office had given our names to Army. It was a good plug for the tiny jewel box of a theater. We had gone to the Mayfair over the Christmas holidays and Cary was totally captivated by the tiny theater, which reminded him so much of his days in vaudeville.

Given Cary's wariness where the press was concerned, I expected some kind of explosion when this item found its way into print. But Cary shrugged it off.

'I *will* do "Albert and the Lion" for them one day,' he announced happily. 'No one does that routine better than Archie Leach from Bristol!'

But his reaction was much less jovial when other reporters picked up the item and tried to expand on it, delving into who I was and my former occupation as a nanny. In short order the *Chicago Tribune*, the San Francisco *Chronicle* and the New York *Daily News* ran items about Cary and me in their gossip columns.

But it was the first mention of our relationship in the English newspapers that caused an almost volcanic eruption from Cary. On Janaury 28, 1974, the London *Daily Mail* headlined: 'The Latest Girl (After Jennifer) in Cary's Life!' It was a fairly innocuous story, mentioning my visits

Cary was born in the upstairs front bedroom of this modest home at 15 Hughenden Road in Bristol, on January 18, 1904.
(Maureen Donaldson)

Bottom: I was born in the upstairs front bedroom (center) of my parents' modest home at 3 Fireman's Cottages in Muswell Hill, London, on September 27, 1946.
(Courtesy of Margaret Avery)

Cary's mother, Elsie, the most important woman in his life. She 'left' him when he was ten, when she was committed by Cary's father to a local mental institution, and Cary never lost his sense of abandonment.
(Pictorial Parade)

Bottom: This is Fishponds today, the sanitarium to which Cary's mother was committed in the Spring of 1914. When she was released in 1934, the first thing Cary remembered was how 'perfectly normal' she seemed. He also told me that when he bent down to kiss his mother, whom he had not seen for so long, 'she pushed me away'.
(Maureen Donaldson)

Top: It was 1964, the Beatles were at the top of the charts, and my friend, Val Sumpter (third from right), and I were right in the middle of it all – literally.
(Rex Features/RDR)

Cary with Deborah Kerr in *An Affair to Remember.* After I met Cary at a film festival in Sun Valley, Idaho, I went back to my room, turned on the television, and found a scene from this movie playing.
(Courtesy of 20th- Century-Fox)

Top Left: None but the Lonely Heart (1944) earned Cary a second Academy Award nomination, although he found the movie painful to watch because it reminded him of his own troubled childhood.
(RKO Radio Pictures)

Top right: My photo assistant took this picture of Cary and me at home in Beverly Hills in 1977.
(George Rodriguez)

Bottom left: Cary with Dyan Cannon, his fourth wife and the only woman to give him a child – his beloved daughter, Jennifer. This picture was taken in July 1966, when the three travelled by ship to England to introduce Jennifer to Cary's mother.
(Pictorial Parade)

Bottom right: Cary and me in Sun Valley, Idaho, in August 1973. Cary was sixty-nine years old, and I was twenty-six and an associate editor for Rona Barrett's stable of fan magazines.
(Globe Photos)

Tea on the terrace was not always served on a silver tray Cary loved plastic cups, courtesy of Western Airlines, for everyday use!
(Maureen Donaldson)

Bottom: Cary's time with Jennifer was precious because it usually was so limited – he had her on weekends and one month in the summer. Here we are together in Palm Springs.

Cary refused to have any pets in his own home, but he loved to watch Jennifer with animals. She had a special bond with them.
(Maureen Donaldson)

I took this shot of Cary and his longtime maid, Willie Watson, in his bedroom. Willie loved Cary unconditionally and also became my dear friend.
(Maureen Donaldson)

Top: Jennifer, Willie and me cutting loose in my Beverly Hills apartment, which I kept throughout my years with Cary. Jennifer loved rock music but Cary refused to play it around the house. *(Elsie Payne)*

Cary celebrating his seventy-first birthday in 1975 at the Palm Springs home of his friend Dunes Hotel owner Charlie Rich. I ribbed Cary mercilessly about his wildly-colored jacket. *(Maureen Donaldson)*

to Cary's house in Malibu. The part I loved the best, of course, was about my alleged 'dark good looks [and] a model's figure.' Words like that can swell a girl's head rather quickly.

I hadn't put my purse down before he practically flung the newspaper in my direction.

'I want to know precisely what you had to do with this story,' he demanded.

'And hello to you too,' I said, trying to catch my breath. 'What's this about?' I picked up the newspaper and glanced at the story. A girlfriend had already phoned me from London and read the story to me, as had my parents, so I recognized it instantly.

'You know perfectly well,' Cary snapped. 'I told you I don't want publicity. I told you you wouldn't like it. And I told you to keep your parents' mouths shut!'

I flew into a rage. He could question my integrity, but not my parents'. Because I worked for movie magazines, a certain amount of suspicion about me was only natural. But for him to attack my parents for something I knew they had absolutely no part in infuriated me.

'My parents had nothing to do with this, Cary, and you know it. This all started with Army Archerd's column, and he's your friend. I don't know the man.'

Contempt flooded his eyes. I had seen this look before — the night at the beach and the night he woke up frightened in bed. He was mulling over what I'd just said.

'Then it was Rona,' he stated. 'She thrives on this kind of thing.'

'Oh, Cary, give the woman credit for a little sense! If she were going to do something about us, wouldn't she report it on her own show rather than give it to a reporter in London? In fact, she hasn't asked me once about you. Unlike you, she respects my feelings.'

'You have a point there,' he said as he turned to look me in the face once again. 'Then it must have been you.'

'That makes even less sense. Would I risk what I have here with you for the sake of a few lines in a newspaper? Christ, Cary, if I wanted publicity, I could get it on my own!'

I started gathering up my purse when his hands grabbed mine to stop me.

'Don't Cary,' I said sharply. 'I cannot believe you do not trust me. You obviously have me confused with someone else ... someone' — I spoke rather gleefully as I plunged the verbal knife — 'like Vicki Morgan.'

Cary didn't say a word. He was standing opposite me, cold and impassive.

'*There's* someone who needs publicity,' I rushed on. '*There's* someone who deserves all your trust and love, even if she is sleeping with another man. Even if she is the mistress of another man!'

'Stick to the subject,' he said blankly. 'And I'm afraid you don't know what you're talking about.'

'I'm afraid I know exactly what I'm talking about, Cary. I don't work for a magazine called *Rona Barrett's Gossip* for nothing, now do I?'

'I suppose not,' he said, sounding defeated but also sad.

'Then what do you think this woman wants with you that she's not getting with Alfred Bloomingdale? Could it be your connections in the film industry — the only thing Bloomingdale really doesn't have, at least to the extent you do? *You* think about *that*....'

He reached over to touch my shoulder. 'Calm down, dear,' he said gently. 'I hope you understand I just have to be very careful.'

'Are you ashamed of me?' I said, on the verge of tears.

'Oh God, no,' he said. 'I'm talking about Jennifer. Well, what I'm really talking about is my former wife. If there's publicity in the papers about Jennifer's father dating a woman who's over forty years his junior, Dyan might be able to make something of it with the lawyers the next time we get into a row in court about the child.'

That seemed to make sense, but it didn't lessen the shock and sting of the past few minutes.

'You don't think the fact that you're seeing someone like Victoria Morgan might not be more damaging to your reputation — in or out of a courtroom?' I blurted out.

I didn't mean to bring up her name again, but I wanted to take his line of logic to its illogical conclusion.

'Well, Maureen,' he huffed a bit. 'I am a grown man. No one expects me to lead a completely chaste life.

'I certainly hope not,' I said, easing up on him.

'Darling, I really didn't want to hurt you, but you do not realize to what lengths I must go to protect myself from some of Dyan's maneuvers.' From what I had read in the newspapers since their divorce, it seemed to me that Dyan was the one who needed protection from Cary, rather than vice versa.

'You really must understand that not everyone in the press is like you, Maureen,' he continued. 'Some of them can do devastating things to hurt people. I'm speaking from personal experience here.'

After we both calmed down and had a drink, what followed was a long but fascinating account of his skirmishes with Hedda Hoppe and Louella Parsons, the once reigning queens of gossip in Hollywood from the thirties into the early sixties. Louella had wounded Cary in the forties when he married Barbara Hutton. She reported that the marriage was made not in heaven but 'in the bank.' But it was Hedda, a political and moral conservative, who had really gone for a piece of his hide in 1958. Cary had joined a Hollywood junket to Moscow and told a reporter in London on his way home, 'I don't care what kind of government they have in Russia, I never felt so free in my life.'

Hedda hated Cary's enthusiasm for the Russian people and said if he was so enthralled with the Soviet Union, he had her permission to go back there on the next plane. 'I had to rush out with a press release, explaining that I had never felt so free because I was able to walk around Moscow without being pestered by people asking for autographs.'

There was an even deadlier dig at him in a much earlier column when Nöel Coward, the playwright who everyone in show business knew was gay since he made no attempt to hide it, visited Cary when he was living in Santa Monica with Randolph Scott in the thirties. Coward was Cary's idol when he started to carve out a career for himself on Broadway in the twenties.

'Noël Coward and Cary Grant took up where they left off about a month ago,' Hedda reported in a 1938 column. 'I mean, Noël was Cary's houseguest.'

Thirty-five years later Cary still found it hard to believe the extent of Hedda's viciousness. 'She had it in for me,' he said, shaking his head.

When I started to try to steer him away from this subject, Cary could not be budged. The ultimate insult, as far as Hedda was concerned, occurred in 1959 after a magazine had written a feature story on Cary's appeal to women. 'Hedda took it upon herself to write a personal letter to the editor — not for publication, mind you, because she knew I would have sued her. She asked the editor: "Who does Cary Grant think he's fooling? This might surprise you — he started with boys and now has gone back to them!"'

'She really went out of her way to do me an unkindness,' he said.

'But think of all the people who've gone out of their way to help you,' I offered.

'Good girl!' he said, brightening instantly. 'You're absolutely right.'

Besides, I pointed out, not all reporters had a vicious streak like Hedda. There was his good friend Roddy Mann, as well as Hank Grant, who wrote the 'Rambling Reporter' column in *The Hollywood Reporter*, another trade publication.

Not only did Hank share Cary's adopted surname, but he had a lovely laid-back quality that permeated his daily column. Cary was particularly fond of the names Hank would use as the sources of his items. For example, he'd report: 'My Beverly Hills spy, Austin Tayshus tells me he spotted Doris Day at Nate 'n' Al's on Beverly Drive.' Or: 'My Arab spy, Sheik Aulegg, reports that Shirley

MacLaine has turned down a chance to do a sequel to *John Goldfarb, Please Come Home*.'

Cary would literally spend hours trying to devise a new name for a Hank Grant 'spy'. He was proudest of Hank's Hong Kong spy, Ho Lee Kau.

Just the mention of Hank Grant's name and his network of spies would bring a smile to Cary's face on any day, even a day as dark as this one.

But he was not through with the press and information that could somehow be used against him.

'It could be as simple as your stopping at a girlfriend's place on the way up here today, let's say,' he explained. 'You call me to see if I want anything at the store, I tell you yes or no, and then you say, "Good-bye, Cary." Right there, your girlfriend has a story. It will get back to Rona or someone else in no time, because your girlfriend likes knowing something about you that nobody else knows. Trust me about this. I know what I'm talking about. You are going to have to learn how to be very, very discreet — for both our sakes.'

I knew he had a point, but I knew at the same time there was more than a slight amount of paranoia mixed in with his apprehension.

'Cary, I know you're only trying to protect me and Jennifer and you,' I said. 'But you can be only so careful. I do not make it a practice to discuss you at the office or with casual friends. But no matter how angry you may get at me for telling you this, I must discuss you sometimes at least with little Dee, my best friend. You do not make it easy for a girl to love you, and you know what I'm talking about.'

'Oh, she's all right,' Cary said, though he had met Dee only once at that time. She had dropped me off one night at Cary's after my car had broken down at work. 'I get a good feeling from her— she's someone like Charlie Rich in my life. You can trust her and I'll tell you why. She comes from money, doesn't she?'

'Yes,' I said, startled. 'Yes, she does. How would you know that?'

'Oh, darling, one can always tell. And if she comes from money, then she has no motivation to sell you out. But if I were you, I'd be very careful what you tell the rest of your friends about us. Please be careful.'

9

BRINGING UP BABY

IT was Dee Joseph who first suggested to me that the waves of mistrust that already had begun to lap around the edges of my relationship with Cary might have very little to do with me and a lot more to do with his previous relationships with women, especially Dyan.

At first I resisted the idea. Cary's image and undeniable charm blinded me. He looked perfect; therefore he had to be. At least that's how I saw him then, in my youthful naïveté. And as insecure as I was at the time, I didn't need much to convince myself I was somehow responsible for these eruptions of mistrust and suspicion. If only I were more beautiful, he wouldn't think that way, I told myself. If only I were more clever and cultured, like the other women he had known before me.

The fact that he talked constantly about Dyan was intimidating enough. It could put a chill on our warmest conversations. But what I couldn't ignore was how hostile he was when he talked about her. It was on holidays and special occasions that the depth of his resentment first became clear to me.

The first Halloween I spent with Cary and Jennifer, I helped make her a little tramp costume, which she loved. Cary was in seventh heaven because he was allowed to have Jennifer on this night which meant so much to little children. Cary and I helped Jennifer and one of her friends get ready, and then we drove them a couple of miles to the heart of Beverly Hills, where each year a family decorated its home to resemble the creepiest haunted house. Nothing is ever done halfway in Beverly Hills and this house was no exception. Black crepe paper, skeletons and ghosts were hanging from every nook and cranny. Of course, Jennifer and her friend loved it. Then we took them trick-or-treating in the neighborhood. As Cary and I watched from the car, the children went from house to house demanding a treat lest the owners be tricked.

In very little time Jennifer and her friend had amassed a big bag of goodies. They couldn't wait to go home, spill everything on the floor and assess their take. But as the children began to do just that, Cary told Jennifer: 'Now, dear, please remember you can have only a few pieces now. I'll save the rest for later.'

I found his concern touching, but Jennifer wasn't exactly thrilled. She wanted to devour it all in one sitting as most kids do. But she accepted his wishes easily enough. Then she went in to show Willie what she and her friend had collected that night.

Later, after Jennifer had been picked up for her ride back to Dyan's home in Malibu, Cary's vulnerability regarding Jennifer began to surface.

'You don't think I was too harsh on her, do you?' he said, as we lay in bed together.

'What do you mean?' I said.

'You know, about not letting her have all that stuff at once.'

'Oh, don't worry, Cary,' I said. 'She's a very bright little girl. I'm sure she understands you were doing it for her own good. Besides, I don't think she was upset in the slightest.'

'But you don't understand, Maureen,' he said, now sitting up. 'I *have* to worry. I'm just not in a disciplinary position where she will do what I say. I have her so little of the time. So she's constantly around my former wife and you know she's not going to learn anything about responsibility from *her*.

'Jennifer's mother has late-night parties and smokes marijuana and God knows what else. Beg your pardon, I *do* know what else — I hired a detective to take a close look at what was going on at my former wife's house and it was not a pretty picture, I can tell you that. I mean, the child's meals aren't even served on a regular basis. And her bedtime is unscheduled as well. What can I do against all that?'

He seemed truly at a loss, bewildered. As for me, I was stunned. The thought of hiring a detective seemed, in the best light, unnecessary and, in the worst, excessive.

Now wound up, Cary continued on. 'I have to hang in there as long as I possibly can so Jennifer has someone she can always count on. I have to show her that men can be constant. That's why I'll fly at a moment's notice to be at Jennifer's side when I'm given any extra time with her. But my former wife even makes that impossible. She doesn't have a regular lawyer now, so I am completely at her whim. My lawyers will call to switch weekends or something so I can have Jennifer, but all they can do is leave a message at Dyan's house. It's utterly impossible!' he said, throwing his hands up.

I knew Dyan represented an emotional minefield, but since he'd brought up the subject, I had to ask one question.

'I hate to sound stupid, Cary,' I began quite tentatively. 'But it's clear you love Jennifer and I'm sure you loved her mother at one point. Isn't there any way for you two, for the sake of the child, to put aside your feelings and do what's best for Jennifer?'

He laughed bitterly.

'If only you knew what lengths I have had to go to just to ensure that I could see Jennifer for as little as I do now.'

With such bait before me, I had to bite.

'What do you mean, Cary?'

'Well, just think about a few things, Maureen. Think about the fact that Jennifer even has a home at all. Do you know it was I who forced Jennifer's mother to buy that house at the beach after I complained to the court — and rightfully so, I might add — that Jennifer did not have a proper home?

'Do you know it was me who fought the idea of a divorce in the first place? Do you know that I promised

Dyan I would come out of retirement and make a picture with her if she would drop the divorce action? And do you think, even after our divorce, the fact that Dyan's first film [*Bob & Carol & Ted & Alice*] was produced by Mike Frankovich, a good friend of *mine*, is a coincidence?

'You know,' he said sadly, 'I've done everything I could to keep Jennifer somehow near or in my life.'

'But Cary,' I responded, 'think of all the options you have that all the other fathers who've gone through divorce don't have. Think of all the things you can give her. I mean, you *can* drop everything at a moment's notice, as you said, to be by her side. Most father's can't just drop their work and do that.

'I'm not saying it's a good situation, but you do have some advantages over most people. You're not completely powerless.'

Cary managed a weak smile.

'You are a dear girl,' he said as he kissed me. 'You always manage to put the best face on things. And thank God, you always somehow manage to make me feel better.'

He turned over, took his Seconal and went to sleep. But I couldn't go to sleep. In my mind I kept hearing the conversation we'd just had, over and over again.

Then, in the morning, Cary told me about a dream he'd had that was just as disturbing.

'I was on the beach,' he said, 'and I saw these two huge turtles wrestling with a man. The turtles were so much bigger than he was. They had to be twice his size. And the poor man couldn't wrestle free from the turtles.

'"That man's in trouble," I heard myself saying. "He's really in trouble." But as soon as I saw the turtles start ripping the flesh from him, I knew there was nothing I could do, nothing anybody could do for that man.

'And then I thought: "No, Cary. It's just a show. That's all it is. Just a show." But it wasn't. Because as I got closer, I could see the sea was turning red. The man was dying and there wasn't anything he or I could do about it.

'The last thing I remember thinking was: "I must not

let Jennifer see this. If she does, it will destroy her. She must not see this."'

Unfortunately, Jennifer saw — perhaps the proper word is *felt* — a lot more than Cary suspected. I knew this because I often slept next to her in the bedroom, in one of the two single beds there. And we discussed everything. (My staying in Jennifer's bedroom also defused Cary's fears that Dyan would make trouble for him in court if she suspected I was 'sleeping over' with Cary instead of Jennifer.)

Without meaning to, Jennifer touched a cord deep within me, especially one evening just after Thanksgiving when she told me she wanted to have a sister named Stephanie.

'Isn't that a pretty name?' the child asked me. 'I think that is so pretty.'

She told me she would do all the things with Stephanie that she did with me and her younger friends. They could ride her horse, which was stabled in Malibu Canyon. They could make plates. Cary had bought Jennifer a plate-making kit that allowed her to paint or print anything she wanted permanently on the surface. She'd already given me a plate that said: 'I like you, Maureen, from Jennifer' with the date on it. (I still have that plate, just as Cary prized all the plates she made and gave to him.)

Then she said something that made me catch my breath.

'Maybe if I had a sister, Mommy and Daddy wouldn't fight about me so much. There would be two of us and they could each have a little girl.'

I frantically searched my mind for something to say.

'Well, you know, Jennifer,' I began haltingly, 'the reason your daddy and mummy both want you is that they love you so much.'

'Yes, I know,' she said halfheartedly. 'But they don't love each other, do they?'

Out of the mouths of babes, I thought to myself.

'Sometimes, it's hard to love each other,' I said. 'People

change, Jennifer. I'm sure you've had a friend you really liked but then she changed — or maybe you changed in some way — and you still liked her, but in a different way. Do you know what I mean?'

'But Mommy and Daddy don't like each other, Maureen,' she said softly. 'They won't talk to each other.'

'The important thing,' I rushed on, 'is that they both love you very much and they both want you to be with them all the time and it makes them unhappy not to have you with them all the time.'

She seemed to accept that for the moment. But now I was beginning, in some way, to feel the massive pain Cary had to feel in being separated from his only child. I hoped I would never have to explain to a child of my own why his or her parents could not be together.

Cary, not surprisingly, probed me constantly for details of my conversations with Jennifer, but I always spoke in the broadest possible terms. I always tried to convey her perspective on things — it was nearly impossible for Cary to understand anything she did from her viewpoint — but that was the extent of it. I felt her privacy had to be protected at all costs. She had lost so much in the tug-of-war between her parents; she had to feel safe and know that everything she told me was just between 'us girls.'

And Cary kept demonstrating that he simply lacked the ability to see things through a child's eyes. I realized how clouded his vision was one weekend at the beach.

Jennifer and her friend Hillary were playing restaurant. They set up a little stand near the back of the house where they served sandwiches and lemonade they'd made in the kitchen. The price for each sandwich was twenty-five cents. Jennifer and Hillary would hawk their food all afternoon as people on the beach walked by. By the end of the day they had managed to collect a couple of dollars and were wondering aloud how they were going to spend it.

'But what about your expenses?' Cary said to the girls.

'Huh?' they said, looking up in puzzlement.

'The expenses, girls. You know, the bread and butter

and the peanut butter and jelly, all that. Someone has to pay for that.'

'But Willie got that stuff at the store, Daddy,' Jennifer protested.

'But I paid for it, dear,' he said.

The girls still didn't get his point. I did, of course, and pulled him aside. 'Oh, Cary, they were just playing and having such a good time. It's only a matter of two or three dollars anyway.'

'You're just as bad as she is,' he said, anger starting to suffuse his voice. 'Look, she has to be taught that I have to be repaid out of her profits.'

'But they don't understand that, Cary,' I protested again. 'They're children. There's plenty of time for that later.'

'I was a child when I learned the importance of money. You can never be too young,' he said sharply.

'Here you go, Daddy,' Jennifer said, instantly ending the argument by handing over the money. 'You save it for something special.'

'Well, thank you, dear,' he said, a bit embarrassed. 'But you've missed my point. I just want you to understand that it costs something to make money.'

'They were your sandwiches too,' she said.

'Yes, dear, that's true too. But —'

'I'm sure there'll be a better example when she's a bit older,' I interrupted, hoping to put an end to this 'lesson.'

'Ah, perhaps you're right,' he said, reluctantly giving up.

I smiled at Jennifer. I could tell by the way she looked back at me that she understood she'd done the right thing by handing over the money to her father.

If Cary could sometimes be insensitive, he more than made up for it at other times with his love and concern for his child. Jennifer occupied almost his every waking moment. He was always asking if she had her jacket and shoes on before she went outside. Such 'little things' proved not to be idle concerns, either.

One afternoon up at Beverly Grove, Jennifer and I were

kicking a ball around the yard when it went into the brush nearby. Jennifer began to rush after it, but she was wearing only sandals so I stopped her. 'I'll get it,' I said as I went after it into the tangle of ferns and weeds.

I was reaching down for the ball when I heard what sounded like a slight rattle. I felt something squirming under my foot. It was a baby rattlesnake. I ran screaming out of the brush and grabbed Jennifer's hand. 'It's a rattle!' I yelled 'Quick! Into the house!'

We ran into the house, where Cary was sitting on his bed going over some papers.

'What on earth?!' he exclaimed.

'There's a snake in the brush. A rattlesnake. Maureen almost got bitten!' Jennifer breathlessly informed her father.

'Maureen,' he began to scold me, 'how in the world can you go into the brush without your boots on? What would have happened if you had been bitten and Jennifer went in there after you?'

'I would have left her all my record albums!' I said rebelliously. Jennifer burst into laughter, delighted.

'Really, girls,' Cary insisted. 'You know it's not even safe to go near the brush without your boots on. Try to be more careful next time!'

'I promise to wear my Wellies,' I said, realizing he did have a valid point. My 'Wellies' were the Wellington boots I had bought in my days at the ranch with my ex-husband.

Fortunately, there were much less hectic moments that demonstrated the extent of Cary's devotion to Jennifer.

Sometimes they were triggered by the simple act of Jennifer's playing. Cary would just stare at her in wonder. Many times tears would well up in his eyes. He never said a word, just silently wiped them away. The pride and love in those tears was unmistakeable.

The depth of his feeling for her was also obvious when it came time for Cary's home movies. Cary frequently tape-recorded Jennifer playing or talking, and he was just as diligent with a home movie camera. He had been filming her from the day of her birth, so she would later have a complete record of her childhood. When Cary was in a particularly good mood, he loved to pull out the projector and show his home movies of her.

Jennifer saw them so often she was bored with them. But Cary never lost his obsession with Jennifer's 'performances'. Here was Jennifer at the beach. Or playing with her horse. Or swimming in Palm Springs at Charlie Rich's estate. I grew facinated with Cary's fascination with the home movies. He would sit there for hours, rapt while Jennifer fidgeted. Occasionally he would throw in some other home movies — there was some particularly hilarious footage from a boating trip with Howard Hughes filled with one mishap after another that I came to love — but for the most part it was always Jennifer.

Cary was especially careful to document Jennifer's birthdays and all the holidays. The first Christmas I spent with him and Jennifer in Malibu was unforgettable for the amount of emotion he had invested in the event.

He didn't show it in the number of presents he bought Jennifer — he gave her only a few. I remember a sweater and a bracelet among them. He was determined not to spoil her. And he certainly did not express it in the traditional trappings of Christmas — his tree was actually an artificial plastic one, purchased years before at a discount store.

I saw Cary at his fullest and his happiest in the afternoon, when the turkey was in the oven, with the spirit of Christmas wafting throughout the house. Jennifer was happily playing. I occasionally checked on the turkey (Cary had given Willie the day off) and on Cary, who was sitting in a chair reading. Under the circumstances, this was the closest he could come to the warmth and togetherness of a real family on such a day, because he knew Jennifer would have to return to Dyan's home within a matter of hours.

But for now he was positively merry throughout the meal, urging Jennifer and me, 'Eat! Eat! Eat!' After we finished and I had cleared away most of the dishes, he put a record on the turntable. I was still in the kitchen cleaning up when I heard a familiar voice coming faintly from the bedroom.

It sounded like Cary! To my knowledge, he'd never made a record, though I knew he had sung on Broadway and managed a song or two in his early movies like *Suzy*.

After listening a few more seconds, I *knew* it was Cary, though it was more of a recitation than actual singing, similar to the way Rex Harrison talk-sang in *My Fair Lady*.

'Is that you?' I asked as I walked into the bedroom.

Cary nodded his head as the record continued.

It was a 45-rpm single Cary had recorded in the summer of 1967 — the summer Dyan had filed for divorce. It was called 'Christmas Lullaby'; the lyrics were by his good friend singer Peggy Lee, and the music by Broadway veteran Cy Coleman. The song described the quiet joy a devoted father felt as he watched over his sleeping daughter on Christmas Eve. It was touching in its simplicity and the feeling Cary packed behind every word.

'Would you like to hear it again?' he asked Jennifer and me. We both agreed eagerly. 'I've heard it before,' Jennifer informed me, but time had done nothing to dampen her enthusiasm.

Soon Jennifer had to go home to Dyan, but the record kept playing in my mind. I knew it was also having its impact on Cary's thoughts.

'Here,' he said, handing me the record. 'I want you to have it. You seem to like it.' It was the best present I could have gotten.

'Cary, I *love* it,' I said, trying not to cry.

'I did it for Jennifer,' he explained. 'When I recorded it, I was desperately trying to get her mother to reconcile with me but I didn't know if I could pull it off. I had the privilege of spending Jennifer's first Christmas with her, but I didn't know if I would be allowed to be with her for her second, in 1967. So that summer I finally gave in to the people at Columbia, who'd been asking me to record some Christmas songs. At least I could do that and be with her in spirit.'

'What happened the second Christmas, Cary?' I asked him.

'Actually, I did manage to persuade Dyan to reconcile with me for the holidays. But we didn't make it past New Year's. She went ahead with the divorce. And you know how the rest of it turned out.'

I certainly did.

Knowing this, I was determined that Cary's seventieth birthday, which was just a couple of weeks away, on January 18, 1974, would be a joyous occasion. I knew the key to that joy would be having Jennifer at his side for the day, but I didn't dare get in the middle of Cary and Dyan's always delicate negotiations about such matters. But I would do everything else to make it a day he would never forget. Willie was equally determined, and we developed a formidable battle plan.

Willie would make a roast lamb with all the trimmings and I would bake him a cake. But our plans began to unravel on the morning of his birthday, a Friday. He was in Las Vegas and planned to fly into Los Angeles later that afternoon and then drive to Malibu. But when I talked to him in Las Vegas, he was desolate. Dyan would not give him Jennifer for the day.

'It's not even that,' he explained to me on the phone. 'I wouldn't want her to miss school or anything like that. But you would think the child could at least ring me and say, "Happy birthday, Daddy"? I just don't understand....'

'The day's hardly begun,' I admonished him. 'Give her a chance, Cary. I'm sure she'll call you. Besides, have you seen *Variety*?'

'No,' he said.

'Well, you should. A lot of people want to wish you a happy birthday, that's all I'll tell you. I'll see you later tonight in Malibu, Cary.'

'Maureen,' he said, sighing, 'I don't mean to sound unkind, but I'm not going to be much fun tonight. Really. All I want to do is forget this supposed milestone. It has no significance to me if it has no significance to my daughter.'

'Stop saying that,' I said as I hung up the phone, 'and I'll see you later!'

I phoned Willie and asked her if there was anything we could do on the Jennifer front to ensure that she'd make a phone call to her father. 'Jennifer knows this is a special day for her father.' Willie said. 'God knows you've told her and I've told her. If she doesn't call, it would be for a very good reason. If that child can get near a phone, she will call. I just know it, Maureen.'

In the meantime I had my magazine's photo department mount a huge blowup of the full-page ad that had run that day in *Variety*. It read:

Dear Cary Grant,

   The millions of people the world over who are indebted to you for so many lovely movie memories, all of us who work in Hollywood who are grateful for the prestige you have brought to our industry, and those of us privileged by the gift of your friendship join together today to send you our gratitude, our affection, and our very best wishes for a happy seventieth birthday.

It was unsigned but expressed the thoughts of thousands. I put a big red bow across the enlarged ad, and both Willie and I signed it with a red Magic Marker. No matter what mood Cary was in, I knew he'd get a kick out of that.

When Cary walked into the beach house around seven, he was not about to celebrate anything. Willie and I had put the *Variety* blowup in the entryway but it failed even to raise a smile. We were positive that when he walked into the living room he would be stunned by the exquisite table setting and the tempting meal.

But he took one look at it, sighed and said, 'I appreciate the effort. I really do. But I want to spend tonight quietly, girls. I suggest you put the food away, because it will just go to waste. And I hate to see anyone waste perfectly good food.'

Before we could say a word, he had already closed

himself in the bedroom, where he began to unpack and put away his clothes. Then the phone rang. Willie picked it up. 'Mr. Grant's residence,' she said.

Then I saw a look of relief flood her face. 'I am so happy you called, dear. He just walked in. I'll get him right now.'

'Jennifer?' I silently mouthed to Willie. She bobbed her head to indicate yes.

Oh, thank God, I cried to myself.

A few minutes later, a different Cary emerged from his room. He was almost floating, he was so happy. Willie had begun to put the food away, but he grabbed her and whirled her around.

'What in the world are you doing?' he said, laughing. 'This is supposed to be a party, isn't it? Let's eat!'

He sat down and dug in. He was ecstatic Jennifer had called to wish him a happy birthday. 'I could tell it was a bit awkward for her,' he said. 'She sounded nervous, so I didn't keep her long. But she did call. She did make the effort. She *does* love me!'

'Mr. Grant,' Willie volunteered, 'that's one girl who really loves her father. There's no doubt about that!'

'Absolutely!' I joined in as I handed him a large gift-wrapped box, my present to him.

'You are both so patient with me,' he said as he took the box and shook it. 'I just get so wound up sometimes. I have so little control over my own daughter's life.'

'Cary,' I said, 'every child can tell if he or she is loved, really loved.'

'You're right about that, you are,' he said, pulling off the wrapping absentmindedly. 'They certainly can tell, can't they?'

'Absolutely,' I said, almost making it sound like a jury foreman's verdict.

'Then I don't have a thing in the world to worry about, do I?' he asked. He took the lid off the box.

'Not a thing,' I told him.

'Well, there is one thing,' he said slowly. A knot tightened in my stomach.

'And what's that?' I said.

'What,' he said, holding up the new cream silk bathrobe I'd given him, 'should I do with *this* tonight?!'

10

ROOM FOR ONE MORE

I HAVE the Symbionese Liberation Army to thank for providing the catalyst that convinced Cary to allow me into his life on a more intimate scale than ever before.

On Monday, February 4, 1974, the SLA kidnapped Patty Hearst from her home in Berkeley, California. The 'urban guerrillas' broke down her door, beat up her boyfriend, and bound and gagged Hearst before tossing her into the trunk of an SLA getaway vehicle.

By Tuesday, February 5, Cary was paralyzed with fear that the same was destined to happen to Jennifer. She too was the daughter of rich and famous parents. And she too would reap enormous attention in the media.

Unfortunately, I did nothing to allay Cary's fears when I walked into his house that evening, because I pointed out just how vulnerable she was in his houses at the beach and Beverly Hills. At the beach, Cary's and Dyan's homes were inside The Colony, which did have a guard in a gatehouse posted outside the exclusive compound. But Cary's rented home there had no alarm system at all.

And the house on Beverly Grove was even less fortified, in my opinion. Cary had only a wooden gate to keep people out and a simple padlock to keep it shut at night. Anyone could leap over the gate with the slightest exertion.

The front door of the house itself had a deadbolt lock, but the rest of the house was not protected by an alarm system, which was available in those days at a cost of between $5,000 and $10,000. Jennifer's well-being was certainly worth more than that.

'Ah, but you don't understand,' Cary argued when I pointed out how unguarded his home was. 'There's the vault which can be completely sealed off, so if anyone came in here and tried to grab Jennifer or me, all we'd have to do is run into the vault and shut the door. From there, I could signal the police.'

'That's fine as far as it goes, Cary,' I said, 'but what happens if someone grabs you or Jennifer *before* you get to the vault?'

'Then I'd shut myself up in the bedroom. I can lock the connecting doors,' he said smugly. There were at least three separate entrances to Cary's bedroom, which could be locked from the inside. But it still seemed foolish not to have any kind of alarm system as another precaution, especially when he could afford it so easily.

Cary thought quite carefully over what I'd said and admitted I might be right. 'You can't be too cautious.' From that day forward, he would instruct architects and contractors working on the other parts of the house to make preparations for the installation of a fully equipped alarm system. Up until then his idea of protection had consisted of making sure he never left the house empty. If Willie or his secretary couldn't be there when he wasn't, then he would ask me to house-sit. (If I wasn't available, he'd allow only two of my friends — Dee Joseph and my neighbor Bobby Birkenfeld, a music publicist I trusted completely — to assume those duties.)

Because Cary felt safer with me around him, I began staying up at the house almost every night instead of just once or twice during the week. (Weekends were still spent in Malibu near Jennifer.) With me on the premises on such a regular basis, that more or less cut Vicki Morgan out of Cary's life. And *that* made me feel much safer.

Beverly Grove was the first home Cary had really tried to make a home. He had purchased it in the thirties and used it largely as a warehouse for his belongings over the years. Before he moved back into it in the late sixties, he'd always lived in larger homes with his wives. After his divorce from Dyan, Cary was determined to make the house suitable for father and child. But because of his perfectionism and more than occasional indecision, work had not progressed very far by the time I moved in. Only the two bedrooms (and bathrooms) for Cary and Jennifer were complete. The rest of the house, including the kitchen, remained in a state of transition.

As I mentioned before, it was hardly your typical movie star's mansion. As you entered the front door, you faced a generous living room. To the left was the kitchen and to the right were the bedrooms and baths for Cary and Jennifer. Cary's bedroom was a surprisingly modest affair decorated in shades of green and brown. The king-sized bed had a comfortable brown leather headboard and was covered by a cream bedspread. We slept under a green electric blanket and, beneath that, his monogrammed white sheets.

On both sides of the bed were bookshelves. On one side, he kept a photograph of Jennifer in a beautiful silver frame. There was also a photograph of Jennifer as a baby in Dyan's arms, as well as pictures of his mother and Cary as a little boy. On the other bookshelf rested a round gold frame with a picture of me in it. He also kept the honorary Oscar he had received in 1970 as well as the Italian David di Donatello award for his performance in *North by Northwest*.

Cary said these momentos always filled him with 'happy thoughts.' I was pleased to see I was already part of that exclusive circle capable of evoking such thoughts. The bedroom also featured two black leather chairs on either side of a round coffee table with a black leather top. His closets were electrically controlled and would snap open at the touch of a hidden button.

The bedroom opened onto his office, where Cary spent most of his day. Next to that was the terrace, where we usually ate our meals if the weather was good, which was most of the time. Breakfast did not begin our typical day. First Cary had to consult each day's message in *Daily*

Word, a publication of the Unity School of Christianity in Missouri. Each day of the year was assigned a line of scripture. For example, 'All things are possible to him who believes' from Mark 9:23 might serve as one day's inspiration. The daily message was three or four paragraphs devoted to that thought with a key word — in this case, 'belief' — boxed in red in the upper left-hand corner of the page.

'It's a nice, positive way to greet each day,' Cary told me when he first showed me this tiny pamphlet, sent out to its audience for a nominal fee on a monthly basis. Very quickly I learned to look forward to reading each day's entry in *Daily Word* with Cary.

After this bit of inspiration, Willie would bring in coffee and sometimes toast, along with the morning newspapers. Cary loved to glance through them and would set his sights on the oddest bit of information. No matter how trivial the 'news' seemed to be, Cary would mark items to be included in his files. And as many of his secretaries could attest, the maintenance of Cary's voluminous files was a full-time job in itself.

Cary clipped coupons. He clipped news items. He clipped stories from magazines. He clipped stories about himself. He clipped everything. Some people are born to dance; others are born to wander. Others are born to greatness. Cary Grant was born to clip. In fact, he told me he even 'met' Dyan first through a clipping — it was an ad in a show business paper promoting her appearance on an early sixties TV series, *The Aquarians*.

He had a paper-cutting machine with a creaky handle that he used constantly. In fact, Cary used it so much that I often joked: 'I swear, you're going to cut off your blasted hand someday!'

Off I'd go to work in the morning and there'd be Cary, happily cutting away. Of course, he also attended to a lot of serious business, which required him to be on the phone a great deal. He was constantly talking to representatives of Fabergé, Western Airlines, MGM Grand and other companies for which he served as a member of their boards of directors. And when he wasn't working with them, he was consulting with the architects, building inspectors, contractors and others who were occupied with getting his house in the shape he wanted. But I have no doubt it was clipping that he loved the most.

His second favorite activity during the day was the care and feeding of The Vault. This fireproof vault was situated right off the front doorway and was his legacy to Jennifer. Not only did it include many artifacts from Cary's life — everything from his old passports to a complete set of his films — but he also devoted much of it to Jennifer's childhood and items he hoped she'd enjoy seeing as she grew up. He feared he would not see her grow into young womanhood, so he wanted her to have this vaultful of memories. And what a treasure chest it was.

Cary packed it with gifts he requested from the rich and famous for Jennifer's future delight, including an autographed baseball from Hank Aaron and a card inscribed to her from Neil Armstrong, the first man to walk on the moon. My contribution was an autographed Beatles picture. But what I found most touching were the mementos from his own childhood that Cary catalogued and stored away for his daughter.

I remember a plum-colored school blazer from his childhood days in Bristol, which he handled with the greatest of care. There was his father's engraved pocket-watch. Then there were the military badges and buttons he'd been given by soldiers in Southampton on their way to fight in World War I. As a Boy Scout, Cary did last-minute errands such as relaying letters for these soldiers on their last day in England before shipping out to France, and sometimes they'd reward the young boy with buttons and badges. Cary told me he'd refused to take money even if the soldiers had it to offer, but he proudly accepted these souvenirs. There were also autographed books from Noël Coward, Cole Porter, Rosalind Russell and many others.

Cary's secretaries hated working inside the vault because it was so tiny — it barely fit them and a stamp-sized desk — but they humored Cary because they knew how much it meant to him and to Jennifer.

In the afternoon Cary ate a light lunch and would usually spend one hour in the sun. The rest of the afternoon would be occupied with more phone calls, more work on the house and of course much more clipping.

When I walked in from work around six, I would be greeted by Cary at the door. But there were nights when I just didn't know *what* I was walking into: If something had gone wrong with the house, or if Jennifer's visiting plans had been screwed up, he would be withdrawn and grumpy. As the years passed, I learned to go into the kitchen immediately if Cary wasn't at the door to greet me, and to check with Willie in order to discover quickly what was bothering him. Willie and I worked out a complex set of signals — because he was usually sitting in the next room within earshot — to let me know if it was I, or Dyan, or Jennifer, or the world in general he was mad at that day.

But most of those first days up at Beverly Grove were good ones, so he'd greet me at the door with a drink in hand — either white wine or vodka with orange juice. We'd sit on the terrace with our drinks and Cary would usually hand me two things: the 'Nut File' and my 'homework.' The Nut File consisted of letters from the 'crazies' who'd written him from all over the world. He took an unusual delight in reading their rantings and ravings. 'You just won't believe this one!' he'd bellow as he handed me one of the more outrageous ones.

Then we would proceed to my homework. This consisted of clippings from various publications that Cary was sure could be of use to me personally or professionally. It might be a feature about someone he thought I should interview, or an article about a disease currently making the rounds I should be particularly careful to fortify myself against.

But the real highlight of Cary's evening came when we settled down to play Spite and Malice, a card game somewhat similar to double solitaire, taught to me by a good friend, Cindy Crowe. It allows you to be pretty vicious in what you're capable of doing to an opponent. The minute I introduced the game to Cary, he took to it like a duck to water. (In fact, many years after we separated, Cary happened to run into Cindy and thanked her profusely for helping to bring Spite and Malice into his life.)

We played for pennies and it was amazing how soon Cary owed me five dollars. He was always a good sport about paying up, but he really wanted to win. It sounds egotistical, but I wouldn't let him. He probably wouldn't have appreciated a 'mercy win' anyway.

Once our game was over, Willie would bring in dinner on the white wicker trays Cary loved. He also loved the cheap plastic plates and cups he'd gotten gratis from Western Airlines ('So functional!' he'd marvel), but I refused to eat off them.

After dinner Cary usually slipped into his pajamas to watch television. I would often join him if I didn't have work from the office to catch up on. Cary's favorite programs were *The Hollywood Squares* and *Concentration*. He was especially fond of *The Hollywood Squares* because he loved the zany humor of Paul Lynde, the fey comedian who occupied the show's center square. Reruns of Groucho Marx's series *You Bet Your Life* were also highly favored. Cary was not eager to see his movies when they were broadcast (there were no videocassettes in those days), but I could usually persuade him with some effort.

Cary made very few phone calls at night and he discouraged me from the practice. He always fell asleep early, while I often couldn't fall asleep until midnight. I would go into the guest bedroom and use the phone there, although I hated to because when I'd lift the receiver a red light would light up on Cary's phone as well. But I often felt the need to catch up with a girlfriend. Cary, as always, was paranoid about my saying anything to a friend that could intrude on his privacy.

Cary's last words to me before he switched off the light on his side of the bed were usually 'Nice Dreams!' or 'Happy dreams!' For the first few months I was with him, he usually added a postscript: a reminder never to sleep on my face. That, he assured me, would cause wrinkles. 'Sleep on your back!' he'd order, and I followed that advice. Maybe that was one of the reasons he looked so magnificent.

What I *did* find less easy to follow were some of Cary's house rules. They included:

(1) No pets. 'Animals carry viruses,' he'd say, and even though Jennifer loved animals, he would not permit them in the house.

(2) No plants of any kind. 'Plants rob us of valuable oxygen.'

(3) No smoking and no eating of any food prepared with charcoal. Both would cause cancer.

(4) No high heels in the house, because they were loud. 'Harsh footsteps!' he'd say disapprovingly when a stranger would come to the house wearing heels. He couldn't wait to get rid of the offender.

(5) No rock music on the radio or turntable. Classical music — Rachmaninoff and Debussy in particular — were favored, with middle-of-the-road performers such as Frank Sinatra and Peggy Lee a close second. But much to my (and Jennifer's) consternation, rock music was *not* to be played. 'Unpleasant noise!' he decreed.

I found this last rule particularly hard to live with. I wasn't into loud, heavy rock but I did enjoy Gordon Lightfoot, the Eagles and the Beatles. One night Cary challenged me to 'prove what's so good about the Beatles,' so I brought a large selection of their albums from my apartment.

I started with 'I Want to Hold Your Hand' and we worked our way through the Beatles catalogue until we reached 'Strawberry Fields Forever.' He listened very patiently but it was a lost cause. 'I'm sorry, dear,' he said. 'I know they're popular. It's just not music in my book.'

But, I protested, he *should* try to learn to appreciate this music because the Beatles were laying the foundation for music Jennifer would be enjoying in a few years. He got my point but he never 'got' the Beatles. I did have enough influence, though, to help him appreciate Gordon Lightfoot — who had written and sung one of my favorite songs, 'If You Could Read My Mind' — as well as a plumpish, diminutive writer-singer named Paul Williams.

Paul's voice resembled something between a rasp and a croak, but he invested it with so much emotion it never failed to strike a chord in me. His songs, such as 'I Won't Last a Day Without You' and 'You and Me Against the World,' were hopelessly corny, even trite, yet they packed a real wallop. After much protesting, Cary began to listen seriously to my Paul Williams albums and even grew to like his singing. 'At least I can understand the words,' he'd tell me. 'Plus, the man has something *positive* to say, hasn't he? And he keeps it simple. I appreciate that!'

Cary appreciated simplicity and moderation in every part of his life, from his clothing to the food he ate. Although he was often on Best Dressed lists and his closets were stuffed with suits tailored especially for him, he liked nothing better than to putter around the house in grey flannel slacks, a cream sweater or cardigan, and dark brown leather loafers handmade for him by Maxwell's on Dover Street in London. After I spotted him on TV in a scene from *Houseboat*, uncharacteristically wearing denim jeans, I told him I thought he looked sexy in them. That's all it took for him to begin wearing jeans on a fairly regular basis around the house.

Cary's most prized possession was a gold chain he wore around his neck. It held not only one of Jennifer's first baby teeth, encased in Lucite ('A marvelous invention!' he'd say), but also three charms representing the three religions of his four ex-wives: a St. Christopher medal from his first marriage, to Virginia Cherrill, a Catholic; a small cross representing his second and third marriages, to Barbara Hutton and Betsy Drake, who were Protestants; and a Star of David for Dyan, his last wife, who came from a Jewish family.

In his drawers and closets there was a special place for each part of his wardrobe. He was exceptionally neat for a man, and he was so demanding he insisted his clothes be cleaned by an outside laundry rather than by Willie.

Then, when the clothes came back from the cleaners, he'd sit right down and check off each item from a list he'd drawn up before sending his clothes down the hill. 'I have to do this,' he once explained to me, 'because people like to take souvenirs.' With his monogram on shirts and sheets, it could be tempting to a serious fan.

Cary was equally fastidious with his grooming. I never saw a stray hair in his bathroom sink. I suspected his concern in this domain had much to do with how 'scruffy' and 'untamed' he used to look back in Bristol after his mother had been institutionalized and he was largely free to run around unsupervised, as he'd told me often.

But there were days he'd prefer to stay in his pajamas all day and not shave. Yet he retained his touch of elegance when he'd ask me: 'Madame, do I have your permission today to forgo the razor?' He was like a small boy asking if he could put off mowing the lawn until another day. Of course, I never refused him.

Cary also did not favor anything fancy in his meals. Nothing pleased him more than eating turkey sandwiches served on white wicker trays while we sat on the bed and watched television. The recipe for those sandwiches had been given him by Doris Day, his costar in *That Touch of Mink.* When I think of Willie, I always think of her in the kitchen making those sandwiches, which consisted of thinly sliced sourdough bread, turkey, a small amount of butter and mayonnaise, a dash of pepper and some watercress. They were tea sandwiches cut into little diamonds. Willie would wrap them in a damp towel and put them in the refrigerator to keep them moist if she didn't serve them to us immediately.

Salmon cakes and lamb chops were also favorites. Sardines on toast were also popular, as were toasted English muffins with a slice of Monterey jack cheese and a dash of Worcestershire sauce. He liked to have his muffin between his main course and dessert, usually ice cream with wafers. Cary did have a sweet tooth — he loved coconut yet detested raspberries — but he never over-indulged. His favorite sweet was chocolate-covered marzipan, which I found in a small shop in Beverly Hills. Just before going to bed, he'd have one or two pieces as his treat. I was more likely to devour an entire bar if he wasn't looking.

Cary loved to have a wine called Setrakian with our dinner. It was an inexpensive, light California white wine that he bought by the case. For his other meals he'd opt for coffee with no milk or sugar. He despised soft drinks and was constantly haranguing me about my temporary addiction to Mountain Dew. The only reason he kept any soft drinks in the refrigerator was that Jennifer loved them, especially Coca-Cola. He reluctantly let her sip to her heart's content, but I always got a lecture. 'Do you know what's in *that*? The chemicals, my God, Maureen!'

Jennifer and I were responsible not only for getting Cary into McDonald's for a cheeseburger one afternoon but also for getting him hooked for long afterward. At first he pretended he liked stopping at the fast-food palace only for Jennifer's sake. But then I noticed he was eating not one burger but *two*. Then he started ordering french fries too. So I started kidding him: 'My God, Cary! Think of the chemicals! What a poor example you're setting for Jennifer!' The child, of course, loved my ribbing her daddy — and he loved her reaction.

Of course, the look on people's faces as Cary stood in line was unforgettable. If people asked him, 'Are you who I think you are!' he'd shake his head but acknowledge, 'I *do* look like him, though. That Cary Grant fellow, you mean?' I usually couldn't resist adding: 'Besides, do you think Cary Grant would eat at McDonald's? *Really*!' Then everyone would laugh at the idea. Sometimes, however, Cary would just send Jennifer and me in for the food, because he wanted to avoid any kind of request for autographs.

We also stopped a few times at Pioneer Chicken, but it never held the appeal for us of McDonald's. I suspect half that appeal came from the fact that those meals were so cheap. Cary was not one to throw money around where food was concerned — Willie's monthly budget for food was only a hundred dollars, aided by all the coupons Cary had clipped for her. But it was still quite a stretch most months, and I secretly augmented that allotment because I was now part of the household anyway. Willie appreciated it, but it was years before I told Cary. His pride would never have permitted it.

Actually, Cary's reputation as a tightwad was deserved in some ways and completely undeserved in others. I hadn't been living with him for very long when he presented me with his monthly phone bill. 'Could you please check off the toll calls you made and tell me to whom you made them?' he asked. I offered to pay half the bill each month or make some other kind of arrangement but he said that was unnecessary. 'I just want to make sure whose calls are whose.'

The implication was not that I was making too many calls; he wanted to check up on his secretaries as well as the people who worked on the house (from the contractor's office and so on). I thought Cary's attitude toward his secretaries in this regard was really petty. He hardly overpaid them in the first place, yet he always protested: 'They make more money than we do!' What's more, he never let them take an hour off for lunch, nor would he allow Willie to make them lunch. If they wanted a soft drink during the day, they had to bring it with them in the morning.

But to outside help he was unfailingly generous. He could be a great tipper. Many times I saw him hand a waiter or even a parking valet fifty or a hundred dollars. 'Well,' he'd say, somewhat embarrassed. 'They need it more than I do, don't they? Plus, they work hard for their money!'

His main complaint usually revolved around not getting proper value for his money. While I was up at Beverly Grove, he had hired a pool man who had made elaborate promises about personally tending to Cary's pool. He supposedly would care for it as no one had before. But two or three weeks after he'd been hired, he was sending a young relative to do his job — and the kid was doing it poorly. Cary was enraged and got the pool man on the phone.

'You promised me personal attention and you're not delivering!' he barked.

The pool man said something to the effect: 'What do you expect for so little money?'

'I expect you to keep your word,' Cary scolded him. 'Otherwise, why did you give it? I didn't force you into a bad deal. If it was something where you weren't going to make a profit, why did you agree to it?'

They bickered back and forth until Cary discharged the man. A few days later, there was an interview with this man in the *Los Angeles Times*. He didn't mention Cary by name but said, 'There's a superstar who's known for his frugality who won't even pay me.'

Cary was terribly upset by this. He went on and on about the 'indecency of the world and people like this. Rather than look inside themselves to find out what's causing their problems, they just blame me.' He then bemoaned the fact that the article failed to mention his considerable contributions to charity. 'Why don't they ever print *that*?'

I tried to explain that such notoriety came with the territory of being a star, but this minus was outweighed by a lot of pluses. 'I know, but it still hurts,' he said finally.

It hurt me to see him wounded in this way, because I, unlike most of the press, had been privileged to see the whole picture. True, Cary would spend only six dollars on a haircut at a little shop in Malibu ('But they do a perfectly decent job!' he protested when I kidded him about it). Also true is the fact that he saved the rubber bands that came around the morning newspapers. And he deeply resented the little chrome strip with the car's brand name on his Cadillac — 'Why should I carry around free advertising for General Motors?' he'd complain.

But there was a truly generous side to him that few people ever saw. Once we were at singer Tony Bennett's house for dinner. During the evening Cary had somehow lost one of his sapphire cuff links that had been given to him by Barbara Hutton. He was momentarily upset but let the loss pass by. Then, a couple of days later, Tony's maid found the cuff link under the couch. Cary was so grateful to get it back, he promptly sent off a check for a hundred dollars to the maid.

And despite his thriftiness and his personal aversion to pets, I saw something one evening at the beach that moved me deeply. We were walking into the Tonga Lei, a restaurant that specialized in drinks with exotic names and silly little umbrellas perched on top of these concoctions. The tropical decorations which looked like something out of a Dorothy Lamour movie by way of an American International beach movie, always delighted Cary.

But as we were parking, Cary saw something that wasn't delightful. A man with a rather flea-bitten dog on a leash was jerking the animal around violently. The poor dog was yelping, not knowing which way to turn to please his master, but this only served to infuriate the man more.

'Look here,' Cary said as he walked up to the man. 'I will give you a hundred dollars right now if you will give me this dog.'

As I joined Cary, I could smell the liquor on the man's breath.

'You wanna buy my dog?' he said woozily.

'That's correct,' Cary said, careful not to challenge the man on his treatment of the animal. This was strictly a transaction between two businessmen.

'Well, I'll tell ya,' the man said, weaving about while the dog still yelped. 'This dog is worth two hundred dollars. Whaddya think about *that*?'

'Why, you're absolutely right!' Cary agreed. 'I wouldn't want to cheat you!'

He reached into his wallet quickly, pulled out ten twenty-dollar bills and handed them to the man at the same moment he snatched the leash out of his hands. We were well on our way toward the restaurant before the man even realized what happened.

'My God,' Cary whispered. 'What are we going to do with this mutt?'

'I don't know,' I said, grabbing his hand, 'but I love you.'

'And what brought that on?' he said, genuinely confused.

'Doesn't matter,' I said firmly. 'But I love you.'

'Good,' he replied. 'Then *you* find a home for this animal!'

11

ROMANCE & RICHES

HOW long would it take for Cary to say he loved me?
I began a mental countdown, but I feared it would take him a long time.

'Oh, how we secretly yearn for love, yet openly defend against it,' Cary had said to the press on more than one occasion.

And there was no denying that Cary's defenses were formidable.

His distancing maneuvers were not promising signs. Yet, I told myself, he *had* invited me to share his home with him. Then there was the fact he'd begun calling me by a pair of nicknames. Most of the time he'd call me Monkeyface, just as he'd dubbed Joan Fontaine in *Suspicion*. On rare occasions he'd call me Precious.

But at the same time there were other signs that were not remotely as encouraging: One afternoon Cary and I were sitting on the terrace at Beverly Grove and he asked me what I was reading. It was *From the Terrace*, John O'Hara's chronicle of one man's search for love and financial success after his father has shut him out of his life.

'What's so romantic about that?' Cary quizzed me after I described the book I was reading.

'I think it's romantic,' I said, 'because it shows there is hope ... that it can take a long time for some people, but you can find true love.'

'I'll tell you what's romantic,' he said. 'Have you ever read a play called *One Way Passage*?' You really should. Now *that's* romantic.'

'How so?' I asked.

'It's very touching,' he said. 'It's the story of two doomed lovers on a ship. He's going to jail, and she's going to her death because she's suffering from a terrible disease.'

'I'm sorry,' I said, 'but I don't see what's romantic about *that*! It's like Ali MacGraw dying of that unnamed disease in *Love Story*. It didn't make *me* cry....'

'But don't you see?' he persisted. 'The boy and girl wanted to change their fate, do anything they could, but they couldn't. There was nothing in the world they could do. The secret is: 'None of *us* really can either, now can we?'

I put down the cup of tea I was drinking. 'Do you *really* believe that, Cary?' I said, distressed.

'Well, of course I do. I just told you I did, Maureen.'

'I don't,' I said, 'not for one second. Because if that were true, you'd still be back in Bristol and I'd be in London waiting tables instead of having tea here with you on the terrace.'

'No, no, no,' he went on. 'You don't understand. It's all been written on a page for us somewhere. Everything we've done. Everything we'll do.'

'Even the day we met?' I asked.

'Of course. Precisely.'

'Then there must be some hell of a writer *somewhere*,' I said, laughing.

Not too long afterward, I got another lesson in life and love from Cary on that terrace. Jennifer was with us and she was practicing some steps she'd learned at school in a square-dancing class. Cary stared at her, totally fascinated. Suddenly he got out of his chair, went into the living room and brought back a portable radio. He turned it to a country-and-western station.

'Okay,' he announced, 'everybody up. It's time to promenade your partner and do-si-do!'

I looked at him as if he were suffering from sunstroke.

'I mean it!' he said, grabbing my hand. 'You too, Willie!' he called into the kitchen. 'We're all going to strut our stuff!'

'Oh no, Mr. Grant,' Willie protested, but he signaled

for her to join us outside. Then he started wheeling Willie around and around as the poor woman did her best to keep up.

Jennifer looked at Willie and her father, then at me and then back at this very odd couple. She was completely enchanted. She burst out laughing.

'Now you two!' Cary instructed, pointing his finger at me and Jennifer.

We locked arms and began to skip around Cary and Willie. We did our best to keep up with those two as they twirled around the terrace, but there was no way we could. Around and around they went until poor Willie begged Cary to stop.

'Mr. Grant!' she yelled. 'I've got to stop or I'll fall down right here and now!'

So Cary scooped up Jennifer in one arm and grabbed me with his other and began rotating us like some demented carnival ride. None of us could stop laughing.

God, how good it was to see this side of Cary. If there was a frightened little boy inside him, there was no denying there was also a lovely, playful one who knew how to enjoy a good time.

A few minutes later, Jennifer went back to the kitchen with Willie. Cary and I stayed on the terrace.

'You know something,' I said, still overflowing with excitement and happiness. 'I love you, Cary. I really do. Especially —'

'Oh,' he jumped in, 'you don't love me, Maureen. You can't. You shouldn't even say something like that. It's ridiculous. A young girl like you ...'

It wasn't said with any malice or hostility this time. But the words chilled me. I could feel the joy of the day evaporating all around me.

'No, Cary. I love you. It's as simple as that.'

'Thank you,' he said, trying to sound kinder but still doing his best to dismiss the thought, 'but I'm sure someday you will find a young man who'll love you as you think you love me — and I will be very, very happy for the both of you.'

I was ready to cry, but I could see Jennifer heading back our way. I cut to the bottom line:

'No, Cary,' I said slowly. 'I love you and I don't care if you don't want to hear it, but it's true. And you know what? Someday you're going to tell me you *love* me the way I love you.'

'Maureen, I didn't mean to —'

'I know I'm right, Cary. Remember when I told you we'd make a great couple? I was right about that. And I'm right about this. You'll see.'

If Cary was reluctant to *say* he loved me, at least he wasn't afraid to show me in other ways how much he cared. One day I got home from work and he couldn't wait to usher me into the bedroom. There, spread all over the room, were piles and piles of Blassport clothes. He'd called up his friend Norman Zeiler and asked him to send a collection in my size.

'When does the fashion show begin?' he asked eagerly. 'I'm waiting!'

I rushed to the bathroom, slipped of my work clothes and ran back into the bedroom in my slip.

'Try this one!' he said, pointing to a beautiful black wool skirt.

'Lovely!' Cary confirmed as I slipped it on. 'Quite lovely!'

I sampled everything from jackets to swimsuits. Many of them were breathtaking, including a cotton skirt in a pale lavender and aqua flower pattern that I have to this day. I was allowed to keep as many as I wanted, which I must admit were quite a few. I also kept some suits I thought were much too old for me — Cary said, 'Oh, you must keep these!' — and today both the suits and I are the right age.

Later there would be many more fashion shows. Some days it would be strictly handbags, with literally hundreds to choose from. Or shoes, my secret passion. Cary's taste was quite conservative, so I was surprised when, on a dress day, he picked a rather risqué black jersey evening dress for me. It was sleeveless and cut to the navel. *When would I get a chance to wear this?* I thought.

The answer came when Cary received an invitation to attend a dinner in Beverly Hills honoring Henry Kissinger. Cary actually hated attending such events because he wasn't fond of getting dressed in black tie. 'A lot of bother!' he'd rant before the event, then ooze charm at the dinner itself.

I looked forward to the Kissinger dinner because I'd heard we'd be sitting next to Johnny Carson, whom I often watched on *The Tonight Show* after Cary went to sleep. It was our first formal evening out since all the hullabaloo in the press about our presence at the Mayfair Music Hall, and I didn't know what to expect.

As we entered the hotel where the dinner was held, a blitzkrieg of flashbulbs ignited in our faces. It instantly put Cary in a bad mood. He started jerking my arm for me to move faster and I had to tell him to slow down or I'd topple over.

Once we were seated, Cary seemed to relax but now *I* couldn't, even when he playfully pinched me on the bottom. We sat at a round table with four other couples, with just our first names inscribed on place cards near each plate. I sat down next to Johnny Carson, who pointed to my place card with his cigarette and asked, 'Maureen what?'

'Maureen Donaldson,' I offered. 'I'm with Mr. Grant,' pointing to Cary, who'd also taken his seat.

'And you're Johnny what?' I said to him, with tongue firmly in cheek. But he loved it. The usual oversized Hollywood ego would have been offended. He was charmed, however.

'I'm sorry, Miss Donaldson,' he said. 'My name is Johnny Carson.'

'And what do you do?' I said, continuing the charade. I caught Cary glaring at me. *He* was not charmed.

Johnny assumed that because I was English I must be unfamiliar with his talk show.

'Oh, I have a talk show — I think you call it a chat show in England,' he explained. 'As a matter of fact, I've been trying for years to persuade your friend to appear on it. Next to Greta Garbo, Cary's at the top of my wish list.'

'Make that your hit list!' Cary said, now relaxing and joining in.

From there the evening went smoothly. The only problem was my nervousness. What would calm me down was the white wine being served, but I'd already gone through my first glass. What was I going to do? I could still hear Cary's warning to me in the car on the way over about being very careful about what I drank: 'People get sloshed at these things all the time and it's so boring!'

While Cary was talking to some of our tablemates, I quietly struck a deal with Mr. Carson: He could have my prime rib — I was too nervous to enjoy it anyway — if he would keep his wineglass near mine and let me drink out of it from time to time. I would let mine stay empty for Cary's inspection. That arrangement got me through most of the night.

Later, when we got home, Cary did something that relaxed me even more — he asked me to dance with him in the moonlight out on the terrace. He turned on his small portable radio and found a station playing a Sinatra song.

We didn't say much. Words would have been superfluous. It was the perfect way to end an evening that had gotten off to such a hectic start. After a couple of dances with Cary, I was practically floating on air.

I came down to earth the next day when local newspapers published pictures of us together: Cary looked annoyed as he held onto my arm, and I had that bizarre, frightened look deer get in their eyes just before they're sent to join Bambi's mother in deer heaven.

'You look like a child!' Cary snapped when I walked into the house that evening. I looked at my jeans and top — my usual work uniform — and stared at him, puzzled.

'I don't mean *now*!' he practically shouted as he handed me a newspaper with our picture. 'Here. This photo. Look at it! I told you to wear your hair up, didn't I?'

Now I knew what had disturbed Cary so much about reports of our being together. It had nothing to do with what Dyan could supposedly make of it in court. It had everything to do with how young I looked. While we'd been getting ready for the Kissinger dinner, Cary had suggested I wear my hair up, but I didn't suspect anything then.

'You have such a beautiful neck, darling,' Cary said as I primped in Jennifer's bathroom. 'I've never seen a neck more beautiful, with the possible exception of Grace Kelly's. Why don't you show it off and wear your hair up?'

With a compliment like that, I'd have been happy to comply, but it would have taken me another ten minutes to get ready. Cary was a stickler about punctuality, so he agreed it'd be best for me to go as I had planned — with my hair down to my shoulders. I was a very young-looking twenty-seven, so the difference in our ages was only more pronounced in the photos from the Kissinger dinner.

Cary could not be persuaded to let the subject go. He dug and dug at it as at an old sore. It did not help when, a few weeks later, an older woman mistook me for his granddaughter while we were dining at a local restaurant.

But I was certain his sensitivity about the difference in our ages would ultimately fade. I shouldn't have been so certain. The issue reared its ugly head once again when we took our first trip to New York together in the spring. It was a quick jaunt on behalf of Fabergé, which was sponsoring a luncheon at which Cary was expected to appear. He did, but not with me at his side.

As we headed into the hall where the luncheon was being held, Cary informed me I would be sitting with George Barrie, the head of Fabergé. I liked George enormously and I knew he liked me — he'd already told Cary he liked me because I didn't 'put on airs' as did some of the other women Cary'd dated.

'Terrific!' I said enthusiastically as we kept walking. 'George is great fun. He'll keep us laughing.'

'No, you don't understand,' Cary said, his voice

suddenly hard and hollow. 'You will sit with George, I will sit elsewhere. You understand, I'm sure. It's business.'

I did not understand, of course. If I was good enough to share Cary's bed, then I should be good enough to sit by his side at any public function. But before I could voice an objection, Cary had already begun moving away from me, practically shoving me into George, who was heading straight for me.

I was on the verge of tears but didn't want to cause a scene. That would only compound the problem. I didn't fool George, though. When he saw Cary walk away and sit down in another part of the room, he quickly put two and two together and did his best to console me.

'He shouldn't treat you this way, Maureen,' he said. 'And I'm going to tell him so later. In the meantime you and I will do our best to ignore him and have as good a time as we can manage. If you feel up to it ... do you?'

'Sure,' I said weakly, forcing a smile.

'Good,' he said. 'Joe Namath is going to be sitting at *our* table, so we'll see who got the short end of the stick, won't we?'

'Right!' I said as I put my arm through his and headed for the table. Broadway Joe was already sitting down but his piercing green eyes were following my every move. He was also part of the Fabergé family, appearing in commercials for its Brut men's products.

George spotted Joe's interest in me and whispered in my ear as I sat down, 'Let's pull a fast one on Cary. If Joe wants to know anything about you, you just tell him I'm pimping for you. That you're here for Cary Grant this afternoon, but an arrangement *can* be worked out for later if Joe's really interested.'

It was silly and childish, but I went along with it in a flash because I'd already been made to *feel* like a whore.

I did my best to charm Joe, and it wasn't long before I was explaining to him that I was 'taking care of' Mr Grant during his trip, but if he wanted to work something out, he could do so with Mr. Barrie. Joe appeared eager to strike a deal, but I lost my appetite for this particular tactic.

I'd been at the luncheon twenty minutes at most when I got up, excused myself and told George I'd be back at the hotel.

Thirty minutes later Cary called the Warwick, where he always stayed in New York, in a suite paid for by Fabergé.

'What do you think you're doing?' he said, his voice so cold it could have frozen the phone line.

'I'm packing, Cary,' I said calmly, trying not to let the emotion show in my voice. 'Then I'm catching a cab to the airport. When I get to Los Angeles, I'll do some more packing and be out of your life.'

'I will be there in thirty minutes,' Cary said, 'Please wait.'

'What's the point, Cary?' I said.

'Don't be foolish,' he said, softening. 'I'll be right there.'

He was, within fifteen minutes. But it did little to console me. I felt cheap. I felt as though Cary had decided I was something to hide. I felt horrible.

Cary did his best to calm me down and listened patiently. But I felt utterly hopeless.

'I don't understand you, Cary,' I said, crying. 'I know I'm not Dyan or Sophia Loren or any of those women. But *no* man has ever made me feel like I was something to be hidden away. If I'm good enough to go to bed with you, why aren't I good enough to be seen with you in public?'

He assured me I was overreacting. He told me he wasn't ashamed of me. In fact, he was proud that a girl so young could love a man of his age.

'That's it, isn't it?' I said, twisting in my hands an oval clock from a table next to my chair. 'You're deathly afraid of what people will think. We've been all through that. Why do you care?

'You should care that I love you. That Jennifer has accepted me. That all your friends have accepted me. The only one who doesn't accept us is *you*. I give up, Cary. I won't fight you any more. You win.'

Again he told me I was overreacting. Again he told me he would never do anything to make me feel embarrassed or ashamed. Again he said that he was proud that I loved him.

But he didn't tell me *he* loved *me*. That came a couple of weeks later, in early April. On April 2, 1974, to be exact. I remember the date because it was Oscar night.

Since our trip to New York, I had been keeping my distance from Cary, even though he was on his absolute best and most charming behavior. I was glad I'd kept my apartment (as I did throughout all our years together) so I would have a place to collect my thoughts, kick off my shoes or just play music as often and as loudly as I liked.

The morning of the Academy Awards ceremony, Cary called me at work and asked what my plans were. I hadn't been assigned to cover the ceremonies that year, so I'd just planned to watch them as I did every year at a friend's house. We'd sit, stuff our faces and generally make fun out of the pomp and circumstance of Hollywood's annual tribute to excess and excellence.

But Cary had a better idea.

'Why don't you get off work early? We'll make up a big batch of sandwiches and watch the program together.'

The opportunity to sit and watch the Academy Awards with Cary Grant was too good to resist.

'You mean you're not going?' I asked him.

'Fat chance!' he said, one of his favorite expressions. 'I hate getting dressed up even when they're giving *me* one of those things.'

I arrived at five so we could watch what I'd always considered the best part of the show — the arrivals of the stars, when reporters awkwardly trip over each other trying to get a better inanity from the passing celebrities than their competition can.

Halfway through this part, I looked in *TV Guide* to see who'd be performing the songs nominated for an Oscar. This was usually another 'highlight,' with blaring over-orchestrations and other offenses against the ear. Then my heart stopped. Dyan Cannon was scheduled to sing 'All

That Love Went to Waste' from *A Touch of Class*.

I turned to Cary and thought I should prepare him for the news.

'Did you know Dyan was singing on the show tonight?' I said cautiously.

'Yes,' he said, not disturbed in the least. 'Why?'

'Oh, I just thought,' I began hesitantly, 'knowing the way you feel about her, you might prefer to watch something else. In fact, if you want, we could go out to a movie and forget the whole show.'

'Don't be ridiculous,' he said. 'I want to watch it. Dyan's not a bad singer, actually. And since *A Touch of Class* is a Brut film, it only seemed appropriate that she sing it. You know, George Barrie did the music and Sammy Cahn did the lyrics.'

So Cary and I were going to watch his ex-wife sing a song about romantic loss, before hundreds of millions of people, complete with music written by one of his closest friends. In Cary's bedroom yet.

I didn't care what Cary said, I needed a drink.

Cary broke open a bottle of Setrakian and filled my glass. He seemed positively merry, as if he didn't have a care in the world. He was either the best actor in the world or completely bonkers.

The ceremony began appropriately enough, with Burt Reynolds telling the audience:

'Right now in New York, Beverly Hills, Bel Air, all over the country, there are cocktail parties filled with people saying nasty, catty, snide remarks....'

'And we're two of them!' Cary hooted at the television. 'Aren't we, dear?'

I laughed uneasily. I wondered just how long his laughter would last. I didn't have to wonder very long.

Dyan's was the first of the nominated songs to be performed on the program. Up to that point I'd been doing my best to join Cary in this atmosphere of forced merriment. Now I needed another glass of wine.

The music began and Dyan was photographed lovingly behind some prop trees and branches. She looked stunning in a white low-cut gown. And she had placed a daisy behind one of her ears for a casual touch.

She started singing, but the first line was garbled because of a problem with her microphone. It cleared up quickly, but not before Cary had snorted '*Ha!*' at the screen. But his laughter was cut short as Dyan proceeded to sing the rest of the song:

> *We were close to it all,*
> *Caught the rainbows we chased.*
> *Then we watched the sky fall,*
> *All that love went to waste.*
>
> *What we had was the end,*
> *It could not be erased.*
> *That's the pity, my friend,*
> *All that love went to waste.*
>
> *If we only could have guessed*
> *That it couldn't stand the test.*
> *We'd have played it all for jest*
> *And been each other's guest.*
>
> *We'd have smiled and strolled away*
> *While it still was light and gay,*
> *But now here's that rainy day.*
>
> *We walked away tall,*
> *Faced what had to be faced.*
> *And we both may recall*
> *That though it's all gone,*
> *It's through and done,*
> *We had some laughs,*
> *And had some fun*
> *That lingers on,*
> *And couldn't have gone to waste.*

I didn't dare look over at Cary while Dyan was singing, but when she finished I turned and saw a single tear roll down his cheek.

The show went on, but Cary sat silent and expression-less for what seemed like hours. I didn't know what to do or say.

Finally he turned to me and said: 'You know, the daisy used to be my favorite flower.'

I grabbed his hand and held it hard. I knew he'd hate it because he detested any show of 'cheap emotion,' as he used to put it, but I also knew he'd still be comforted.

He smiled, trying not to let his eyes meet mine.

We pretended to watch the rest of the program with the high spirits we'd generated earlier that night. But they vanished again when Peggy Lee came on to sing another nominated song, 'The Way We Were.'

Another song about romantic loss from another friend of Cary's. The irony, coupled with the masochism in the air, was unbearable. I had to have yet another glass of wine. Lee sang the song so languidly it seemed as if she were in slow motion.

I occupied myself throughout the rest of the show keeping tabs on how many people on the program Cary knew personally. There was Edith Head, who won the Oscar that night for Best Costume Design for *The Sting* (she had clothed Cary in *To Catch a Thief* and other films). There was Katharine Hepburn, who made her first (and, to date, last) appearance on the Oscar program, present-ing the Irving J. Thalberg Memorial Award to producer Lawrence Weingarten. There was Alfred Hitchcock (who'd made so many films with Cary, including *Notorious* and *North by Northwest*) drolly presenting Lew Wasserman, the pasha of Universal Studios, with a humanitarian award.

Cary had little to say about them. But two people did not escape comment: One was Connie Stevens, who'd been engaged to dance the theme song from *Live and Let Die*. After she wriggled through the number, supported by a multitude of chorus boys clad in silver lamé costumes that looked like discards from *Flash Gordon*, Cary proclaimed: 'Thank God they had the good sense not to let her *sing*!' The other was Charlton Heston, who'd been chosen to copresent the Best Actress award with Susan

Hayward. 'My God,' he said tipsily, as he watched Heston read the list of nominees, 'there's something *dead* on his head!'

For me, the highlight came when Telly Savalas was brought onstage to sing another nominated song, '(You're) Nice to Be Around' from the movie *Cinderella Liberty*. God knows why Savalas had been chosen, but he put the song over fairly well. He was only a couple of lines into it when I recognized the tune.

'My God, Cary,' I said, moving closer to Cary on the bed, 'that's a Paul Williams song. I've heard it before.' There was no mistaking its message:

> *Hello*
> *Such a simple way*
> *To start a love affair.*
> *Should I jump right in*
> *And say how much I care?*
> *Would you take me for a madman*
> *Or a simple-hearted clown?*
>
> *Hello*
> *With affection*
> *From a sentimental fool*
> *To a little girl*
> *Who's broken every rule.*
> *One who brings me up*
> *When all the others seem to let me down.*
> *To one who's nice to be around.*
>
> *Should I say it's a blue world*
> *Without you?*
> *Nice words I remember*
> *From an old love song*
> *But all wrong*
> *'Cause I never called it love before.*
> *This feeling is new.*
> *This came with you.*

I know the nicest things
Never seemed to last,
That we're both a bit
Embarrassed by our past.
But I think there's something special
In the feelings that we've found
And you're nice to be around.

I was suddenly sober and said a silent prayer, thanking God for Paul Williams. Here, finally, was a song about romantic *possibility*, not loss.

I turned to Cary and said:

'Didn't I tell you Paul Williams was good?'

Cary got my message as well as the song's.

'Hello,' he whispered, touching my hand so gently.

'Hello,' I sighed.

'You are nice to be around.'

'You too.'

'Not all the time,' he laughed.

'Me neither,' I said.

'I know. I'm so glad you're here.'

It was my turn to say 'I know.'

'Do you know I love you, Maureen?'

'I know.'

'I really love you,' Cary told me.

The countdown was finally over.

12

WHEN YOU'RE IN LOVE

I WON something even more precious than Cary's love that night. I was given something by Cary that he'd give me only one time for any kind of extended period: peace. Peace for month after happy month. Suspicion and hostility faded away that spring and all through the summer. In this season of our relationship, not only did we reach an equilibrium we would never match again but more and more barriers fell between us.

For now, Cary's trust was complete. Nothing could overthrow it, not even a newspaper report in late May that just a few months earlier would have sent him into cyclonic rage.

On May 28, Dorothy Manners led off her column with this:

'It continues to tickle Hollywood that Cary Grant continues to date slim and pretty Maureen Donaldson, British-born writer. What causes the chuckles is that publicity-shy Cary's favorite lady of the moment works as an associate editor for a Hollywood magazine run by TV gossiper Rona Barrett. Nope, I haven't heard Rona predicting marriage — even with her front-row seat at the romance.'

After I got home on the day this item was printed, I found that Cary had circled it and included it in my homework. But he seemed as 'tickled' as the rest of Hollywood. Alongside the Manners story, he wrote:

'How much do you think we should charge Rona for that seat?'

As Cary's trust grew, so did his passion for me. He began to lose some of his inhibitions and that sense of holding back I'd felt earlier. Previously he'd been embarrassed to take a shower with me, but sometimes in the late afternoon on weekends I'd take his hand and lead him into the water. As always he professed to be ashamed of his 'chicken skin,' but I wouldn't hear of it.

His skin was a beautifully burnished brown, and it remained supple and sexy. One afternoon, after I'd persuaded him to join me in the shower, he paid me one of his highest compliments.

'You know,' he said as he lathered my body, 'there's been only one other woman I made love to this way. I never thought I would again....'

I hoped he wouldn't mention her name, because I didn't have to be told who it was. Every instinct I had informed me it was Dyan, the woman who'd gotten under his skin more than any other. Fortunately he didn't say her name. It would only have intimidated me, particularly at such an intimate moment.

Cary was just as considerate at those moments he let me know he wanted to make love. (Usually I was the one who initiated things, by rubbing my leg against his.) This modest, shy man would come out of the bathroom, not clad as usual in his bathrobe but with a towel around him. He knew the sight of his chest always excited me. He would cast a sideways look at me, his face somewhat flushed. If he was feeling particularly eager, he'd position the towel in such a way that I could get a slight glimpse of what was underneath.

One evening, when I felt especially close to him, I urged him to release every feeling he had inside him.

'Don't be afraid,' I whispered. 'Don't hold anything back. I want you to give yourself to me, darling. I won't hurt you. You can trust me.'

And he did. He became not more aggressive, as some men might at such an invitation, but much more gentle, losing himself in the moment. There was a tenderness he had only hinted at before. I had a boy in my arms, not a man, and he trusted me enough not to crush or suffocate him. It was in these moments I knew Cary Grant loved me, and I'd never felt so secure with him. My arms provided a temporary cocoon within which this deeply troubled, immensely complicated man felt safe. Knowing I could provide this gave me a strength I felt for the first time with any man. Finally, we were a couple. A *real* couple.

He felt free enough to tell me anything. Nothing was too trivial or too shameful. And I felt the same freedom with him. We developed an ease, a fluidity that amazed both of us, though we rarely discussed it for fear we'd somehow ruin it. It got to the point that I could kid him (and vice versa) without fearing he would take it all the wrong way.

'I dreamed wonderful dreams last night about you,' Cary told me on many a morning. 'But I've forgotten what!'

'Typical,' I'd say, poking him in the ribs. 'But don't worry, I'll help you remember.'

Cary never failed to surprise me. He was, as he had once said about himself, 'a series of contradictions.' Fortunately, I shared one of his contradictions: his desire, on the one hand, to have people around him in the house — he hated being there with no one else around — yet, on the other hand, to feel free enough to go off by himself and read, clip or whatever. He needed the warmth of human bodies nearby but also needed to be alone much more than most people.

I understood this need completely. There were many afternoons and evenings when Cary and I went off by ourselves to different corners of the house, secure in the knowledge that the other was nearby.

Today this kind of need is referred to in psychospeak as 'needing space.' In those days we referred to it as 'our solitary side.' It didn't mean, of course, that we didn't do many things together in or out of the house.

One of our favorite activities was spending Sunday mornings with the zany British comic Tony Hancock. Thanks to radio, he came into the house for an hour and a half by way of his famous programs that had been taped in the fifties. Though Hancock had died in 1968, he lived in our mind's eye all over again as his bulging eyes, jowly cheeks and shaggy eyebrows faced all the indignities that the world hilariously tossed his way.

Cary loved Hancock's brand of comedy, and I think he felt a special bond with him because Hancock had rocketed to fame in Britain in the early fifties with the radio program *Educating Archie*. The former Archie Leach also felt a kinship because Hancock's specialty (what one critic called the portrayal in countless situations of 'the collapse of the grand into the ungrammatical and baffled') mirrored what had become Cary's specialty in movies like *Bringing Up Baby*, in which his pompous, stuffed-shirt character was reduced to sputtering distress by the stubborn whirlwind of a woman played by Katharine Hepburn.

Hancock's humor reminded Cary of the vaudeville routines he saw back in Bristol as a young boy, and as a fledgling actor later in New York. Cary loved the corny, knockabout humor that pervaded these routines, and he was constantly quoting lines from them to me.

Once when were were watching a Fred Astaire movie on television I commented: 'Fred Astaire is so good. He must've been born dancing.'

'Must've been hard on his mother, don't you think?' Cary said dryly.

If someone introduced himself to Cary and said, 'How do you do? he'd always answer: 'I don't!'

If someone exclaimed: 'Oh, brother!' he couldn't wait to reply: 'Oh, sister!'

If someone said, 'That should strike a happy medium,' he'd offer: 'Oh, please don't! Mediums are abused enough as it is, don't you think?'

Cary's love for this type of humor also had a bawdy side.

One night we were sitting in bed reading, when he put down his book, turned to me and ordered:

'Say "terrified"!'

'Excuse me?' I said, confused.

'Say "terrified,"' he repeated.

'Terrified,' I said patiently, putting down my book.

'Now say "tissue,"' he continued.

'Tissue,' I said.

'No, no,' he said. 'Say them together.'

'Okay,' I said, sighing. 'Terrified tissue.'

'Faster. Say it faster!'

I said it so fast it came out sounding like 'Care if I kiss you?'

'Don't mind if I do!' he said, proud of himself. Then he leaned over and bestowed a kiss. (It was a routine from one of his films.)

This schoolboy glee mixed with risqué corniness surfaced on another night.

'I guess I'll turn in now,' I said, for once going to bed before he did.

'Into what?' he asked erupting into laughter.

But the one routine I heard over and over again I first heard one evening when we were sitting on the terrace watching the sun go down.

'It's so nice out,' I said, staring at the crimson streaking across the sky.

'Then I think I'll leave it out!' he bounced back.

This became a running joke between us, and it shamelessly greeted panoramas from Bristol to Boston. It was a side to Cary that I cherished because it not only contrasted so outrageously with his sophisticated screen image but also brought out the little boy in him.

I was also privileged to see that side of Cary in his almost fanatical love for baseball. He fell in love with the game while touring the United States with Bob Pender soon after he came to this country. Cary and the other boy acrobats frequently shared the same trains and hotels as the New York Giants when the team was on the road. Over fifty years later Cary was a big Los Angeles Dodgers fan.

Fabergé had arranged for season box seats at Dodger Stadium for Cary, and he rarely missed a game. Of course, I wanted to share Cary's love for baseball, but it mystified me at first. The nearest equivalent for me was an English game I'd played called rounders. But the strategy and terminology were still mysteries to me until one afternoon we were invited to sit in the box of Dodger owners Walter and Peter O'Malley. A gruff, elderly man sat down next to me and began speaking with a twisted syntax that left me even more puzzled.

'Maureen, this man can explain a lot to you,' Cary said as he introduced me to Casey Stengel, the baseball legend with the leathery face. Not only had he played for the Dodgers, when they were in Brooklyn, at the beginning of his career, but decades later, as manager, he led the New York Yankees to four World Series wins against his former team. Now in his eighties, Stengel lived with his wife, Edna, in Glendale and still loved the game.

Casey took his assignment that afternoon very seriously as he began to give me the basics of the game. But I found it hard to keep up with him, considering the convoluted way he spoke.

'Darlin',' he rasped. 'You gotta pay attention or you're gonna miss your strikes and pop flies!'

'I hope I don't pop *my* fly!' Cary joined in, making matters worse.

Eventually, however, I got the hang of it and even learned what 'base on balls' meant, though it always retained a slightly bawdy implication to Cary and me.

Most of the time we brought Jennifer with us, and it was heartening to see Cary so gentle and patient with his young daughter as he tried to explain the intricacies of the game to her. This display of paternal devotion and forbearance was more thrilling than anything I ever saw on the Dodger playing field.

Cary also surprised me with his passion for 'Dodger dogs,' plump hot dogs in a generous bun which he always ate. The first time I saw him buy one, I assumed it was for Jennifer. I couldn't believe it when he popped it eagerly into his mouth.

'Cary!' I almost yelled. 'What are you doing?'

'Oh, I'm sorry,' he said, 'I should have given you first bite!'

'No, I'm not talking about that!' I said, still stupefied. 'I'm talking about all the times you've yelled at me for having soft drinks. "Do you know what's in that?" you say. And all the times you've ranted and raved about food cooked with charcoal.'

He gulped down a piece guiltily.

'Do you know what's in *that*?' I demanded, waving my finger at the part of the hot dog that remained in his hands.

'Oh, I know,' he said lightly. 'But baseball's not baseball without a hot dog.'

As I've said, he was a man full of surprises and contradictions. As for Jennifer, baseball wasn't baseball without a Coke. One afternoon I'd spent what seemed like ages waiting in line for Cokes for Jennifer and me, plus a beer for Cary.

When I finally got back to our seats, I placed my Cokes down on the ledge in front of our seats as I put away my purse. Suddenly everything toppled down on the people sitting below us. I was horrified and afraid to get up to look down at the damage, but I did. Two men and a woman were staring up at me, positively drenched with the sticky soft drink, now drying rapidly on them in the hot sun. One of the men began shaking a fist at me, yelling: 'Thanks a lot! Thanks so much!'

I was too humiliated to speak, but Cary took matters into his own capable hands. He stood up and looked down at the still-dripping group.

'Oh!' he said in his most charming tones. 'I'm so terribly sorry! I can't imagine what happened. We'll get you a towel or something!'

The woman in the group was the first to recognize Cary. A big smile began to flood her face.

'Oh, Mr. Grant,' she cooed. 'I didn't know it was you. Oh, please don't worry. Accidents happen.'

Then the men started buzzing with recognition.

'So sorry to bother *you*!' one of them said as he issued a partial salute toward Cary.

Now they were apologizing to us when, just seconds before, they had been ready to lynch me. Cary had that effect on people. Then he shot me a little smile that said: 'What do you think about that?'

Cary also loved the racetrack, but I rarely went with him. Having had my own horse during my days at the ranch in Chatsworth gave me a keen appreciation for the animal's power and strength, so I really couldn't bear to see a horse whipped into winning — which is what it all amounted to in my eyes — as I watched the horses straining to get around the racetrack.

The only thing I really enjoyed at the track was the company of Jean Kerkorian, Kirk Kerkorian's wife. We got along like a house on fire after we met there one weekend. She was so down-to-earth, and her warmth contrasted sharply with Kirk, whom I found distant and preoccupied. He wore his hair in an odd kind of pompadour that, combined with his dark Armenian looks, made him a real character in my eyes. I knew he had a brilliant mind because Cary had told me how Kirk, a former boxer and pilot, had parlayed ownership of a charter airline in the late forties into ownership in the seventies of not only his own movie studio (MGM) but also a string of hotels in Las Vegas, including the mighty MGM Grand.

But I thought Cary's friendship with Kirk strange when I remembered that one of Cary's other best friends, Howard Hughes, was one of Kirk's mortal enemies. The two had become locked in lethal financial combat in the mid-sixties when Hughes was trying to buy up every hotel in Vegas, while Kirk took over ownership of Caesar's Palace and built a new palace, the International. How could Cary be friends with both? I chalked it up as another one of Cary's inconsistencies.

Besides, I truly loved Jean. She had a Cockney accent she took no pains to disguise. She was what she was, and damn proud of it. Jean had two beautiful daughters, Tracy and Linda, and she had instilled in them her disarming lack of pretense. Nothing could disturb this woman's composure.

One evening at a particularly proper dinner party in Beverly Hills, Jean and I entered an unspoken agreement to shake things up. We felt honor-bound to do so because we were surrounded by a platoon of old-money society women who refused to crack a smile for fear of disturbing a jowl. Cary, Kirk and the other men had retired to another part of this elegant home, so they did not have to suffer through the attack of inconsequential chitchat and veiled zingers to some present and some absent.

One woman especially irked Jean and me: Her hair had been teased so strangely and so violently it looked like an angry tumbleweed. But it was her voice that annoyed me most. It had that monotonous quality particular to those people who've spent their entire lives listening only to the sound of their own voice.

The woman was droning on and on about some recent catastrophe in her life, allegedly caused by her cook's incompetence, when Jean cut through the conversation:

'You should have your cook make spotted dick!'

Everyone at the table stared at her in disbelief.

'What did you say?' the woman with the tumbleweed hairdo inquired haughtily.

'You ... should ... have ... your ... cook ... make ... spotted ... dick!' Jean said merrily, enunciating every word in the cultured tones of the best King's English.

I burst out laughing because I knew what spotted dick was: an English pudding with raisins in it. But to American ears it sounded rather obscene.

I glanced at Jean and winked.

'But without raisins,' I said, 'it's not spotted dick, if you know what I mean.' Nudge, nudge. Wink, wink!

The women at the table were now lost somewhere between mystification and anger, so Jean finally told them just what spotted dick was. They were not amused.

But Cary was, when I told him the story on the way home.

'As the actress said to the bishop, "Serves them right for being so *stiff*!"' was his verdict.

13

ALICE IN WONDERLAND

THAT magnificent summer of 1974 also proved liberating for Jennifer.

Cary had been living just a few doors down from Dyan in Malibu for years so he could be close to his daughter. But after I entered the picture and our relationship really kicked into gear, he began to spend less and less time at the beach house and more and more at his own home on Beverly Grove, however incomplete it was. Then something happened that none of us could have predicted — the landlord raised Cary's rent in Malibu from approximately $1,200 a month to $2,000. Cary decided the increase simply wasn't worth it and promptly moved out of Malibu.

For Jennifer this could mean only an improvement. Sometimes in Malibu she had come to resemble a walking apology as she was torn in two directions at one location. Now she could be with her mother at the beach without ever worrying if her father was watching. And in Beverly Hills she could be completely in Cary's environment. She could separate the two worlds in her mind and have the best of both, without either closing in on her.

You could see the change in Jennifer as she tasted this new freedom. She was much less nervous and hesitant around her father. Before, she sometimes seemed bound by an invisible leash which had wrapped itself around her in the pressure she felt to please her father. Now she seemed to free Cary as she freed herself, becoming much more affectionate and attentive towards him. Not surprisingly, Cary himself started blossoming as this process unfolded.

He still worried about Dyan's influence on Jennifer, particularly when he heard she was taking Jennifer to a commune up in Monterey. 'There're drugs and black people and God knows what else,' he worried aloud. I had to laugh because he sounded like a racist member of the John Birch Society. Fortunately, he never pressed his concerns with his lawyer or Dyan beyond expressing his disapproval in general terms.

Personally, I found Dyan's journey of self-discovery — a journey that had begun shortly after her traumatic separation from Cary — both encouraging and exciting. Conventional answers were just not making it in the unconventional world of 1974; the country had been almost instantly turned upside down by the Watergate scandal. Richard Nixon resigned in August to avoid being impeached. If you couldn't trust the President, whom could you trust? The only answer seemed to be: yourself. More and more people turned inward as the outside world collapsed.

Wherever Dyan's journey took her, I knew she'd find her way home. After all, she had Jennifer with her for much of the ride. I hoped someday I would have a child as loving and special by my side.

In addition, Cary's concerns about Dyan supposedly using drugs struck me as hypocritical. After all, wasn't he the one who'd reaped the headlines in the late fifties when he admitted taking LSD? Wasn't he the one Dyan accused in her divorce suit of taking LSD on average once a week?

One day when Cary started speculating about what Dyan was doing up in Monterey, I mentioned this contradiction.

'But you don't understand,' Cary said, 'LSD is a chemical, not a drug. People who take drugs are trying to escape from their lives. LSD is a hallucinogen, and people who take it are trying to look *within* their lives. That's what I did.'

The difference between a drug and a chemical seemed basically one of semantics the way Cary explained it, but I encouraged him to tell me precisely what he felt LSD did for him.

'Well,' he said, warming to the subject, 'let me put it this way — I'm now seventy years old and I have lived a lot longer than you have, Maureen. And I know that two things changed my life: First, there was LSD, which helped me look within myself. It was painful and there were days I literally could not get off the floor, it hurt so badly. But once I faced what was inside me, I eventually forgave myself and the mistakes I'd made, and I forgave my parents and the mistakes they'd made.

'The second thing was the birth of Jennifer. LSD was my rebirth. Jennifer was the birth of a new me, the one who was forced to stop thinking of only me, me, me, and to extend his boundaries a great, great deal ... far beyond me, do you understand?'

I did, but I wanted to know more. How in the world did someone as conservative as Cary get involved with something as radical as LSD was in the late fifties and early sixties?

'First of all, you have to understand it was legal in those days,' he began to explain. 'And it was Betsy, bless her, who set me on the path. She was a very educated girl, much more than a mere actress. She was the one who helped me stop smoking. She hypnotized me one night right out of it. I know it sounds crazy, but she did. I never did smoke a cigarette after that.

'She was always very interested in psychology and she mentioned several doctors who believed in the wondrous effects of a hallucinogen called LSD 25. That's what they called it in those days. There was a doctor named Mortimer Hartman, and he's the man who saved my life. I am not exaggerating. I was so confused and lost when I began seeing him.' (Cary would express his gratitude to Dr. Hartman in his will with a bequest of $10,000, though he had not been in touch with him for years.)

As Cary described the effect of his first sessions with

LSD, I'd rarely seen him so excited and enthusiastic.

'The first breakthrough came when I realized I was the one responsible for the cycles of my life. I was repeating the same mistakes and patterns over and over again. It became so clear to me one day when I was twisting myself all over the sofa in the doctor's office. I heard myself saying aloud, "Why am I turning around and around on this sofa?" "You don't know why?" the doctor said. "No," I said, very annoyed, "but I tell you this: It better stop soon." And the doctor said, "Cary, it'll stop when *you* stop it."

'And of course, he was right. It was as if a light finally went on inside my brain. It was a revelation. *I* had to take command. *I* had to take complete responsibility for my own actions and stop blaming my mother and my father and everyone else. And then I said, "Look, I'm un-screwing myself, aren't I?" And that's what happened in more ways than one.'

Cary described this self-illumination as a 'release' and a 'discharge.' In his mind he could see himself going through birth and pushing through his mother's body.

'You see,' he almost whispered, 'I finally realized that for all the pain I thought my mother had caused me, I had caused her pain too. When I broke through this way, I lost all the tension that I'd been crippling myself with. I lost all my inhibitions.

'The day this all became clear to me, I lost it all, but I gained something more. Myself. And on that day I shat all over the rug in the doctor's office and I shat all over his floor.'

He laughed a little, somewhat embarrassed. But I could sense the pride he felt. He had the conviction that this was *the* shining moment of his life, next to Jennifer's birth. He had that magnificent assurance all true believers have, whatever the cause.

And like all true believers, he was eager to share his faith and joy. 'I would love for you to try it,' he said. 'It's illegal in this country now, but LSD is still legal in a couple of countries. We could go there and I would be there for you, just like Betsy was for me. Did I tell you she went to every session with me and waited outside the doctor's door to make sure I was all right?'

This invitation contrasted with the position he usually gave to the press. 'I would never recommend LSD to others,' he said over and over, 'but I will say that it worked for me.' But he did recommend it to me. Frequently.

But I was extremely reluctant to take it. Like many of my generation, I smoked marijuana and I liked it. I was hardly a pothead, but I found its occasional use relaxing.

Cary and I had begun planning a trip to New York and then England for the fall and I seriously considered trying LSD while we were in Europe. But one night he said something that stopped me. It was during another of his enthusiastic endorsements. The speech about LSD rarely varied: the rebirth ... the unscrewing of himself ... taking responsibility for all his actions ... forgiving himself and everyone else.

But during this session he added something that made me never want to hear about LSD again.

'LSD made me realize I was killing my mother through my relationships with other women. I was punishing them for what she did to me,' he said matter-of-factly.

'What do you mean?' I asked, but I think I already knew the answer.

'I had to face the fact that psychologically I killed every woman I'd been with since my mother deserted me.'

'But,' I said, 'LSD helped you to stop that. . . .'

'Of course, that's my whole point!' he said impatiently.

The whole discussion made me uneasy. After that I always did my best to turn the conversation away from LSD whenever he brought it up. He caught on quickly and rarely urged me to take the substance. I realized he wanted it to act as a passport to a world few people experienced, and his sincerity touched me. I decided to re-double my efforts to show him *my* world, a world that would help him strengthen his ties to Jennifer, who was growing up fast before our eyes.

My key was singer Alice Cooper, whom I'd interviewed

during my days with *Teen* magazine. He was the complete opposite of his stage persona, which consisted of snakes and guillotines and anything else capable of offending Mr. and Mrs. America. Behind the makeup, he was actually a gentle soul who became one of my best friends. While people who didn't know either of us well read something romantic into our relationship, we were what the British call 'good mates.' We could talk to each other and, more important, we understood each other without holding judgment over each other's head. I looked far beneath Alice's ominous appearance and learned to love the shy boy from Arizona he really was, while Alice likewise delved beneath my sometimes cheeky, sometimes happy-go-lucky surface.

As I mentioned earlier, Jennifer was fascinated with the mere fact I knew someone as exotic as Alice. When I mentioned this to Alice, he started giving me autographed pictures and drawings he penned on the spur of the moment to give to her. She was speechless with delight, but Cary initially refused to understand the attraction Alice held for either of us.

'Maureen,' he'd protest, 'I know you like him very, very much and he seems quite thoughtful and all that. But once you scratch off all that hideous makeup, what you've got is just a homely man.'

But Jennifer and I persisted. Since Alice was my friend, I wanted Cary to meet him. I knew if they met face to face Cary would drop his resistance within a matter of minutes. But I couldn't persuade Cary to invite him to the house, although Alice lived nearby in Benedict Canyon.

Yet with Jennifer's enthusiasm for Alice, Cary's objections to the man were slowly but surely chipped away. I got an inkling of this when I told Cary about my first photo shoot with the singer. Alice had suggested I try photography as an adjunct to my writing. 'If it's as expressive as your writing,' he said generously, 'then you should have something. And how can you go wrong with me? Who would know a good picture from a bad one?' he said laughing.

One afternoon I stopped by Cary's house before going on to Alice's for my shoot; Cary had a surprise for me. It was a trilby hat, one Spencer Tracy had given him. It was dashing and extremely photogenic.

'Why don't you try this on him?' Cary suggested. 'It might give you something different.'

'Thank you,' I said on my way out the door.

'And be sure to tell him hello from Jennifer and me.'

I knew he was really extending himself with all of this. I rushed back to the door and gave him a kiss.

'That's good-bye and a thank you from *me*,' I laughed.

That was the start of a running gag between Cary and Alice. Every time I ran into Alice, I gave him Cary's regards. And every time I saw Cary after seeing Alice, I gave him Alice's regards. But Cary was still entirely confused as to what appeal Alice could have for someone like Jennifer or me.

I vowed to rectify that. If Cary wouldn't meet Alice socially, perhaps I could persuade him to see Alice in action onstage. It was tongue-in-cheek Grand Guignol theater. Groucho Marx had gotten the joke and had even invited Alice to his home for dinner. George Burns had invited Alice to play golf. If these classic comics could give Alice their personal seal of approval, surely I could convince an old vaudevillian like Cary to give him a try.

But it was like persuading Zsa Zsa Gabor to undress. Cary would have none of it. Then one day I said, 'You mean you really don't want to see what Jennifer's going to see the first chance she gets? You don't want to understand what she sees in him?'

That did it. But he refused to go to any of Alice's concerts in the Los Angeles area. There was no way, as he put it, that 'I'm going to give this chap free publicity when I don't even know if I'll like what I see — which I strongly doubt!'

We waited months until there was a concert scheduled for San Diego. Cary insisted he go incognito, so I disguised him as best I could in the 'style' of a more than slightly seedy agent. I wrapped sunglasses around Cary's eyes, a gold chain around his neck and a checked jacket around his shoulders. The trilby covered his gray hair. Sharkskin pants from a girlfriend's brother completed this too-trendy-for-words picture.

Cary rather enjoyed this tasteless and tacky getup. What he enjoyed less was the ride down to San Diego. It was a two-hour drive (I drove because Cary was an awful driver), and he complained every mile of the way. 'I can't believe I'm doing this for a man named Alice, or is it a boy named Sue?' he needled me.

Alice's manager, Shep Gordon, had given me a pair of tickets in the press section, but I switched them outside the concert with two kids who had tickets much farther away from the stage. I told no one I was bringing Cary to this event; the last thing I wanted was for my colleagues in the press to discover him in those ridiculous clothes. I also thought some distance might give Cary a more benign view of Alice's activities onstage.

I will say that Cary did his best. He wore earplugs and he sat through the entire show without one word of complaint. He sat through the 'beheading' and the contortions with the snake and the rest of the highlights of Alice's set. Afterward I told Cary we couldn't come this far without saying hello to Alice, finally face to face.

'If you think I'm going backstage and letting photographers get pictures of us together — because you know there will be photographers there; there are *always* photographers backstage with someone like him — then I'm afraid you're more misguided than he is. Besides, what do you think I could say to him? I *enjoyed* it?'

Driving back to Los Angeles, I congratulated Cary for being such a good sport otherwise. He'd made an extraordinary effort to please me and/or Jennifer.

'Now at least you can tell Jennifer you've seen Alice,' I said cheerfully.

'Oh, I don't know about that,' he said as he stifled a yawn. It was midnight, far beyond his usual bedtime.

'What do you mean?' I asked.

'If she knew I'd gone to see Alice, it might encourage

her to do the same thing.'

'You really hated it, didn't you?' I said, trying not to sound disappointed.

'It's ...' he said, struggling for words, 'you know what it's like? Remember I told you about the time I took LSD in my doctor's office and shat all over his rug and floor?'

'Yes ...' I said.

'Well, now I know how that poor doctor felt!'

Cary and Alice continued to send each other their regards through me for years after that night, but that was their first — and last — time together in the same room.

Our efforts to raise each other's consciousness may have failed, but Cary and I were soon going to take a real trip that would change my perception of him forever.

14

THE TOAST OF NEW YORK

ONCE a year Cary returned to Bristol to visit the man he called 'my only living relative' and 'my favourite cousin': Eric Leach. In October we took off for Bristol, but first we stopped off in New York City.

Cary was especially eager to make our second trip to New York together a happy one after the disaster earlier in the year at the Fabergé luncheon with Joe Namath. Though he was going to conduct a little business for Brut in the city (just as I was going to conduct some interviews for the magazine), Cary's first priority was showing me a wonderful time.

'What do you want to do there?' Cary asked me with boyish enthusiasm a few weeks before we took off.

'You're going to think I'm the corniest creature on earth,' I warned him before making my request.

'No, I won't,' he insisted gallantly. 'I am yours to command.'

'Well,' I began somewhat shyly, 'do you remember how you and Deborah Kerr were supposed to meet at the top of the Empire State Building in *An Affair to Remember*, but she never made it?'

'Yes.' he said, not yet catching on.

'Remember how Deborah tells your character, Nicky, that she thinks the hundred-and-second floor is "the nearest thing to heaven we have in New York"?'

'Right,' he said.

'Well,' I sighed, 'I want to go to heaven with you!'

Cary laughed and agreed instantly.

And we went in style. For our first trip to New York, we'd flown on a Western Airlines jet, but this time we took the private Fabergé jet, a Grumman G2, one of the most expensive aircraft in the world. Close to one million dollars had been lavished on the interior alone, with such luxe items as a small kitchen and a television. The whole situation reminded me of the scene in *That Touch of Mink* in which Cary, playing a rich playboy, sends a Boeing 707 to fly poor working girl Doris Day to Bermuda. When she gets on board, she discovers she's the only passenger!

Caviar and champagne were served and I felt like a princess. And I could see the joy in Cary's eyes as I lapped it all up. 'Stick with me, kid!' he said without having to say a word.

The royal treatment continued once we reached New York and took a limousine to Cary's penthouse at the Warwick Hotel. It was within walking distance of Brut's offices on the Avenue of the Americas. The apartment had been given to Marion Davies as a gift from 'Citizen' William Randolph Hearst, and many of the original furnishings — including wooden beams and elaborate mirrors from San Simeon — were still intact. The rooms evoked a kind of faded glory that contrasted greatly with Cary's salad days as a young actor in the city. The penthouse's best feature was a generous terrace which allowed the sun in, despite the profusion of sky-scrapers nearby.

The first night in New York, Cary kept his promise to take me to the top of the Empire State Building. He waited until it was late and then we rode the elevator all the way up. When we got out at the top floor, there were only a few people staring off into the night. They were too wrapped up in each other to notice the gray-haired man with the black horn-rim glassed and the scarf covering much of his face. He was tightly holding the hand of a British girl who seemed more interested in looking at him than at the skyline.

'Thank you,' I said, squeezing his hand. 'I feel like I got something Deborah Kerr didn't.'

'You did,' he said. 'A cold!' The brisk night air was all around us. But I couldn't feel the chill.

We didn't say much that night. We didn't have to. We were both content with each other and the world.

The next day we busied ourselves in the morning with our professional duties. But the afternoon was all ours and Cary had scheduled a personally guided tour of the New York he had once known and loved.

Yet there was one part of New York he *didn't* love — the smell in the streets. He complained constantly about it and had his own solution for it — he would spray the air with Brut cologne every chance he got. Some people were not amused, but I was, as Cary did his part to beautify New York. Cary also professed little fondness for Brooklyn — he had rehearsed in a park there with the Bob Pender troupe after he came to New York in 1920. 'What an uncharming place,' he decreed.

Manhattan, however, could still move Cary with its brash and brutal pace. We climbed into a company limousine and began to retrace some of Cary's steps in the city he first saw as a sixteen-year-old boy. As we went down Fifth Avenue, he recalled taking a trip on an open-top double-decker bus up the same thoroughfare so many decades ago.

'The first thing I loved about America was how fast it all seemed,' he remembered as our limousine wound its way through the afternoon traffic. 'The second thing was the ice cream. There were so many flavors, many more than they had in England at the time. Then I made the greatest discovery of all — it was something called a banana split. There was no such thing in England!'

He ordered the limo to take us to Sixth Avenue between Forty-third and Forty-fourth streets. He pointed to the surrounding detritus and sighed.

'Do you realize this used to be the site of the world's largest theater?' It was the Hippodrome, where the Pender troupe appeared in a revue called *Good Times* with more than 1,000 people onstage, aided and abetted by nearly 800 behind the scenes.

'Today you cannot imagine the size of it,' he continued, with awe rising in his voice. 'It really was *show* business. There was a finale with scores of swimmers diving into a million-gallon tank!'

He also described his first 'home' in America — the theatrical hotel on Forty-sixth Street off Eighth Avenue where Cary stayed with the Penders and the rest of the boys in the troupe. They shared a long 'railroad' apartment with, as Cary remembered it, 'rooms leading into the others like cars on a train.

'That's where I learned to cook,' he continued. 'I became an expert at making beef stew. We all had to pull our weight and depend upon each other to get things done. It was like a real family. I even learned how to sew and iron.'

On Sundays Cary had the day off, and he loved to go to the East Side, specifically Sutton Place, where the mansions and apartment buildings fascinated him.

'I did fantasize about living inside one of those places,' he admitted sheepishly. 'I really did. The people inside those places just had to have magical lives. Wasn't I naive?'

Then he told me about the first girl he fell in love with in America. She was Gladys Kincaid, a member of the Hippodrome corps de ballet.

'She had beautiful eyes and blonde curls. She reminded me of Mary Pickford. But I never really had the guts to talk to her. I would just stare and stare at her like some moon-faced boy. Can you believe it?'

As a matter of fact, I could.

Then he ordered the car to take us to Broadway and Forty-seventh Street.

'You see that corner?' he said, pointing near the Palace Theatre. 'I used to look for work there with actors. That was our hangout!'

It was two years after *Good Times* had closed and the Pender boys had toured the vaudeville circuit. Cary decided to stay on in New York while most of the others had made their way back home to England.

'I was eighteen years old,' he said.

'Weren't you frightened?' I asked.

'Fat chance!' he laughed. 'Too stupid to know better, but I made out. I wasn't bad-looking and I got a lot of free meals.'

At one dinner party he met the owner of Steeplechase Park out on Coney Island. Cary was so broke he made the man an unusual proposition: He would cover the boardwalk on stilts (a skill he'd picked up during his Pender days), wearing a red and green uniform, and advertise the park for the sum of five dollars on weekdays and ten dollars on weekend days. 'It was *not* fun,' he insisted.

But it had served its purpose. Cary had enough money to finance his career for the rest of the year. He was in the process of making the switch from vaudeville performer to young leading man. After several years he achieved that transition, but Cary would never forget the struggle.

'I lived in nothing better than upholstered sewers when it got tough,' he recalled. 'But I got through, like we all do. And I had some good friends along the way.'

He told me a charming story about Fred Allen, the acerbic comic who once observed that you could take all the sincerity in Hollywood, put it in a flea's navel and still have room to spare. It was 1929 and Cary was very nervous about appearing in a play called *Wonderful Night*.

'I was, frankly, worried I wasn't going to be so wonderful,' he said, snickering. 'I was caught up in myself until I ran into Fred on the way to the theater and he grabbed me by the arm and took me downtown to the Woolworth Building. We got to the observation tower and he pointed through the fog to Broadway. We could barely see it, it was so tiny. I suddenly got a very good perspective on how small I was and how small my problems really were.'

Two years later he took off for Hollywood with a friend, in his pride and joy — a Packard. 'And after I got some good wishes from Billy "Square Deal" Grady at the William Morris office, I left for Los Angeles from right outside the Palace Theater, very near that same corner where I'd hung out looking desperately for work several years before. Funny world, isn't it?'

Now Cary asked the driver to take us by the Winter Garden Theater, a few blocks away from the Palace.

'Do you know who Al Jolson was?' he asked me as the limo pulled up near the theater. 'He was a legend. Great singer. There was nobody bigger in the twenties. *Nobody*. One day I was walking by the Winter Garden and I saw the men putting up Jolson's name in lights. Something shot right through me and I started crying. I think it was the realization that this was exactly what I wanted, what I had to have. And Jolson had gotten there and won that acknowledgement, because he was the absolute best.'

'Umm,' I said, burying my head in Cary's shoulder. 'The best. The very best.'

He didn't pull away, and let me share the moment with him. Of course, I realized how much more he had let me share with him that afternoon as he lovingly opened the door to his past.

The next day, as I scurried about on more business for the magazine and Cary occupied himself at Fabergé, Willie let something slip when she called to check up on us. Thank goodness I happened to be back in the Penthouse.

'Maureen,' she said, faintly scolding me, 'I've got to ask you a question — what's more important to you: Cary or that magazine?'

I didn't consider them mutually exclusive, so I asked Willie what prompted her question.

'Well, I talked to Mr. Grant this morning and I got the feeling he feels somewhat ignored.'

'Ignored?' I repeated. I was shocked. I told her about the flight and the trip to the Empire State Building and the previous day's tour of New York, Cary Grant style. 'How could he feel ignored? Besides, he has his own business to do.'

'I know,' she said, 'but I'm just telling you the feeling I get. You know he never comes right out and says something, but when he mentioned some of the interviews you're doing, I got the feeling he wished you didn't have to do all that stuff.'

I thanked Willie and put down the phone. I couldn't let anything tarnish this time together even slightly. It was to be our last night in New York, and I wanted to make it something Cary would never forget.

It was five in the afternoon and he was due back at the penthouse at seven or seven-thirty. Cary had mentioned something about having dinner with Norman Zeiler, so I called Norman at his office and begged his forgiveness. I had a surprise planned for Cary that required our staying in for the night. Would he mind? Of course not, he said as he wished me well.

I rushed out to Bloomingdale's and dashed through the gourmet section, picking up Brie, caviar and fruit. Then I gathered up a score of candles and a bright red-checked tablecloth. I bought some wine on the way back to the Warwick.

When Cary walked through the door of the penthouse, he could see how much attention he was going to reap from me that night. I came to the door wearing the sexy black jersey dress he had given me.

'We're going to see Norman on another trip,' I said as I handed Cary a glass of wine. Then his eyes widened as he caught sight of all the candles and the picnic I had spread out on the floor.

'I thought we'd just stay indoors and do our best to entertain each other,' I whispered.

He smiled with pleasure. 'Let me get out of this,' he said, indicating his suit, 'and I'll join you. I can't wait!'

Cary practically flew into the shower and emerged within a matter of minutes. He walked back into the candlelit room wearing nothing but the cream silk dressing gown I'd given him for his birthday.

'Sit down and eat,' I urged him as I took his hand and guided him to the floor. Now he was sitting next to me.

'I have everything here you want,' I said.

And his eyes told me I was right.

Then we satisfied our appetites as we never had before.

15

ARSENIC AND OLD LACE

W^E flew into London in high spirits, not letting the wet weather dampen our enthusiasm.

After checking into the Nine Kings Suite at the Royal Lancaster in Bayswater, where Cary always stayed in London, we barely had a chance to unpack before Cary whisked me off in a cab to a fish-and-chips shop on Elizabeth Street near Victoria Station.

It was a very modest establishment, a few doors down from a bus terminal. Cary had the cab wait as he picked up a couple of orders of skate with chips. (Skate is a whitefish from the North Sea.)

'This is the first thing I want the minute I get to London,' Cary said happily as he shoved an order into my hands. 'They can't get this right at all in the States, can they?'

After one bite I had to admit the meal had been worth the trip across town. The steaming mass of food was the perfect reintroduction to the simple pleasures of the country I hadn't been able to visit for almost a year. I tended to get nervous if I couldn't see my parents once a year, as well as catch up with some old friends from my 'swinging sixties' days.

I wasn't the only one who had formed a special bond with London at an early age. The city had also played an important part in Cary's young life after he moved away from Bristol and toured the English provinces as part of Pender's Knock-About Comedians.

He then played London and the Gulliver circuit of vaudeville theaters. Cary was still a teenager when he scrambled on top of an open-air bus and the top deck of a tramcar for the first time. It was these vehicles that took Cary through London's districts that helped him really get to know and love the city.

As Cary and I headed back to the Royal Lancaster, he mentioned these early journeys, and I proposed we take a similar one the next day on one of the double-decker buses still making their way through London.

At first Cary pooh-poohed the idea, saying he'd be recognized and that would start the proverbial chain reaction of autographs he always dreaded. But I said if he could fool a stadium of Alice Cooper fans in San Diego, he shouldn't have any trouble getting around London. Besides, we had a completely free day to ourselves in London before motoring down to Bristol. I had no professional obligations and just wanted to stop and say hello to my parents. Cary had one early-morning meeting for Fabergé that could be quickly disposed of. Why not spend the day enjoying the city as he had so long ago?

By the time we got back to the hotel, I had successfully persuaded Cary. We would reserve a company car, a Daimler, which we would use when we weren't traveling by double-decker.

'I know where I want to go first!' Cary announced gaily when he came back to our room after his morning meeting. 'Brixton!'

'Brixton?' I said skeptically. 'Why?'

'That's where the Penders' home was,' he informed me.

'Fine with me, Cary,' I said hesitantly, 'but how long has it been since you've been to Brixton?'

'Oh, I don't know,' he replied, 'quite a few years, actually. Why?'

'Well, I don't mean to discourage you, but it's probably changed a good deal from the days you lived there with the Penders. Actually, it's known as a pretty rough district.'

From my days in London, I knew the once suburban landscape of Brixton had turned into a melting pot of races and rough places.

'You mean it's not safe?' he asked.

'Not exactly, but since we have the car, we should be fine.'

So off we went to South London, and it wasn't long before Cary had guided the driver to a crumbling house on High Street. 'I think this is it,' Cary said as we got out of the car.

As Cary remembered it, the Penders' home had a long walk out front and a small garden in the back, and this place fit the bill. It was hard to picture Cary in something this forgettable and common, but he seemed to be happy to be back here as details began to flood his mind. He recalled the dormitory-type rooms where all the boys in the troupe slept, and the limbering-up exercises they did in the garden out back.

Cary also remembered the daylight air raids over Brixton during World War I when he lived there. He said he and the other boys found the raids exciting until something happened at the house next door that forever changed their minds.

'The lady of that house was as thrilled with the air raids as we were,' he said. 'One day she went out during the shelling, right up to her front gate to get a better look through her trees, when she was decapitated by a shard of shrapnel!'

On that unhappy note, I begged Cary to bid Brixton a quick farewell. This was supposed to be a *fun* day. Off we headed for Muswell Hill and the fireman's cottage where my parents had lived for over thirty years. I could just imagine the reaction of our neighbors when we pulled up in the Daimler. 'What has Maureen Payne got herself into this time?'

I saw my mother peeking from behind the curtains as the car came to a stop. She opened the door slightly and signaled for us to come in; the coast was clear. And so Cary Grant stepped into my past as he entered our tiny living room, where my father was now waiting with a gin and tonic for his guest.

'Pleased to meet you, Mr. Grant,' my father said. 'I'm Jim Payne and this is my wife, Elsie.'

'I'm so honored to meet you,' Cary said.

'Sit down! Sit down!' Daddy said eagerly, pointing to our little sofa and chairs. 'I can't tell you how proud we are to have you in our home.'

Cary couldn't have been more charming, putting them completely at ease, which wasn't easy with my mother as nervous as she was. After all, Mummy had to serve lunch. Cary had requested one of his favorites — beef stew — and she was frightened she wouldn't pass muster.

But she did, with flying colors. We spent most of lunch talking about the advantages of English food over American. Cary was convinced that dairy products are far superior in England than in the States. 'Too many chemicals in everything,' he sniffed about American milk and cheese. 'And American cream is not real cream. You have to come here for that!'

He then began enthusiastically quizzing Mummy about the dishes she most liked to make. When she mentioned a sausage dish, toad in the hole, he made her promise to make it for him on his next trip. Next Cary asked her if she made bubble and squeak, that inexpensive dish consisting of leftovers such as potatoes and greens fried in a pan until cooked to a golden crust.

When Mummy said she had also mastered bubble and squeak, I knew she'd won a permanent place in Cary's heart. He finished the meal with a special invitation:

'Maureen told me you're coming to Los Angeles to spend the holidays with her this year,' Cary said. 'Would you do me the honor of spending Christmas with me and my daughter, and Maureen?'

I thought Mummy was going to burst with pride.

'Oh yes, Cary!' she gushed, now on a first-name basis with him.

'I think that would be splendid,' Daddy chimed in.

I was virtually in tears because I knew how much it

would mean to them. This was their first trip to America, and being invited to spend some time with Cary Grant made it all the more special.

My feet were barely touching ground as we said our good-byes and got back into the car. 'Piccadilly!' Cary ordered as we waved to my parents and sped toward the heart of London. When we got there, Cary told the driver we would meet him in two hours at Victoria Station.

We were right on Piccadilly and, although the tourist season was over, the street was still crowded with people. We decided to window-shop for a while and hadn't gone very far when I spotted a model of a red double-decker bus at an outside vendor's stand.

I bought it for Cary — it couldn't have cost more than a pound, if that — and placed it in his hands.

'Now you never have to wait for a bus,' I said as I winked at him. 'You've got your own!'

He cupped it in his palm carefully.

'I thank you for such a wonderful remembrance,' he said, sounding as if I'd handed him the crown jewels. 'I will always keep it.'

His gratitude seemed out of proportion, considering the modest nature of the gift. It puzzled me but at the same time it touched me. I was about to say it was nothing, when Cary caught sight of a real double-decker and whisked us aboard. We stepped up to the top deck, where fortunately the front row was empty. Staring straight ahead, Cary would be showing only the back of his head to the other passengers. There was no danger of anyone recognizing him here, especially since I paid for the ticket when the conductor collected the fare.

Cary looked eagerly at the sights of London whizzing by us and kept pointing out people and little shops that caught his eye. It was as if he were seeing it for the first time. I suspected it had been a long while since he had seen London this way instead of through the tinted glass of a limousine.

When we arrived at Victoria Station, Cary was determined to have tea and currant buns. We pushed our way through the hundreds of people streaming through the station until Cary found a small coffee shop. Like the fish-and-chips place the night before, it was nondescript and built strictly for function. But you would have thought Cary was dining at the Ritz.

He marveled at my mother's beef stew. He marveled at the tea in this shop (that too was better than its American counterpart). Most of all, he marveled that no one had recognized him all afternoon. With his overcoat and a huge scarf wrapped around him, it didn't seem too implausible to me.

But then I spotted an old dear staring at Cary from across the room. She had a flowered hat with a daisy listing rather forlornly to one side. Her face was heavily creased with time. She got up and began to smooth and straighten her simple dress.

I feared the worse as she prepared to come over to our table, but Cary stopped her in her tracks when he put his finger to his lips as if to say: 'Sssh! It's our secret that I am who you think I am and I'm sitting here having some tea.'

She took her seat again, occasionally sneaking a look our way. But she respected our privacy and I appreciated it greatly. So did Cary. When we were done, he got up, walked over to her and expressed his gratitude.

'I just wanted to tell you how much I appreciate your leaving us alone,' Cary told the woman. 'Because if you had come over, then other people would have, and it would have started a chain reaction and I wouldn't have been able to enjoy my tea. I thank you very, very much.'

She was at a loss for words.

'Are you really him?' she said weakly. 'I mean, Cary Grant?'

'Yes, I am,' he said, 'and I'm pleased to meet such a considerate fan. I'm presuming you *are* a fan?'

'Oh my, yes,' she said shyly. 'I wish I could tell you how many years. My friends will never believe I ran into Cary Grant at Victoria Station.'

'Then it'll just be our secret,' he said as he bent down and kissed her hand.

I'm sure she never forgot the experience. His kindness and self-deprecating brand of charm could take my breath away.

When we finally got to Bristol, I heard something that took my breath away in a very different manner. The trip down in the car had been pleasant and picturesque enough as we took in the verdant countryside like voracious tourists. The view from the Grand Spa Hotel where we checked in was even more spectacular. About a mile from the center of the town, the hotel (now called the Avon Gorge) is perched three hundred feet above the river Avon and I couldn't stop staring down at the limestone cliffs from the terrace of our room.

'You see that,' Cary said, pointing to a massive structure spanning the gorge.

'Yes,' I said, impressed by its size.

'That's the Clifton Suspension Bridge and we're going to walk across it — now!' he said enthusiastically.

And that's just what we did after we unpacked. On our way out of the hotel, a porter stopped us. 'I thought you'd want to see that, Mr. Grant,' he said as he pointed to the Union Jack which had been raised at the hotel to show someone special was 'in state.'

'Thank you very much!' Cary chirped as he tipped the porter royally. Cary took my hand in his and we walked up a rolling green hill to the bridge. My hand was still in his as we began our trek across the 245-foot-long structure. Halfway across, we stopped to enjoy the view.

'My mother used to love to take me to this bridge,' Cary said. 'She came from Clifton, you know, and was quite proud of the fact. She also took me up there!'

Now Cary was pointing to an observatory on a hill high above the bridge. I didn't have to ask where we were going next. When we reached the top, we could see the entire city below us.

'After we visit Eric and his wife, Maggie, I'm going to show you Bristol,' he told me.

'I couldn't have a better guide,' I said, looking forward to the personally guided tour.

It was about two in the afternoon when we pulled up outside Maggie and Eric's modest home on Weston Crescent in Horfield, a few miles from the heart of Bristol. It reminded me of the fireman's cottage I'd been brought up in, but was a bit grander. There was a pocket-sized garden out front and more shrubbery in the back. The house itself was small but cozy and Cary's cousins did their most to make me feel at home.

We had tea and sandwiches, probably just as Dyan had done when she first met them ten years before. I knew I couldn't be the first woman Cary had introduced to them, but I was treated like a long-lost relative. I found their warmth and hospitality overwhelming, but I got the feeling Cary couldn't wait to get out of the place after about an hour. I picked up his cue and we left. Perhaps he was just as eager to show me the rest of Bristol, I told myself as we got back into the car. Then Cary corrected that impression.

'They're very nice people,' Cary began, 'but Eric rubs me the wrong way sometimes. After all, he's content just to sit there and drink his beer and let the day pass him by.'

Eric was a retired sales manager so I was confused.

'But isn't he retired?' I said. 'On the way over here didn't you say he's seventy years old?'

'Well, yes,' Cary allowed, 'but he could be out working. He just doesn't work hard enough. I give them money, you know. Helped them buy the house, in fact.'

'I'm sure you're pleased to be able to do that for them,' I said, hoping to put the conversation back on the jolly track we'd been pursuing for so many days.

'Definitely!' he said, brightening. 'Don't misunderstand me. I love them both dearly. Why else would I come here each year to visit them? It's not like a walk down the block, is it?'

'It certainly isn't!' I agreed cheerfully as I tried to put his ambivalence about Eric behind us. 'Where are we headed?'

'Fifteen Hughenden Road,' he said.

'And where's that?'

'Where I was born,' he whispered.

We got there within minutes because it was also in Horfield. It was an attached house on a narrow street near the end of a cul-de-sac. There were scores of other homes — terraced, with graystone exteriors — on the same side of the street with the exact same appearance. The effect was something like a flattened-out accordion. Fortunately, a lovely park was nearby, where we saw some children playing.

Cary got out of the car so he could give his first home a close inspection. The occupants weren't there and the curtains weren't drawn, so he peered in.

'You know what's funny?' he said, more to himself than to me, I thought. 'It is true what they say. Sometimes I can't remember what happened yesterday, but I can remember things from my life here that are so clear and so vivid.

'The thing I remember most is how cold that upstairs bedroom would get. There was an eiderdown that always slipped off the bed. There's nothing worse than waking up in a cold home, is there? That's why I love California. It's so warm. I love Bristol, but I could never live here because of the cold.'

I took ahold of his arm and it seemed to warm his memory as much as it did his body. He remembered one of his first toys, a fort with lead soldiers ... buying coconut-and-jam tarts at a tuckshop, or sweetshop, nearby ... reading comics such as *The Gem* and *The Magnet* and the Greyfriars stories by Frank Richards ... and hitting a neighbor's window with a cricket ball.

When Cary had grown up in Bristol, masted schooners still sailed the river and gas lamps and horse-drawn trams dotted the streets. As we visited other places that had meant so much to Cary's youth, I realized how much of him had been forged in this ancient seaport city of wood and stone.

We stopped at the second home he'd lived in, another small, two-story affair carved out of stone, this time on

Seymour Avenue. He had moved there at the age of seven. Later, after his mother had been institutionalized, Cary and his father moved to a three-story, three-bedroom place on Picton Street.

'This was my grandmother's house,' Cary said as we got out in front of a house on a very narrow street in the Montpelier district. 'She was a cold woman. But no one had an easy time of it, especially my father. One time the landlord came to the door for the rent, and I'll never forget the shame on my father's face. He didn't have it then.'

Cary had happier memories of the schools he attended, which we also visited that afternoon. Bishop Road Junior School had been his first school; now it was called Bishop Road Primary School. It was a cold, imposing edifice made of stone with a red brick roof. The Horfield Prison was nearby. 'That gave the school a special appeal in our young eyes.' Cary smiled.

But it was his grammar school, Fairfield, for which he reserved his warmest memories. It was a much grander school built of stone and red brick on a triangular site where three streets meet. To the immediate north was a railroad which Cary recalled from his days at the school: 'One day I was whistling and I thought the sound coming from my mouth was what was causing this piercing whistle. Actually, it was a train going by. The vanity of youth!'

He also recalled breaking off part of his front tooth on a slide on the ice-covered schoolyard. 'We didn't have any money, so I went to a dentist's school and got them to pull the rest of the tooth for free.' Fortunately, time took care of the gap.

'Either you were a hitter or you got hit,' Cary said about his schooldays. Cary must have been a pretty heavy hitter: he told me a story about a teacher confiscating a slingshot. 'It could have been Miss Craigie; she was Scottish and I had a crush on her.'

As we continued our tour of Fairfield, Cary remembered some of the ways he first made money: 'My pocket money was only a shilling a week, so I had to do something. I worked in a chemist's shop in Stokescroft and, before that, I took tickets at a roundabout on Redland Green.'

Then Cary decided school was over. 'Let's go to Fishponds!' he instructed our driver.

My heart sank. I knew Fishponds was the colorful name given the rustic district where hospitals and sanitariums were located. The driver had mentioned it during the course of our day's travels. Many of the structures, he said, had been built by prisoners from the Franco-Prussian War.

It had been such a lovely trip, I prayed Cary would not spoil it now.

'Are you sure you want to do this?' I whispered to Cary as the driver approached Fishponds.

'Sure!' he said, almost gaily.

I kept my mouth shut and hoped for the best.

When we got there, I was impressed by the acres and acres of lush green grass. Even the stone buildings looked less intimidating than Cary's first school near Horfield Prison. This was far from the snake pit I had pictured in my mind.

'Why, it's beautiful!' I said, trying to disguise the relief I felt.

'It is, isn't it?' Cary agreed.

He asked the driver to go as slowly as possible so he could take in every inch of the place, but without a pass we couldn't stay long.

Cary sounded disappointed, though I couldn't imagine what would be gained by staying in such an emotionally loaded location.

'Show me the Hippo!' I demanded. The Hippo was the Hippodrome Theatre, near the center of Bristol. Cary had worked there as a callboy after it was built in 1912. Here he'd gotten his first smell of greasepaint, and much happier memories had to reside there for him.

'Okay,' he joined in merrily, 'but first the docks! And we can't forget the Theatre Royal, either.'

We left Fishponds and headed for the center of Bristol,

where boats and ships were docked. When we got there, we began walking over the cobblestones. Cary told me this is where he had first dreamed of sailing for America.

The docks were awash with more memories for Cary, but before he could share any of them with me, the river-front was full of something else: cats. Scores of them. They seemed to come from every direction.

'Quick!' he said, grabbing my arm. 'We better leave!'

'Leave?' I asked as I bent down to touch one of the black cats twirling itself around my legs.

'Because those animals are infested with fleas and God knows what else! If you don't leave this second, I will not allow you back in the car.'

He wasn't kidding, but I burst out laughing.

Then he realized how harsh he'd sounded and started chuckling as well. 'If you'll leave right now, I promise you the best fish and chips you've ever had!' he said, pulling me along.

It was a deal, and we headed for our next stop before Cary could keep that promise. It was the Theatre Royal in the very oldest part of Bristol on King Street. Cary per-suaded the day manager to let us have a look inside. (It didn't take much for Cary Grant to persuade anybody to do anything.)

The theater was a tiny jewel box like the Mayfair Music Hall in Santa Monica. The foundation had been laid in 1766, and it was now the oldest working theater in Britain.

Cary had come there as a boy, decades before the birth of Cary Grant in Hollywood. But I was no longer interested in history. My stomach was growling, so I reminded him of his promise. We pulled up near a fish-and-chips stand on St. Nicholas Street and gorged ourselves. Cary had been right — this was gastronomic perfection, even if it was covered in grease.

I felt like a hippo when we pulled up in front of the Hippodrome. Between the driver and ourselves, we had shared *five* orders of fish and chips! Unfortunately, among the first things I saw as we entered the theater were some fish designs on an auditorium door.

Cary and I looked guiltily at each other and then laughed. But we stopped laughing when the person kind enough to show us around mentioned that the Hippo was threatened with extinction, as many giant old music halls and movie palaces were in the mid-seventies. (Fortunately, a local group salvaged the Hippo from the wrecking ball and it remains open to this day, mostly for touring plays and musicals.)

A science professor's assistant at Fairfield who worked part-time as an electrician at the Hippo had been the conduit for Cary's introduction to both the Hippodrome and show business.

'I was obsessed with the Hippo,' Cary said as we went backstage and peered into dressing rooms and storage areas. 'My mother was at Fishponds by this time, so places like this became my home away from home. I also used to go to the Empire in Old Market, where I got my first job in the theater.'

He nearly ruined his career in show business when a magician, The Great David Devant, appeared on the Empire's bill. One day Cary was assisting the man who worked the center arc light in the balcony.

'All I had to do was hold that lamp steady when he needed to be relieved for a moment, but I bollixed it up,' Cary recalled. 'The lighting man decided to have a smoke and told me to hold the spotlight precisely at the center of the stage. I didn't know then that if you let the light wander, it would destroy one of Devant's best illusions.

'I was so wrapped up in watching The Great David Devant that the not-so-great Archie Leach let the light wander and exposed his trick, revealing two mirrors under the table. They never let me back into the Empire, but I persuaded the management of the Hippo to let me work for nothing, or darn close to it, as a much more attentive callboy!'

Our second day in Bristol started out full of promise as we first stopped at the House of Lewis on College Green, a men's apparel shop Cary loved. Then we made our way to Broadmead, the shopping district near the center of town.

Cary wanted to check on a couple of department stores there to see if they were fully and properly stocked with Fabergé products, and he wanted to pick up a few things for Jennifer. Cary may have been born to clip, but I was born to shop, so I was in the best possible mood. Cary was feeling no pain either, especially after we took a short break to have some draft ale at a pub. (Beer was another thing Cary insisted the Britons did much better than the Americans.)

Then we walked into the local Marks and Spencer, a chain of department stores in England well-known not only for the quality of its products but also for the good prices on everything from sandwiches to shampoo. This store was located in an outdoor shopping mall.

Cary and I were idly searching for bargains and souvenirs, entertaining ourselves with the notion of what people would think if they knew Cary Grant shopped at Marks and Spencer, when we heard a little boy crying nearby.

Cary's high spirits vanished in a second, and he seemed distracted and tense.

'That little boy has lost his mother,' he said. 'We must find the manager. You stay here with him and I'll get help.'

I asked the little boy if indeed he was lost and he shyly nodded to indicate he was. But how could Cary have known that? The boy had been crying but hadn't said a word.

As I was pondering Cary's mind-reading ability, the boy's mother appeared on the scene.

'Geoffrey, there you are!' she said, relieved. 'I've been looking all over for you!'

By the time Cary got back with the clerk, mother and child were gone. When I told Cary this, he said, 'Good!' and thanked the clerk brusquely. He was in a foul mood, but he should have been pleased that the boy's mother had shown up so quickly.

'Let's get out of here,' he snapped as he took the two baskets we'd been using for our shopping and deposited them on the floor. 'We're going back to the hotel.'

' *What?*' I said, totally confused. 'We were going to shop this afternoon and it's not noon yet, Cary!'

'Fine, then,' he said, his voice cold and unpleasant, 'you stay here and I'll have the driver pick you up at four or five.'

'That doesn't make sense, Cary. I want to be with you. That's the whole idea,' I protested.

'Well, if you want to be with me, I'll be back at the hotel.'

The drive back to the Grand Spa was lethal in its silence. I tried to talk Cary out of his mood, but it was useless. He just stared out the window and wouldn't say a word.

When we got to our room, I asked him what was the matter.

'Nothing's the matter, Maureen. I'm just tired. Why does something always have to be the matter?' he said, annoyed.

'But darling,' I said, moving closer to him on the bed where he was sitting. 'Something *is* wrong. One minute we're having a great time shopping and the next minute you can cut the atmosphere with a knife. What happened inside that store?'

'Oh, you know how moody I can be,' he said, trying to brush me off. 'And I really am tired. Let's take the afternoon off and just have dinner here in our room tonight. By tomorrow I'm sure I won't be so grumpy.'

He was better in the morning, but he still wasn't the lighthearted man I'd spent the rest of the trip with. He appeared to be making a sincere effort to have a good time, but it was futile. We visited the Bristol Zoo and resumed our shopping in Broadmead that day, but his heart wasn't in it.

I couldn't stand it. It was oppressive and profoundly upsetting. Surely it would be better to get what was bothering Cary out in the open than to let it fester this way.

We ate again inside the hotel and again I tried to pry

out of him what was disturbing him so deeply. And again he evaded me.

It was our last night in Bristol before returning to London and then the United States. We decided to turn in early. I was half asleep when I thought I heard Cary say something, but it was barely audible.

'Did you say something?' I said, still not quite believing I'd heard anything.

'I'll tell you,' Cary whispered.

'Tell me what?' I said, not fully awake.

'What happened in Marks and Spencer,' he said softly.

I started to turn on the light, but his hand stopped me. He had his back to me and I waited for him to turn around and face me. But he didn't.

'It was my mother,' Cary began, 'I was thinking of my mother when I saw that lost little boy.'

I didn't say a word.

'My mother used to love taking me shopping with her on Saturday mornings,' he continued. 'It's one of the first things I remember. And she always held me close, holding my hand. We usually went to Castle Street.

'But one day we went to Marks and Spencer in Broadmead. It couldn't be the same store we went to the other day — it's too new — but I do remember it was a Marks and Spencer. We went inside and I just loved the place. I couldn't have been more than four or five years old, maybe even younger, because everyone seemed so tall.

'The thing I loved most was the penny bazaar and I rushed over to see what I could get with my money. I didn't see anything I wanted at first so I started to go down another aisle when I noticed my mother wasn't anywhere to be found. I must've let go of her hand in my excitement and now she was gone. Just like that. I was frightened and I wanted to cry. But I also wanted to be a big boy so I didn't cry. And I thought she would be back.

'But she didn't come back, not right then. So I did start crying and people kept rushing by. And I kept crying and people kept going by. I'm sure somebody would eventually have helped me, but to the little boy I was, it seemed that hours had passed.

'Then I felt somebody grab my hand. Hard. It was my mother! I was so happy but my happiness was short-lived. She knelt down and looked me right in the face. "You see, Archie," she said, "nobody wants you. Nobody came for you, did they? I'm the only one — *the only one* — who cares about you. Nobody else. And don't you ever forget it, because the next time you let go of my hand and wander off, I won't come back."'

I was crying. And I wasn't crying just for him. I was crying for both of us because, during those last few moments, I finally understood and felt more about Cary's early life than I ever had before. I understood how Elsie had insinuated herself into every relationship Cary had had with a woman after her, including our own.

It explained his mistrust and hostility during those early months after we'd met and made love for the first time. And it explained his obsession, even his love/hate, for Dyan. 'Hate,' I'd once read, 'comes from unfinished love.'

I don't know if Cary cried that night. At least I didn't hear him. He'd told me the whole story with his back to me. I put my hand on his shoulder gently.

'It sounds so small, Cary,' I said as I rubbed it, 'but I am sorry.'

'I know you are, dear,' he said, 'and I do appreciate it. I do.'

His free hand reached up to pat mine.

'I'll tell you one more thing,' he said.

My heart skipped a beat. What frightened me was how calm he was, how damn calm. When he had first told me about Elsie down at the beach in Malibu, it was as if he'd released a torrent of emotion he could not hold back. This time he was preternaturally calm as we lay in the dark, hundreds of feet above the river Avon.

'The last time I saw my mother,' he said, 'after she had been released from Fishponds, the first thing I did was bend down to give her a kiss.

'And she pushed me away.'

I reached over and put my arms around him, holding him for as long as I dared. But I knew someone else had a much stronger hold on him.

Cary invited Roddy Mann to fly back to the States with us on the company jet. During an interview conducted in flight, Roddy asked Cary how his trip back home to Bristol had been.

'I thoroughly enjoyed it,' Cary said. 'I'm always nostalgic for it. However long you live abroad, your heart is always in the place where you were born.'

He also said the favorite part of his trip had been drinking pints of wallop — beer — with his favorite cousin, Eric.

16

THE WOMAN
ACCUSED

'DON'T you see?' Cary was insisting. 'She killed him — and she almost killed me too.'

Cary was talking about his mother. Since our return from England, it had become his favorite topic of conversation. After that night in Bristol he'd become obsessed with making certain I understood how and what he felt about her. When he talked about Elsie, there was almost always a sense of immense feelings barely being contained … feelings not totally loving and not totally hostile, but mixed up into a powerful combination.

I was initially confused, for several reasons. First, there was my own relationship with my parents which, while not perfect, was certainly more consistent and consistently loving than Cary's relationship with his mother and father. In addition, I was bewildered by what he had told me just a few months before about LSD opening a brand-new world to him, a world in which he learned to forgive his parents as well as himself. He did not sound very forgiving.

Even more confusing was the fact that the details he provided fluctuated as much as his moods. One day he said Elias James Leach and Elsie Kingdon Leach were real churchgoers who followed Episcopalian Protestant teachings. The next day he was certain that there was Jewish blood on his father's side of the family, but nobody talked about it and nobody ever really went to a synagogue or church of any kind.

One day he remembered his mother clinging to him constantly, never letting him run free. The next day she emerged more benignly, a concerned mother still haunted by the loss of her first son. But even the death of Cary's older brother, John, was struck by this kind of double vision. Some days he repeated the story he'd told me that night in Malibu about Elsie's accidently catching the boy's hand in a doorway, which led to his death from gangrene. Other days it was from tubercular meningitis (which is listed as the official cause of death on the child's death certificate in Bristol).

About one detail, however, Cary was always consistent — and that was the memory of his parents fighting. 'They constantly fought. Elsie had lived in Clifton,' Cary said, 'kind of the Beverly Hills of Bristol, and she looked down on the part of town where we lived. It was by no means a slum — it was a good, working-class neighborhood — but it wasn't Clifton and she never let my father forget it. Ever.

'They were always arguing about money,' he continued. 'There just never seemed to be enough of it. That's all they talked about. And she made it seem like it was his fault. He was a tailor's presser and a damn good one, from what I hear. He even moved away once so he could take a job for more money, but it didn't prove to be practical in the long run.'

The Leaches also argued about where they should take their son to the movies. 'My mother insisted on taking me to the Picture Palace on Claire Street. It was so posh they served tea. But my father liked to take me to a theater that was like a big barn. I remember seeing a serial called *The Clutching Hand* there with him, week after week after week.'

As Cary grew older, he became the prime topic of dispute. 'My mother wanted me to be a pianist and she insisted I take piano lessons from a very mean old lady. But my father would argue that I should be out playing with boys my own age.' One of the fondest memories Cary had of his father involved a Sunday outing to a civic meeting at a meeting hall, where his father accidentally knocked some marbles out of young Cary's hands while they were sitting high up on a tier of wooden steps. 'He burst out laughing as each one of my aggies went *clonk, clonk, clonk,* down the stairs!' Cary still remembered with relish.

But surely, I would insist, he had to have some happy memories of his parents *together*?

He could recall only one. It was the Sunday afternoons when they would sit in the garden under an apple tree and have a late lunch. Cary and his parents sat on a trestle table and would admire the plants his father had brought to life in their garden. 'He had a vegetable garden he was so proud of,' Cary said. 'He also planted fuchsias and hollyhocks and lilies of the valley. It was beautiful. I think those were the most peaceful times we had.'

But typically, this golden memory was mixed with resentment. 'Have you ever asked yourself why we rarely eat at the table in this house?' Cary said, referring to a plain wooden table that sat mostly unused. 'I'll tell you why. My mother had to control everything, including our meals. I used to be fined two pence for each stain I left on the white linen tablecloth she'd put out for Sunday lunch. I was scared of dropping my food because I knew what it would cost me.'

'Control' was the key word Cary used in describing his mother. He remembered her beauty, particularly her black hair and lovely skin. But he remembered most what he called 'her will to control. She controlled what I wore. She controlled how I ate. And it wasn't until many, many years later that I realized she had this tremendous need to receive the love and affection she sought to control.'

Young Cary also had no control when his mother was committed to Fishponds by his father in the spring of 1914. Cary was not told the truth; instead, he was told she'd gone to a nearby seaside resort for a rest. When she didn't come back, his feelings turned from confusion to anger and then resentment. And it was very clear, sixty years after his mother's disappearance, that Cary still felt the loss acutely. But his interpretation of the tragedy disturbed me.

'It was her way of rejecting society and of rejecting my father,' Cary declared repeatedly about his mother's stay at Fishponds. The implication, of course, was that she had rejected young Cary as well. But I continually argued with Cary on this point. How could any form of mental illness be judged a conscious choice? It was a horrible loss — and one that I could understand made Cary feel abandoned and deserted — but it was not one Elsie had deliberately planned.

'You make it sound like something she did against you, Cary,' I would argue, 'but she did it against herself as much as she did it against you and your father. After all, the woman lost her husband and her son and her home. Fishponds is a beautiful place, I know, but I'm sure she'd have preferred to be in her own home with her own family if she could have.'

I had switched from defending Dyan, a woman I barely knew, to defending Elsie, a woman I had never met. This defense, unfortunately, served only to infuriate Cary to the point that one of us would have to drop the subject. But one day I must have pushed him too hard. And what he told me convinced me never to pursue the subject ever again.

Cary asked me if I remembered what he'd said about his being a psychological killer of women, an insight he had learned during his sessions with LSD.

I told him I did. I would never forget it.

'Good,' he said impassively. 'Because it was true. But I learned from the master of psychological killers, the best there was.'

The master, he said, was his mother. His father was an alcoholic and had begun drinking when Cary was a boy. According to Cary, it was 'his only escape — the only way he could get away from my mother and her constant complaints about money and everything else.'

After Cary's mother went to Fishponds, after Cary found a life in the theater and went to America, after Jim Leach began living with another woman, Cary's father still drank. Cary wrote his father faithfully when he was in

America, but he heard from him only intermittently. 'There would be years when he wouldn't answer my letters and postcards and then there would be others when he would. I don't think I fully understood why.'

But he did in November of 1933. Cary was making his first trip back to Bristol since he'd become a star. He had made fourteen films in a two-year period, starring opposite the likes of Marlene Dietrich and Mae West. He was not yet the superstar he would become in the late thirties, but he certainly was well-known. He planned to return to England in triumph with his future wife, Virginia Cherrill, and his best friend, Randolph Scott, at his side.

But the triumph turned into disaster.

'My father attacked me,' Cary said sadly. 'I thought he would be proud of me. I thought I'd done pretty good for myself. And when I first arrived in a fancy car and loaded with gifts, we did have some good times celebrating. But after a few times together, that all changed. One day I showed up and my father had been drinking. I tried to take him to a pub to share a pint with him, if he was in the mood to drink. But he wouldn't have it. He wouldn't drink with me. He said he could tell I thought I was too bloody grand for the likes of him.'

While Cary was still struggling with the realization that his father was an alcoholic, he received an even bigger shock: His father — 'in the most indelicate terms imaginable,' Cary remembered — informed his movie star son that his mother had never gone away. She had always been in Bristol. In the local county home for mental defectives.

'I went crazy myself,' Cary recalled. 'Why hadn't he told me the truth? It had been almost twenty years since she'd gone to Fishponds. Why hadn't he written me and told me? It's the least he could have done. My God, I had told the press she was *dead* because that's the only thing I could think after all these years.'

Cary's reaction to this traumatic visit was understandable — he began to drink. Instead of staying in England for a few weeks as he'd originally planned, his visit turned into months. He said it got so bad he had to be dried out in a sanitarium outside London.

'I was trying to escape too, you see? When word started to leak to the press, the studio released some statement about my suffering the after-effects of a concussion that had occurred while filming a movie in America before my trip.'

Two years after that bitter reunion with his father, Cary was informed by a lawyer's letter that his father had died and, as Elsie's legal next of kin, Cary now had to decide what to do with her.

Cary flew to Bristol and saw his mother for the first time in over twenty years at Fishponds. 'She seemed perfectly normal,' he said, 'maybe extra shy. But she wasn't a raving lunatic.'

But this reunion was not destined to be a happy one either.

'I told you what she did when I bent down to kiss her,' he said. 'She was not a loving woman. That's why my father drank, I assure you. That's how she killed him.'

Elsie spent the rest of her life in Bristol, first in a home Cary bought for her on Coldharbour Road in Redland. But she'd always wanted to go back to Clifton, and she finally made it back when Cary put her in a nursing home there, overlooking the Avon Gorge.

Over the years mother and son worked out an uneasy alliance that saw Cary making an annual pilgrimage to visit her each February for her birthday. 'She did not know how to give affection and she did not know how to receive it either. I tried to give her so many things, but her answer was always the same: "Why would I want that? Don't spend your money on me!"'

But I did detect a grudging admiration in Cary's voice as he described a small, wiry woman in her later years, searching the secondhand stores and antique shops of Clifton for a bargain or two.

'They'd knock up the prices when they saw her coming,' he laughed, 'because they knew they would have to go through this process of knocking down the price for her. But she didn't want any favors from anybody. She did her own shopping and marketing until she went into the nursing home. She didn't want to owe a soul. And that's how she died too.'

It was the closest thing to love I ever heard him express for his mother.

If the press asked Cary about his mother, he invariably told a very charming story about a hip, humorous woman. When Cary's hair started to go gray in the fifties, he said, his mother began to scold him.

'Dear, you really must do something with your hair.'

'Why, what's wrong with it?' he'd inquire.

'It's so white, dear. You should dye it. Everybody's doing it these days.'

'Why should I? Does it make me look old?'

'No, dear,' he'd quote her, 'it makes *me* look old!'

It was a dear story.

It may even have been true.

For Cary's sake I hoped it was.

17

HOLIDAY

GIVEN Cary's unhappy memories of his parents, I wanted him to share some of the joy I'd been privileged to experience with *my* Jim and Elsie.

Christmas 1974 provided the ideal occasion, when my parents arrived in mid-December to spend the holidays with me. I turned my apartment in Beverly Hills over to them and it wasn't long before the three of us were conspiring to give Cary and Jennifer a proper English Christmas. Personally, I was even more motivated when I remembered something Cary'd told me during the previous year's holidays: He had never really celebrated Christmas fully and sincerely as an adult until Jennifer's birth.

Although Mummy and Daddy had already met Cary once, they were still nervous as I drove them up to Cary's house Christmas morning.

'Now, Mummy,' I said, 'please remember Cary is a strict non-smoker, so don't pull out a cigarette. He'll give you a lecture about ruining your health.'

She said not to worry, but my father was feeling contentious.

'If I don't like him,' he offered, 'I'm going to tell him to buzz off because I don't need his coppers!'

'Oh, Jim!' my mother scolded him. 'Now stop it — you're going to make Maureen nervous. Besides, you sound as if you haven't met the man. You told me you liked him when he came for lunch, so why wouldn't you like him *now*?'

I'd heard Daddy's coppers speech for years. His patient friends had dubbed him 'Honest Jim' in recognition of his boast that he had never owed a penny to any other human being on the planet. Daddy hated the mere idea of credit cards and mortgages. So he refused to buy a house because he couldn't stand the thought of owing even a bank some coppers. I knew Cary would appreciate Honest Jim's frugal nature, so I really wasn't worried how they'd get along.

I wasn't even worried about Cary, for that matter, because he'd been whistling with happiness all week. Dyan had decided to let him have Jennifer for Christmas afternoon and evening as well as for much of the rest of the holidays.

When we arrived, Mummy and I headed for the kitchen while Cary offered Daddy a drink. Daddy had his usual gin and tonic and Cary had an unusual vodka with orange juice — unusual in that he rarely drank before six in the evening. But he obviously decided to make an exception for the holiday.

It wasn't long before Cary and Daddy were on a first name basis again, with Cary inviting Daddy to make himself comfortable at the bar whenever he felt like it.

'You know where it is, James!' Cary said.

While Mummy and I took care of the Christmas dinner as best we could in Cary's still-incomplete kitchen, Honest Jim won his way into Cary's heart even further by telling him how he handled members of the British press who called the house from time to time seeking some tidbit about my relationship with Cary.

'But I don't tell them a thing, Cary,' Daddy said. 'I remembered you told Maureen to tell us to say, "No comment," and that's just what I do.'

'Good going!' Cary said enthusiastically.

'That's all he will say,' Mummy said, joining in between visits to the kitchen. 'If they ask whether we've met you, all Jim says is, "No comment!" If they ask what we think about you two, all Jim says is, "No comment!"

'One time a lady came to the door and said she was from a London paper and said she had a question, but before she could ask it, Jim said: "No comment!"

'Then the lady said it was quite a trip out to Muswell Hill. Could she use the bathroom for just a minute? And Jim said: "No comment!"'

Cary rocked with laughter. 'I see I have to tell you something only once!' he said, patting Daddy on the shoulder.

Then Jennifer arrived and she couldn't wait to open her presents. As in the year before, Cary did not over-whelm the now eight-year-old child with gifts, in his deter-mination not to spoil her. But Cary was wildly generous with my presents. There was a handsome set of luggage and a transistor radio, as well as a handbag and an umbrella for Mummy and a cashmere sweater for Daddy.

They gave Cary a photo album for all his photos of Jennifer, while Jennifer was given a copy of *Black Beauty*, fitting for her love of horses. I gave Cary a silver photo frame, while Cary paid $1,000 toward the purchase of a new car for me. My Triumph had been breaking down on a regular basis, but I had been reluctant to give it up because it was my way of holding on, in some small way, to Britain.

After we had all exchanged presents, Cary brought out a big box that wasn't wrapped.

'Okay, everybody,' he instructed, 'let's not waste all this perfectly good string and wrapping paper. Into the box for next year!'

Mummy and Daddy exchanged a quick look but didn't say a thing, dutifully putting what material they had into the container. Cary's frugality could challenge even my father's.

Dinner was next, and Mummy and I served roast turkey, with all the trimmings, plus mince pies and custard. The taste was a bit foreign for Jennifer's young palate, but Cary loved it. He was so thrilled he began waxing nostalgic about an early Christmas on Hughenden Road back in Bristol.

'We had a stone larder,' Cary recalled, 'and my mother used to hang up the Christmas puddings from the ceiling. I can still see the white cloths covering the puddings as I stared up at them. It was with such anticipation!'

It was a wonderful night for us all and the next day — Boxing Day to us Brits — was even better. Cary lavished a few more gifts on my parents, but that wasn't the end of his surprises that day. While Mummy and Daddy were carefully storing the holiday string and wrappings, Cary winked at me and Jennifer and disappeared into his bedroom for a few minutes.

When he emerged, he was resplendent in top hat and tails. Jennifer and I burst out laughing. He pointed a cane at us and said:

'No laughing until I'm done!'

Then, with my parents openmouthed in amazement, Cary launched into a rendition of 'Top Hat' at the Steinway.

He sang it all the way through and obviously was having as good a time as his audience. Jennifer was especially tickled, clapping continuously. I was so touched. He could do the damnedest things at the damnedest times. As for my parents, they couldn't have been more delighted if the Queen Mother had personally invited them home for gin and tonics.

Before Cary did his next number, he poured champagne for all of us (except Jennifer of course).

'This one you'll like, Jim!' he announced merrily as he began to pound out 'Maybe It's Because I'm a Londoner' on the piano. As with his first song, Cary's voice was strong and full. The man just loved to perform.

Then, as corny as it sounds, we all surrounded the piano and sang Christmas carols. When we were finished, Cary handed me a beautiful bound diary.

'This is from Jennifer and her father,' he said, 'so you will remember this day and we hope many more days with us.'

And the next few days with Cary, Jennifer and my parents were indeed memorable. Cary had dedicated himself to showing Jim and Elsie everything he loved about Los Angeles and the rest of southern California. There was an uproarious visit to the members-only Magic

Castle in Hollywood, a nonprofit club operated by and dedicated to magicians. Cary had never lost his love of magic, which went all the way back to the days he 'exposed' The Great David Devant at the Empire in Bristol. The mischievous little boy in Cary surfaced once again at the Magic Castle bar, where he seated my mother on a stool. As she sipped her drink, she and the stool slowly went all the way down to the floor. Then Cary told her to try a stool next to that one. Of course, that one went sky high.

There was more fun at Disneyland — where a guide took us through a secret entrance at the back of every ride so we wouldn't have to wait in line — as well as Chinatown and historic Olvera Street in downtown Los Angeles. Trips to Palm Springs and Santa Barbara also continued the royal treatment Jim and Elsie were accorded.

Perhaps the most tender moment during these glowing holidays occurred when we visited the Old Towne Mall, a shopping complex in Redondo Beach. Cary loved the place because it had a million and one things to distract Jennifer and keep her entertained. By now, I suppose none of us should have been surprised to discover Cary jumping up and down on a waterbed in a showroom, but we were.

Jennifer squealed in delight and ran to join her father on the mattress. So there they were, the nearly seventy-year-old Cary Grant and his eight-year-old daughter, bouncing up and down like two kids on a trampoline. If only I'd brought a camera with us that day!

Once the excitement was over, we stopped for fish and chips on the pier. As we finished eating, Cary asked Mummy and me if we'd mind if he took Daddy for a 'pint of wallop' at a bar at the bottom of the pier.

After we gave our permission, Cary and Daddy retired for their drink. Later that night Daddy told me what had happened.

Once they got inside the establishment, Daddy insisted he was going to buy Cary a beer. Cary thanked him because, as he said, 'it's not very often people think to buy me anything.'

They were enjoying their brew when Cary began to talk about me to Daddy. He said that I had brought joy into his life and he was especially pleased that Jennifer and I had such a special rapport.

'I suppose I should be embarrassed,' Cary continued. 'Here I am talking to you about your daughter and how I love her, and you are younger than I am, James!'

My father didn't know what to say except what he *always* said where I was concerned:

'The only thing that's ever mattered to me is Maureen's happiness. If you make her happy, Cary, then I don't care what anybody thinks.'

Cary seemed happy to hear that.

'You know,' he said, 'I will always take good care of Maureen. I care very much about her.'

Daddy didn't doubt that for a second.

'Then let me ask you something,' Cary whispered, drawing Daddy closer in the din. 'What would you think if I asked Maureen to marry me?'

'Have you asked her?' Daddy said.

'No. I wouldn't before I asked you what you thought.'

'Then I'll repeat what I just told you — Maureen's happiness is all that matters to Elsie and me. If she thinks she'd be happy marrying you, then that would make us very happy.'

Cary then thanked Daddy and bought him another beer.

When Daddy told me about his conversation with Cary, I didn't know what to think. It certainly sounded as if he were asking Daddy's blessing to marry me. But how did I feel about marriage to this emotionally scarred man? He could be so wonderful, as he had been during the past couple of weeks, but he could also be disturbing, even irrational, at other times. There was also the matter of my career to consider. I didn't want to remain a fan-magazine writer all my life, but being a full-time wife to a retired legend was not what I had in mind either. And being Mrs. Cary Grant would be a full-time occupation, given his negative feelings about wives who worked. 'Women can't run a home and a job too,' he said chauvinistically. 'I'd rather they stayed home and raised families. That's what nature designed women for.'

These concerns were still much on my mind one night a week later when Cary and I were in bed. My parents had flown back to England, overjoyed and exhausted. I couldn't thank Cary enough for the way he opened his home and his heart to them.

'I owe you a lot for making them so happy,' I told him.

'Oh, you really don't owe me a thing,' he insisted gallantly. 'It was my pleasure. Really. They're wonderful people and they know how to have a good time.'

That was high praise indeed from Cary. It was his official seal of approval.

'Can I ask you something?' Cary said as he rolled over to face me. Some part of me was expecting him to ask me to marry him and I didn't know what to say. I guess I would just have to lay out my concerns and see where that took us.

'Of course,' I said nervously.

'You know I love you, don't you?' he began.

'Yes,' I said.

'And you know I would never do anything deliberately to hurt you.'

'Right,' I said.

'Then I know you will accept that I ask you this with love,' he continued.

Here it was. But why did he make marriage sound like something awful? It didn't make sense.

'Maureen, do you know you're adopted?' he said finally.

I could not believe what I was hearing. Surely I had had too much wine with dinner.

'What did you say, darling?'

'I asked you,' he said, slightly impatient, 'if you knew you were adopted.'

I felt as if my head were going to crack open and the contents would shoot into space. He had to be kidding.

'Are you insane?' I said after a few moments.

'What did you say?' he snapped.

'You've got to be kidding, Cary. I mean, I *hope* you're kidding. Why would you even ask me that? You know they're my parents. I've seen it on my birth certificate. And my father showed you the room I was born in at Muswell Hill and even the steps he sat on while he was waiting for Mummy to give birth to me, for God's sake. Don't you remember that?'

'*What did you say?*' he said, angrily snapping off each word. He had gotten up in bed and was now staring at me.

'I asked you if you were nuts, because what you said makes no sense whatsoever, and I'm *livid* that you would even think that!'

'So you think I'm insane?' Cary said. He was sitting right across from me but he couldn't have sounded more distant if he'd lived in Timbuktu.

'Well,' he continued, 'if I'm insane, then you're crazier than I am, because you're the one who's in bed with a madman!'

I knew Cary was a master of diversion but his hostility didn't feel like part of a diversionary tactic.

'I want to know why you said that about Mummy and Daddy,' I said, getting up and off the bed.

'I'm mad as a hatter,' he said sarcastically. 'I'm cuckoo as a cuckoo clock. Crazy people say crazy things. Don't you know that?'

'You're not answering my question,' I said.

I began to pace furiously in front of the bed. I thought it might help me get my bearings.

'Well, if you're interested in the truth — which you obviously are not, Maureen — then you would know that I asked it out of my love and concern for you.'

'What does love have to do with a question like *that*?' I demanded.

'Because, my dear,' he said haughtily, 'I love you enough to tell you the truth. I love you enough to want you to know the truth.'

'And just how do you "know" I'm adopted? Have you

had detectives looking into my background, like you had them looking into Dyan's windows?'

'Ha! No one told me. I know it. Anyone could tell by looking at you and then looking at them, especially your mother. She is not your real mother, Maureen. Trust me. Look into this. Ask her for the truth.'

'Cary,' I said, trying to remain calm. 'I don't think you know what you're saying and I —'

'Don't ever make the mistake of thinking I don't know what I'm saying, Maureen. I have lived many more years than you and I don't say things idly.'

I couldn't stay by his side. I was shaking with anger. I went to sleep in Jennifer's bedroom, but I couldn't sleep. I left in the morning without saying a word to Cary.

What could I say?

18

ONLY ANGELS HAVE WINGS

'IT'S as if he unconsciously feels he must follow something lovely with something awful,' I was telling Dee Joseph the next day. 'Perhaps he's known so little real happiness, he mistrusts and tries to destroy it.'

With this ridiculous notion about my 'real parents,' Cary had ruined the lovely Christmas we had all shared. Why? I knew that notion said much more about Cary and his relationship with his own parents than it did about me or my parents, but it still disturbed and hurt me.

What also disturbed me was the way Cary wore his misfortune in this domain as a kind of badge of honor that only he could wear, whose true significance only he could understand. When Cary had felt compelled to discuss his mother and then his father with me, it was as if he were inviting me to get closer. But when I did, he took an almost perverse pride in shutting the door on me just at the moment he was really opening up. It was clear that on some level Cary really did want me to understand, yet on another he wanted me to stay away and maintain my distance. These were his wounds and they were essentially his alone to make better — or worse. Cary let me in close enough to be a witness to his pain, but never close enough to be a balm.

It was a painful, frustrating role.

There was something else that bothered me. It was not a huge issue but was, in its way, just as revealing. Not surprisingly, it involved the issue of control. Cary had put

$1,000 toward a new car as my Christmas present, but I had no say in the color (yellow) or the make (Datsun) or even the equipment. If I was going to be responsible for paying at least $4,000 more over the years on that vehicle, I naturally expected some kind of say on these matters. But Cary had picked the make ('Japanese cars are better mechanically') and the color ('Yellow is much safer; it can be seen at night') without one word to me.

I told him I thought it was wonderful he'd spent that much money on me and that he obviously had been thinking of my safety, but I would have appreciated having been consulted about the make, color and so on if I was going to be responsible for paying most of it off. I was extremely careful in the way I put this to him, because I knew how sensitive he could be. But he turned on me anyway.

'You are an ungrateful child!' he almost shouted.

'No, Cary, I'm not ungrateful for what you tried to do. I just don't think you understand that if I was going to have to pay for most of this car, then I should've been able to have some say in the color or the make or whatever.'

'You are ungrateful!' he repeated. At that moment, I could hear him also saying it about his mother and Jennifer.

'No, Cary, I am *not* ungrateful,' I repeated, standing up to him as best I could. 'If you had bought me the car outright, if it had been pink polka-dot under those circumstances, I wouldn't have said a thing.'

'One day you will thank me that I didn't indulge you,' he said. He was hurt and didn't understand a word I'd said.

'Oh Cary, please understand,' I said gently. 'I know how much you indulged my parents. And there have been many times you've indulged me too. I know that and I love you for it. But don't you see my point here? I don't want to make you angry or hurt you, but we have to be close enough and honest enough with each other to discuss something like this.'

'I suppose so,' he said, subdued, 'but I want you to

understand *my* point. I can't spoil you, Maureen. It would only be crippling you, don't you see? I won't be around here forever. You have to face that. And I want you to be prepared to do things for yourself and not depend on me. I know you resent me now, but one day you won't. You'll be grateful I didn't indulge you that way.'

'Cary, I don't hate you,' I said, trying to soothe him. 'I love you. Sometimes I don't understand you. And just as you want me to see *your* point — and I do — I hope you'll try to see mine. That's all.'

Soon two things happened that made my problems with Cary look infinitesimal by comparison. Cary, Jennifer and I had gone to Palm Springs to celebrate Cary's seventy-first birthday and it was a wonderfully relaxed, carefree time.

Then we got a phone call that stopped our merriment. Willie was calling Cary to ask for a few days off to care for her mother, who was dying. 'Anything you want,' Cary said, concerned. 'Is there anything any of us can do?' Willie said there wasn't, but we cut short our trip and rushed back to Beverly Hills to be at her side. Now it was time for us to lend support to this marvelous woman on whom we had all leaned so much. Willie was embarrassed by the attention, but I could tell she was touched.

And in the middle of February there was an even more devastating blow. Bobby Birkenfeld, my neighbor who occasionally house-sat for Cary, had made an awful discovery — he was suffering from a brain tumor. He was due to go into UCLA Medical Center for an exploratory operation in a few days and was deeply worried. I took some time off from work to be with him and look after all the little things he shouldn't be bothered with as he faced such a big operation.

Cary couldn't have been more supportive and understanding. He even invited Bobby up to the house for a chat. He knew the fears Bobby, who was still in his mid-twenties, had to be facing.

'If you believe it will turn out all right,' Cary told him one afternoon on the terrace, 'then it will. I know that sounds simpleminded, but it's true. Take my word for it, Bobby. I'm a lot older than you and I've been through a lot more than you. That's what it all comes down to. Have faith in yourself and in God and you'll be fine, I promise you.'

'May I ask you something?' Bobby said hesitantly.

'Of course,' Cary said. 'Anything you want.'

'Did you ever think you were going to die?'

I wanted to get up and walk away because I knew I was going to start crying. But Cary shot me a glance that told me to save my tears. They wouldn't do Bobby a bit of good.

'Two times, as a matter of fact,' Cary said. 'The first time was when I was making a movie with the ridiculous title of *I Was a Male War Bride* for Howard Hawks. We did *Bringing up Baby* together and some other pictures. But this picture was unlucky for all of us.

'My costar, Ann Sheridan, got pleurisy. Then when we were on location in London, I got the flu. At least I thought it was the flu. Actually, it was jaundice from hepatitis. I had an infection in my liver and lost forty pounds within a matter of weeks. Everyone thought I was going to die, but I didn't. I knew I had too much to live for. I'd married my third wife, Betsy, and I loved her too much to just go off and leave her alone. Do you have someone now, Bobby?'

'No, not really,' Bobby said, a little embarrassed.

'Don't worry,' Cary reassured him. 'That means you're going to meet someone very soon. It gives you something to look forward to, doesn't it?'

Cary's second brush with death, he told Bobby, occurred in March 1968, just a few days before he was due in a Los Angeles courtroom for the start of proceedings for his divorce from Dyan. He was in New York and it was a rainy night. After dinner with his good friend Bob Taplinger, Cary got into a chauffeured limousine with a woman who worked in Taplinger's publicity firm, for the ride to the airport. Cary was due to take a late-night flight back to Los Angeles.

But on the Long Island Expressway a truck skidded on the wet highway and its spare wheel assembly flew off and slammed into Cary's limo.

'I got the least of it, but I looked the worst of it,' Cary said. 'The chauffeur broke one of his kneecaps and the lady broke her collarbone and fractured her leg. I bled all over the place and everyone thought I had a broken nose, but it was just bruised cartilage and some cuts on my face. I also had a pair of fractured ribs.

'But as the ambulance took me to the hospital, I could tell by the look on everyone's face that they thought I was dying. And I went along with it. But then I started thinking of Jennifer — she was only a couple of years old. She barely knew me. And I started to get angry. Wait a minute! There was no way I was going to die. I had to see my child grow up to be a young lady, a happy young lady doing what she wants to do with her life.

'So I started giving everybody trouble, first in the ambulance and then at the hospital. Believe you me, they wanted me to get well as soon as possible so I'd get out of there! And I tell you what I did, Bobby. Just two weeks later I walked out of the hospital. And things turned out well for me in that courtroom too, though I wasn't there, of course. I got much more time to spend with Jennifer than I thought I would, considering what my former wife had said about me to the judge.

'You must never, never give up. I'm going to be around to see Jennifer become a wonderful young woman and so will you!'

Cary's pep talk did much to raise Bobby's spirits. And fortunately, the operation was a success. Two days afterward we visited Bobby in hospital.

'What did I tell you?' Cary said as he breezed into Bobby's room, carrying flowers. 'I knew you'd be okay.'

Bobby was so touched Cary would take time to visit him, and it instantly improved the amount of attention he was getting from the nurses. He was also thrilled to get a gift Cary had brought him — a portable radio.

'I know you work in the world of music, so I thought

you should have some here while you get better,' Cary said as he handed the young music publicist his gift.

'Thank you, Cary,' Bobby said, trying not to cry.

'Don't be silly,' Cary replied. 'We don't want our favorite house-sitter to fall behind in his other job, now do we?'

Cary's warmth and consideration could be overwhelming. At such times, he just didn't seem to be the same man who disturbed me with what he'd said about his parents — or mine.

While Bobby was in the hospital, I had another 'operation' to deal with — the overnight repair of the yellow Datsun. I had smacked the rear end of it into a wall near Cary's house one night as I backed down the hill. After all the drama we'd gone through about the car, I didn't dare tell him I'd managed to bang it up within a few weeks. Luckily a friend of a friend knew a body shop where very quick repairs could be accomplished for an extra hundred or two.

Cary never caught on, thank God, or I never would have heard the end of it. And of course, I didn't want to upset Cary while he was being so solicitous toward Bobby. My guilt deepened when my brother, Dave, paid me a visit from Paris. Like my parents, he was shown an incredibly good time by Cary, with much the same agenda — Disneyland, Magic Castle, Chinatown . . .

Cary even made my brother's departure from Los Angeles something unforgettable. Dave was running late and had to catch an afternoon flight back to Paris or he would have had to stay over for at least another couple of days. While Dave and I scrambled around my apartment, where he'd been staying, Cary seemed unusually calm.

'Don't worry,' Cary said, 'I'll get you there on time — and even if I don't, I'll have them delay the plane for you.'

'What?' Dave said, as astounded as I was.

'Oh, yes,' Cary said nonchalantly. 'I'm on the board of Western Airlines and I'm sure if I call your airline and explain the problem, they'll hold the flight back a few minutes as a courtesy.'

The man could work miracles. But we'd still have to

rush like crazy. Once Dave was all packed up and ready to go, Cary put the pedal to the metal and off we hurried to the airport in his Cadillac. I've already told you what I thought of Cary's driving, so you can imagine how nervous I was, but I hoped for the best.

Yet I had to start worrying when Cary began running red lights.

'Cary,' I said as delicately as possible, 'since you called them to hold the plane, you don't have to rush and run the lights.'

'I'm not running any lights,' he said. 'What in the world do you mean?'

Was Cary so determined to get Dave to the airport on time he couldn't see the traffic lights?

On we raced toward the airport, with Cary still blithely running red lights. I was terrified we were going to hit somebody or get hit. At the least we would get a ticket and Dave would not make his flight. But none of this seemed to concern Dave — he was sitting in the backseat, his arms folded and a giant grin plastered across his face.

He liked speed-racing, Cary Grant style. I'm sure he thought it was some new American fad.

Somehow we made it to the airport in one piece, but we were late. After Cary brought the car to an abrupt halt at the unloading zone, he motioned me to the wheel.

'Here,' he said, 'I'll take Dave into the terminal. I'll get him past everybody in a jiffy.'

'But he has to check in and —' I sputtered.

'Don't worry,' Cary interrupted. 'We'll get him on that plane. I'll just do the Cary Grant thing so no one holds us up.'

'The Cary Grant thing?' I said blankly. What in the world did he mean?

Then Cary cocked one eyebrow quizzically. I'd seen the gesture a hundred times in his movies. I wanted to reach out and kiss him, but there wasn't time.

A few minutes later Cary came strolling out of the terminal. He had a huge grin on his face.

The Cary Grant thing had worked its charm one more time.

19

LADIES SHOULD LISTEN

SINCE the beginning of 1975, the tabloids on both sides of the Atlantic had been flying high with reports about my 'imminent marriage' to Cary.

The *National Enquirer* unveiled a cover story about '71-Year-Old Cary Grant's Secret Love — She's 28.' Cary, of course, looked great in the photo the *Enquirer* ran, but my cheeks were so chubby I told my friends I looked like Ann Miller's illegitimate daughter. My embarrassment was compounded when a shot of then President Ford was released to the wires showing him reading that particular issue of the *Enquirer* in the White House.

London's *Daily Mail* had a much more flattering shot of me, but my heart sank when I saw the headline for its story: 'Cary to Marry Again ... to Win His Daughter Back!' Not only was it not true, it also brought Jennifer's name into the middle of our relationship. Unfortunately, more papers picked up the same story, with the very same angle.

It got so bad that a mutual friend got Joyce Haber, entertainment writer for the *Los Angeles Times*, to quash the marriage reports. Here's what Joyce wrote on March 13, 1975:

'Since everyone has been asking me, I can tell you that Cary Grant's steady date, Maureen Donaldson, is telling her friends there's nothing to the rumors that she and Cary will marry. So there!'

Cary did not seem bothered in the least by the

published reports we were on the verge of marriage, not even when Jennifer was brought into this particular rumor mill. But I felt there was no point in misleading anyone, the press included. I still had the same questions and doubts that concerned me after Cary's discussion with Daddy at that Redondo Beach bar.

At the same time it was easy to see why people might think Cary and I were on the marital path. It was my friend Dee Joseph who picked up on what was really going on. I got a clue when she asked me a question one afternoon as we were lying around the pool. It was a Sunday and Cary had gone off to the races.

'Maureen, don't you see what's happening?' Dee said. 'This man is grooming you to be the fifth Mrs. Cary Grant. He's changing everything about you.'

'What do you mean?' I said, genuinely startled.

'From your hair to your teeth to the clothes you wear, Cary is taking over your life to make you ready to become his next wife.'

At first I told her she was wrong. As wrong as the time I thought Cary was going to marry me but instead asked me if I knew I was adopted.

'And I'm telling you,' Dee insisted, 'that you are in the middle of being groomed to be his wife. I'm not saying there's anything wrong with it, just that you should be aware of it because that's what *you're* doing and that's what *he's* doing.'

Once I thought it over, I had to admit Dee made a lot of sense. Since the beginning of the year, Cary had taken a much greater interest in my personal appearance. There were many more 'fashion shows' than ever before. There was also a visit to Cary's dentist to fix a crooked tooth. I would have to wear a removable retainer most hours of the day, but Cary couldn't have been more supportive: 'It'll take just a few months and then you'll see the benefit for the rest of your life.' Then there was the matter of my hair. I was beginning to gray early. One day I told Cary I thought I'd start putting a rinse on my hair to hide the gray.

'Oh, no!' he said. 'Gray hair is a symbol of wisdom. Besides, if you dye your hair, you could damage your brain.'

Cary outlined what I came to call the Jean Harlow Theory of Brain Damage. Cary insisted that the movies' platinum blonde had died not from uremic poisoning, but from all the years of dyeing her hair. 'All that poison seeped into her brain and killed her,' he said with great assurance.

When I laughed at his theory, Cary took great offense. 'I know what I'm talking about. Don't forget, I made a film with her!'

That he had — it was called *Suzy* — but it wasn't enough to persuade me about the merits of this theory.

'Well, I'm sorry, Cary, but I happened to see *Harlow* with Carroll Baker and I'll always believe Jean Harlow died of a broken heart.' He was not amused.

He also took quite seriously his attempts to show me the proper way to be a good dinner-party guest. This included everything from how to hold a wineglass correctly to how to say 'hors d'oeuvre.' He insisted that most people erroneously said 'hors d'oeuvre*s*' when they should say 'hors d'oeuvre' to signify one appetizer. When I pointed out that the Random House dictionary said either use was correct, he snippily told me: 'Maureen, I've been around a lot longer than any dictionary. I was going to dinner parties with Noël Coward in the twenties, so I think you can accept *my* word as final on this matter.'

And the dictionary was also part of my grooming or reeducation.

'You should always try to learn one new word each day,' Cary instructed me. 'It gives your mind something to munch on, if you know what I mean.'

I did my best to be a good student. For a time I even took a course in stocks and bonds so I could keep up my end of the conversation when Cary and I went to dinner with his business associates. Unfortunately, most of these people seemed much more interested in *my* business, namely, who was going with whom in Hollywood.

But I did my best to be as attentive to Cary's wishes as possible. He'd lived a life most people could only imagine. He did know more world figures that you could shake a stick at. And he was very sincere in his efforts to open the gateway to a new life for me. Perhaps the most important thing I learned from him was attention to detail. Cary was a perfectionist, and though he could drive me crazy with his perfectionism, it was a lesson that opened a whole new profession to me. Not by coincidence, I'm sure.

I'd begun to take photographs of some of my interview subjects, with the encouragement of Alice Cooper. But it was Cary who started telling me I had 'a real eye' after I took some test snapshots of him around the house.

'I've had thousands of pictures taken of me,' Cary said, 'and I can tell almost immediately if someone has a good eye or not. I'm telling you that you've got the gift and you are doing a disservice to yourself not to pursue it.'

Cary became so persistent he offered to buy me a camera if, for my part, I would take a photography class. Of course I agreed, because I was enormously flattered. The day after he made this offer, Cary bought me a Nikon F2. If he'd bought me something cheap, I would have thought Cary was just trying to be kind. A Nikon meant he was serious.

Cary also gave me my first job as a photographer. I was to photograph all of Jennifer's toys he had in the house, as well as her clothes. He wanted to document everything he could for Jennifer's future perusal in his fireproof vault, or shrine.

It was the best possible assignment I could've gotten, because Cary was a demanding taskmaster. He was so specific that if I shot a picture of one of Jennifer's dresses and it wasn't perfectly centered, it had to be redone. And redone until it was right. 'If it's worth doing, it's worth doing right!' I heard him say on countless occasions. At the time I sometimes resented it. Today I thank him for not letting me settle for anything less than my absolute best.

It was at this time Cary began to ask me if I really

planned to remain an entertainment writer for the rest of my life.

'And what brought this on?' I remember asking.

'It's just that you have a gift and I think you should follow that, unless, of course, you really want to deal with other people's misfortunes for the rest of your life.'

'Gee, Cary,' I shot back, 'when you put it so charmingly, I can't imagine how I'll manage to get my nose out of the gutter!'

'You know what I mean, dear.'

And so it would go. He was relentless. If I was serious about photography, I should forget about Rona Barrett and her magazines.

'Doesn't a free-lance photographer sound like a glamorous job?' he'd say to entice me.

I had to admit it sounded much better than my current job. Cary had discovered a vulnerable spot. Perhaps he'd sensed my general fatigue with interviewing and with my other duties at the magazine.

'And you know I know a lot of people,' he'd continue. 'I'd be happy to call up all my friends and see if they'd pose for you.'

He was pushing. Hard.

'What about this? You know I don't do many interviews anymore —'

'Yes,' I interrupted, 'you've never given *me* one!'

'That's beside the point. But I could agree to do some and tell the papers that if they want the interview, the only person I'll pose for is my good friend Maureen Donaldson.'

That's the arrangement that ultimately emerged, even with *The New York Times*. Cary did the talking; I did the shooting. But it took almost a year before I finally resigned from my job and took up photography exclusively.

It also took me some time to recognize the fact that for Cary it would prove to be a lot less embarrassing to be married to a photographer than to a movie-magazine writer. But I should have gotten a clue in that Dorothy Manners column from the year before, which had snickered about my profession, considering 'publicity-shy Cary.'

Whatever the motivations for my personal and professional grooming, it ultimately did not have the desired effect. Rather than bind me closer to Cary, it served only to make me more independent in the long run. With tooth fixed and stunning new wardrobe, this former chubbette from Muswell Hill finally became confident about her looks. And once freed from my magazine job, I was free to pursue my career on my terms. And that meant *my* terms, not Cary's. If I was going to be a photographer, I was not going to be a dilettante. I turned much of my apartment into an office and photo studio. I also began making my own contacts and connections; I was grateful for Cary's help in this arena, but I didn't want to be completely dependent on him or his friends.

It was in this way that Cary inadvertently sowed the seeds for our breakup a couple of years later. Cary had wanted to change me, but I'd begun to change how I felt about him and our relationship. In most relationships it's hard to pinpoint the real beginning of dissolution. But in my mind, ours began to unravel on a late spring day in 1975 when we met Peter Sellers and his girlfriend, Countess Christina Wachtmeister, whose father is the Swedish ambassador to the United States.

The whole idea of Cary and Peter being friends struck me as odd. Peter was carefree, slightly dangerous, a real eccentric. He communicated with friends frequently by telegram. He also had a habit of getting up right in the middle of dinner — regardless of how few or how many people were with him — and just walking off, already having made arrangements with the management to pay the bill. Cary was too much of a perfectionist for such a loose wire as Peter. As far as I could see, there were only two things they had in common: They both had been born in Britain and gotten their early starts in vaudeville, and much later in their lives, they both had fallen in love with Sophia Loren. Cary pursued Sophia while making *The Pride and the Passion* and *Houseboat* in the late fifties;

Peter wooed Sophia while making *The Millionairess* in 1960. Both attempts were unsuccessful.

But Christina — or Titi, as she urged me to call her — and I had a lot more in common. Though I'd been born in a humble fireman's cottage and she'd come from old money and real power in her homeland, we were both young, attractive and fun-loving. We got along like peas in a pod and were each gratified to find in the other someone who was down-to-earth in the sometimes rarefied atmosphere the men we loved traveled in.

For our first time out together, the four of us went to a Dodgers game. It was a lovely evening, with Cary surprising Peter and Titi by having their names lit up on the Dodger scoreboard. We all agreed to see each other later that week for a day at the races.

I knew something was wrong when we got to the Turf Club at Hollywood Park and Cary refused to have a glass of champagne with the rest of us. I gave him a 'What's wrong?' look but he ignored me.

Then Peter was asked by an official if he'd like to have a tour of the whole racetrack. He agreed and the three of us followed in his wake. Peter was in rare form that afternoon, assuming a variety of accents that kept not only Titi and me but also our guide in stitches. Cary tagged behind us, poker-faced.

'Don't be a wet blanket!' Peter nudged Cary as he tried to persuade him to join in the fun. But Cary would have none of it. Then an Inspector Clouseau fan cornered Peter as we were about to reenter the Turf Club after our tour.

'Oh, Mr. Sellers, my wife and I think you're so wonderful in those Pink Pussy movies of yours!' he gushed about the Pink Panther films.

Titi and I literally started gagging with laughter.

After seeing our reaction, Peter only encouraged the poor man.

'Oh, so you like my Pink Pussy films, do you? Well, you know I've made quite a few.'

'I know,' the man said. 'My wife has seen every one. Every one!'

'Well,' Peter continued, 'which is your favorite Pink Pussy movie?'

By this point Titi and I had to run to the ladies' room or we'd have caused a serious breach of etiquette right then and there.

When we came out and went into the Turf Club, there was Peter gaily chatting to another fan. And there Cary was, sitting with his arms folded and his face a thundercloud. We had a couple more drinks and later dropped Peter and Titi off where they were staying in Beverly Hills.

The second the car was out of the driveway, Cary unleashed a flood of invective.

'I'm never going out with you or with those two ever again!' he snapped.

'Oh, really?' I said, angry at his anger. 'And what do you propose we tell them about tomorrow night? We're supposed to go to the Magic Castle with them, remember?'

'Well,' Cary said, 'I have no intention whatsoever of going anywhere with you two girls! You behaved like *children*, giggling little girls in front of my friends at the Turf Club. And I will not have it!'

'You haven't answered my question, Cary,' I said calmly. 'What should we do about tomorrow night?'

'Either you will take them to the Magic Castle tomorrow night or I will, but it will not be the two of us. You may call them and ask them to make their choice.'

'It's your game,' I said, now red with anger. '*You* make the call. But you should think it over before you do, Cary. I admit Titi and I were silly, but we were just having a good time. Perhaps we were a bit loud, but that was the extent of it. Don't make more of it than it was. I know Peter and Titi had a good time, so why ruin it for them now?'

But Cary refused to listen to me. The minute we got home, he walked over to the phone and dialed Peter's number. Coldly, he gave Peter his choice. I knew Peter picked me as his Magic Castle host, because Cary slammed the phone down.

'You've got the job of chauffeuring those two around!' he said as he walked into the bedroom and shut the door.

For a time, this incident caused a serious breach in Cary's relationship with Peter. Cary and I soon made up, but it was the first significant rumble in the storm that was quickly gathering around us.

In June, Cary and I went to London again. He always attended the annual Fabergé trade fair at the Royal Lancaster as part of his duties with the company. But we'd barely checked into our suite when Cary got a call from his attorney. Dyan had said that if Cary wanted Jennifer for the next couple of days he could have her.

As Cary had told me, there was no distance too great for him to travel if it meant seeing Jennifer. He began repacking and asked me what I wanted to do: I could stay in London and wait for his return in three days, or I could come back with him now and return to England when he did. Since I was looking forward to seeing my parents, I told him I'd stay, see them and do a bit of shopping.

'Are you going to stay with them?' he asked.

'No, I thought I'd stay here,' I said since the room had already been reserved for him and would be kept in his name until he got back, whether he occupied it or not.

'Well,' he said, 'as long as you're staying, I have some things I'd like you to do for me, if you don't mind.'

I gladly agreed and then rode with him to Heathrow to wait for his flight. He was acting odd again, almost as withdrawn as he'd been during our day at the races with Peter and Titi.

'What's wrong, Cary?' I asked as we sat in the lounge. 'Would you like me to go back with you? I don't mind. I'm sure we can arrange a ticket very quickly.'

'I don't want you to do anything you don't want to,' he said with an edge.

'What I want is to make you happy, and in this instance I don't know what that is, Cary. I'll happily go with you if that's what you want ... or I'll happily stay and do your errands and see my parents. It doesn't make much difference to me.'

'It doesn't make any difference to you whether you're with me or not?'

'Cary!' I said, startled. 'You're twisting my words! That's not what I said or even meant to say. Something's wrong. Please tell me what it is.'

Suddenly he brightened and pretended nothing was wrong. 'Maybe it's just knowing that I'll miss you ...' he said.

'So I'll come with you. It's that simple,' I volunteered.

'No, it's too much bother. I'll be back in three days. I want you to have a good time.'

I tried my best to have one, seeing Peter and Titi for dinner. The next afternoon I played tennis with Titi and then went to see my parents and stayed overnight with them. When I got back to the Royal Lancaster the next day, there was a message that Cary had called at about three in the morning London time. I tried to get him then but couldn't, so I went out to do his errands, using a car that had been put at Cary's disposal by Fabergé.

Late that night, I got a phone call from Cary.

'How are you? How's Jennifer?' I asked.

'We're fine. And I hear you're having a wonderful time too.'

I didn't hear the sarcasm coming through the wires yet.

'Oh, yes,' I said enthusiastically. 'I did your errands today, and yesterday I saw my parents and played tennis with Titi. She says hello, by the way.'

'I heard about your parading through the lobby in your pink tennis shorts,' he said. His voice was colder than the Atlantic.

He must have meant the tennis shorts I had with a Pink Panther logo on them. They'd been a gift from Peter and Titi.

'What's wrong, Cary?' I said. 'Didn't you get to see Jennifer after all?'

'She's fine. She knows how to act like a young lady.'

'What *are* you talking about?' I said, feeling the anger starting to choke my throat.

'Don't pretend you don't know what I'm talking about,

Maureen,' he snapped back. 'I've heard about your behavior.'

'Cary, if wearing tennis shorts in the lobby is a felony in England, then they've changed the laws since I left!'

'You know that's not what I'm talking about!' he shouted.

'Just get it out, Cary,' I said wearily.

'I called you at three in the morning — three in the morning — and you weren't in the suite. What are you going to tell me? You were playing a game of tennis?'

'No, Cary, I've *already* told you. I was with my parents. I went to their house for dinner. Why didn't you call there for me? I left a message at the desk saying that's where I'd be.'

'You're very clever, Maureen. But you're not as clever as you think. You're not fooling me. You're not fooling anyone.'

'Well,' I offered, 'if you don't believe me, call my parents. Ask them.'

'Your mother would lie for you, so what's the point? Besides, you were supposed to invite your parents to come to the Fabergé fair and then have dinner with them in the suite, or have you conveniently forgotten?'

'No,' I said, 'I simply wanted to have a good home-cooked meal instead of a hotel meal. You once told me you thought my mother was a marvelous cook, but I suppose you'll tell me I made that up too.'

'I am very disappointed in you,' he said, not budging an inch.

'I would also like to know why you used a Fabergé car to do your shopping when you have your own money for taxis.'

'Cary, I don't believe my ears!' I declared. 'Your sources are awful. Have you forgotten the list of errands you gave me? Well, I've done them! I used *your* car to do *your* work. You're not making sense, Cary! No sense at all!'

'I think we should have a long talk,' Cary said, his voice still frozen and impassive. 'I've asked George Barrie to bring the Fabergé jet to London and pick you up. If you're not too busy, George will come for you tomorrow morning and accompany you on the jet back. I'd like to see you as soon as possible.'

'Could it fly tonight?' I said. 'There's no point in waiting, is there? This trip is ruined.'

'Let me check. I'll leave word if I can't reach you.'

'Cary?' I said, more angry than I had ever been in my life. 'If you can't reach me? You may think I'm a whore, but I advise you to stop treating me like one right this instant. See if your sources can get the plane ready in an hour. I can't wait to see you because I have something to tell you too. It won't take long.'

I wanted to reach through the phone line and strangle him. Fortunately, I had to wait until the next morning for the flight. I called my parents and told Mummy the whole horrible story. I decided to check out of the hotel that evening and spent what was left of it with Mummy and Daddy. I informed a Fabergé attaché of my plans and told him to leave word for the company car to pick me up at my parents' house in the morning. My father picked me up at the hotel and drove me to Muswell Hill.

'Mummy,' I cried as I ran into her arms, 'he can be so cruel. I don't think he loves me. Sometimes, I don't think he could love anyone with the exception of Jennifer. What's wrong with him?'

Mummy listened to me until it was dawn. I couldn't stop talking and I couldn't stop crying.

When the car came for me, Mummy pushed into my hands a bag with dripping sandwiches. She knew it was my favorite kind. The drippings from roast beef put between two slices of bread are my idea of snack heaven. It was Mummy's way of doing anything she could to make me feel better.

I must have looked a sight when I boarded the jet. I had been up all night and I was carrying a little brown bag with grease stains.

A more pitiful figure I could not imagine.

Apparently, neither could George Barrie.

'What happened to *you*?' he said as I took my seat.

'Didn't Cary tell you?' I said.

'No,' he replied. 'Are you all right? Did someone die?'

'No,' I cried, 'just my relationship with Cary.'

20

THE AWFUL TRUTH

BY the time I got to Los Angeles, something had changed in Cary's personal weather.

When I got up to the house, he grabbed me in his arms and said how much he'd missed me.

'But Cary ... ' I sputtered. 'Just two nights ago or the night before ... I've lost all track of time ... you all but called me a whore. You said I disgraced you in the lobby and cheated on you in your suite. I don't —'

'Oh, you're much too sensitive, my dear!' he pooh-poohed. 'I just wanted to see you. You're so tired, you don't know what you're saying.'

I was so tired I thought I'd imagined the whole conversation.

'Look, you're right,' I said. 'I do need some rest. I'm going down to the apartment, where I won't disturb you, and get some sleep there.'

'Why on earth would you do that?' he said, seemingly perplexed. 'This is your house too, you know.'

The last thing I wanted was *another* scene, so I put my bags down and climbed out of my clothes and into Jennifer's bed. I was confused and wary and much too tired to be angry, but something told me I'd be safer there than in Cary's bed.

I slept for what seemed days. I had lost all sense of time. I'm sure I was using sleep to escape. I didn't want to wake up to the reality of what Cary had said on the phone. If I just slept, it would go away.

And so it did, at least for a few days. Just as I was beginning to get my bearings again, Cary invited me to a Dodgers game with Jennifer and him. God, that sounded like fun. And another escape. We went and Cary still acted as if nothing were the matter. Perhaps for him nothing was. We sat in the O'Malleys' box instead of the Fabergé seats in Cary's name. He'd given them to a pair of visiting executives.

The next day there was another Dodgers game but Cary was too busy with legal work. He asked me if I'd like to go with my girlfriend Dee. Great. Escape, Part III.

I told Dee what had happened in London and the hideous phone call. She was strangely quiet. Usually she put in her two cents. But the more I talked the more quiet she became.

Finally, after the game was over, I phoned Cary to tell him Dee and I were going out for dinner. I'd pick him up something if he'd like. He demurred, saying Willie would cook up some leftovers if he got hungry.

Dee and I went to one of her favorite Mexican restaurants, Barragan's, near Dodger Stadium (a Mexican restaurant with an Irish name — just one more of L.A's anomalies). As we slipped into a booth, I could see Dee was upset. I asked her what was wrong.

'I don't know how to tell you this,' she said, struggling with the words.

'What do you mean?' I said. 'We've been friends for too long. You know that.'

'I know, but this is hard,' she said, flicking her cigarette ash nervously into an ashtray. 'You know John, right?'

'John, you mean Cary's secretary?' I said.

She nodded her head. John is the name I'll use here for one of the young men who had taken over after Bill Weaver resigned as Cary's secretary. He was nice enough and he seemed to idolize Cary. Cary's word was law with John and Cary liked having that effect on him. I thought John was kind of weak or wimpy, but he was always pleasant to me. Besides, he and Dee had become friends. They'd met when Dee had been up at the house.

'Yes, I mean John,' Dee said, her eyes nervously scanning the room. 'Well, while you were gone, he told me . . . he told me that Cary came on to him.'

'What?' I said, suddenly alert.

'John told me Cary had come on to him and he didn't know what to do because he was worried if he didn't go along with it, he might lose his job.'

Cary and I made a fine couple — the pansy and the whore. I started to laugh at the thought. I couldn't stop laughing. It was just too funny for words.

'Maureen,' Dee said, grabbing my hand, 'you've got to calm down.'

'Oh, I'm fine,' I said, laughing. I sounded every bit as maniacal as Cary repeatedly accused Dyan of being. 'Just *fine*!'

'It's the last thing in the world I wanted to tell you, but I thought you should know.'

'How could it be true?' I asked Dee. 'I mean, you don't think it's true, do you?'

'I can't say for certain,' she said, still holding my arm. 'It could be wishful thinking. But even if it is, it's unhealthy for Cary and unhealthy for you to be around someone who thinks like that. And if it's true ...'

'I've got to find out,' I said, starting to rise. 'I've got to find out *now*.'

We paid our bill and drove back to Beverly Grove. Dee had parked her car there and now she was getting in it to drive home.

'Oh, Maureen,' she said, 'I don't know what to say.'

'I do,' I said as I bent down to hug her. 'I want to thank you for telling me the truth. That's what I count on in a friend. You're a good friend and I want to thank you for being my friend now if I've never told you before.'

'Are you going to be all right?' she said, worried.

'I will be when I've found out the truth in there,' I said, pointing to the house.

'If you need me, please call.'

'I may have to, you know.'

I walked into the house. Cary was sitting on a stool in the kitchen, but the light wasn't on. He was drinking a glass of wine in the shadows. For a moment or two I couldn't see him. All my eyes could focus on was the chipped and peeling paint in the still unfinished room.

'How was Mr. O'Malley?' he said.

No 'Hello.' No 'How are you?'

'Do you mean Walter or Peter?' I said. 'I saw Peter for only a minute on the way out, Cary, but I thanked him for the other night, when we were in his box with Jennifer.'

'You just had to let yourself be known to him, didn't you?'

'No, he already knew me from the day before,' I said.

'Don't pretend with me, Maureen. What did I tell you yesterday?'

'Cary, all I said was "Hello" and "Thank you for last night" because I knew I'd been so groggy from London and all that. I was worried I hadn't thanked him properly. It's not as if I sat there and had a drink with him or something. It was just on the way out.'

'No, I got a full report on your actions,' he said. His voice was bitter and hard. 'What did I tell you? Didn't I tell you that it was a privilege to sit in the O'Malley box and we should never abuse it like so many other people feel free to do? But no, you had to go rushing in there and show your cute personality to Peter and show off for Dee, didn't you? I told you specifically never to go into the O'Malley box unless you were with me, didn't I?'

'Cary, I didn't go inside the O'Malley box,' I said, trying to reason with him. 'I said hello and thank you and that was it. It took no more than a minute, two minutes at the most, I promise you!'

What the hell was I doing? I was defending a simple act of courtesy. Now who made no sense?

'No!' he said, standing up and knocking over the stool in the process. 'You wanted to ingratiate yourself with them and you just had to do that, no matter what I'd told you, because you're so young and you're so pretty!'

He was standing no more than six inches from me. There was malice in his eyes and I could smell the wine on his breath. *Oh my God, I don't know this man*, I thought to myself. *I don't really know him. This stranger wants to hurt me.*

I started to back away from him.

'Cary,' I said, 'I'm sorry to say that your sources about this are just as good as your sources in London. Either you know me or you don't. Either you trust me or you don't. And let's face it — you don't.'

'You have the nerve to bring up London?' he said. 'You think you're so smart and so cute, but you're not getting away with a thing. I know what you're doing! Cute is not a profession, my dear.'

'I know what you're doing too, Cary,' I said, looking at him directly in the face. 'You're right. I'm not as smart as you are. As a matter of fact, I've been damn stupid. But I just smartened up. Very quickly.'

'And what,' he said, 'does that mean, pray tell?'

'It means I know about you and John. In fact, I'm not the only one who knows about you and John. How long has it been going on? I guess I'm the last to know, aren't I?'

'You are insane,' he said coolly. 'You are. If I were going to bed with a man, do you think it would be with that ... that *creep*?'

He spat out the word. He blinked at me in disbelief.

'Do you know the men I could have?' he continued. 'Everybody thinks I'm a faggot anyway, so you wouldn't believe who lets me know they're available in their sly little way. But John? I'd laugh if it weren't so disgusting, so odious, so repulsive. I'd rather give up sex for the rest of my life than go to bed with *that*!'

He was too indignant to be acting or lying.

He also seemed suddenly sober.

'Why would you say something like that?' he said, now much calmer. 'How could you? I expect you to know better. You're the woman who shares my bed.'

'I didn't say it,' I said, much calmer myself and feeling the relief fill up my every pore. 'I mean, I did just say it but it's John who's really saying it. He told Dee you were coming on to him and he didn't know what to do.'

'I know what to do,' Cary said. 'I'll take care of him shortly. He's dangerous and a liar to boot. But what disturbs me is that you believed it. You really believed it.'

'Like you believe I was going to bed with half of London,' I said ruefully. 'We do make a fine pair, don't we?'

A slight smile crossed the corner of his mouth.

'There's more to this,' Cary said.

'What do you mean?' I wondered.

'You believe all that rubbish about my being homosexual, don't you?'

'Not now,' I sighed, 'but a few minutes ago I would've believed anything, considering the past few days. The whole thing is like a nightmare, Cary. It's my own life and I keep hoping it'll go away. I've been through some rough times, but I never felt that way before.'

'But all it took was one lie and you had me convicted,' he said, shaking his head.

'Are you saying *I* got a fair trial tonight about the O'Malleys? And what happened in London was fair?'

'I'll make you an offer, Maureen,' he said. 'I'll make it only once.'

I looked at him, my curiosity piqued.

'What's that?' I said.

'You can ask me anything you want on this subject and I will tell you the truth. But this is it. That's the end of any questions or any discussion or anything about homosexuality. What do you say?'

'I say I believe you, Cary, when you say John's lying. Do I need to say anything more?'

'Yes, you do. Because I know how the female mind works. You have to be sure. So ask me. Don't be afraid. I assure you I'm not.'

'Please, Cary,' I begged off. 'I'm tired. You're tired. Can I have a rain check on this?'

'No, no rain checks. It's a one-time-only offer. I'll never make it again. And you know you want to ask me, so ask.'

'Okay,' I said, nearly spent. 'There's only one thing I want to know. Have you had any experiences with men or feelings for them since we began seeing each other?'

'No,' he said, looking me directly in the eye.

'Thank you,' I said. 'That's all I need to know.'

'Go ahead,' he proceeded, still looking me in the eye. 'You're not finished. You know you're not. What else do you want to know?'

'Well,' I stammered, 'why do you hire male secretaries who are mostly gay?'

'That's simple if you really think about it,' he replied. 'I used to have female secretaries but they always fell in love with me.'

'And you don't think that happens with the *men*? Cary, what about John?' I laughed.

'You didn't let me finish,' he continued. 'Homosexuals, in my opinion, work more diligently than heterosexual men. It's like having a woman, but not having a woman, if you know what I mean. You get so much more value. So if somebody's going to fall in love with me and be my secretary, I'd rather it be a man than a woman. Besides, a man can carry suitcases and take care of things like that, which you just can't get a woman to do.'

The logic was uniquely Cary's. There was something in this reasoning to offend everyone of every sex and/or sexual persuasion, but I was frankly too tired to protest.

But Cary was not about to let the subject drop yet.

'What do your friends say about me?' he said. He was deadly serious.

'What does it matter, Cary?' I said, trying to avoid the subject. 'All that should matter to you is what I think.'

'I know what your friends say about me,' he went on. 'They say I like men, don't they?'

'No,' I said, hesitating slightly. 'They say you don't like women. And there is a difference.'

Finally, even he was too exhausted to argue. We fell into bed and then into an uneasy silence that lasted for several days. We were struggling to be polite. We were each struggling not to say anything that would upset the other. We were struggling to hang onto a relationship.

It was Jennifer who unknowingly pushed us over the edge. It was a Sunday afternoon and Cary had gone to visit a friend for an hour or two. Willie had the day off, so

Jennifer and I were alone in the house.

'Why does he do it, Maureen?' Jennifer said as she carefully stroked the hair on her doll. We were sitting on the floor in the living room.

'Do what, darling?' I said, not really paying attention.

'Tape us,' she said.

I stared at the tape recorder on a table.

'Oh, that's easy,' I replied. 'Your Daddy loves you so much, he likes to listen to you when you can't be here in person. That's why he likes to tape you when you're having fun or when we're playing. That way you are always around him later. You never really go away. Isn't that nice?'

I thought of the reels and reels of Jennifer's every utterance stored safely away in the vault.

'No,' she said, shaking her head. 'I don't mean the big recorder. I meant the little one on the top shelf near my bed. He puts it there but I'm not supposed to see it. I don't think you are either. He likes to tape us but I don't know why, do you? Couldn't he ask you if he wanted to know what we're talking about?'

I was sweating profusely, with beads of moisture already on my lip. *Dear God*, I said in a silent prayer, *don't make this true. I can live with everything else that's happened but I can't live with this. Cary would not do this to his own child.*

But there was no mercy on that day in June.

'Do you want to see it?' Jennifer asked me. 'He turned it on and put it on the shelf before he left. He didn't think I saw him, but I did.'

'Yes, Jennifer,' I said as I struggled to keep my composure. 'I would like to see it.'

She took me by the hand into her bedroom and pointed to the shelf. I reached over and discovered a tiny tape recorder, hidden among some of Jennifer's toys and books. It was still running.

I put my forefinger to my lips, indicating we should be silent. Jennifer understood and smiled. We went back into the living room, where she went back to playing with her doll. A few minutes later I tiptoed back into the bedroom alone.

I picked up the recorder again. It was still running.

'Cary,' I said as loudly as I could without Jennifer over-hearing me. 'This is why I'm leaving you. Any man who really loves his child would not invade her privacy this way. I love you but this is sick and I feel very sorry for you. I beg you to throw this machine away and forget you ever used it this way. Maybe Jennifer will too one day if you're lucky.'

An hour later Cary returned home. A couple of hours after that Dyan pulled up the driveway and honked her horn. Jennifer skipped out to join her.

I went into our bedroom and began to pack my things in the one suitcase I had left up at Beverly Grove. I'd have to get my other things sometime later.

'What are you doing?' Cary said as he walked into the room.

'I'm leaving you, Cary,' I said calmly.

'And I'm supposed to know what this is about?' he said impatiently.

'You do,' I said as I stuffed things into my suitcase as fast as I could. 'You already do.'

'You mean you're not going to have the decency to explain your actions?'

He started to reach out for my arm, but I backed away. 'Don't worry,' I said as I snapped the suitcase shut. 'You'll hear from me.'

21

KISS AND MAKE UP

CARY had an unusual response to my message. He asked me to marry him.

After I had left Beverly Grove, I went to stay with Dee. Cary called me there, but I wouldn't take his calls. Then I went to stay at my apartment-office; I had my answering service screen all my calls, trying to avoid him.

But late one night I picked up the phone and there was Cary on the line. He said I had been unfair just to walk out without giving him a chance to explain. After the time we'd spent together, I owed him at least that.

I said I'd think it over and get back to him. But before I had a chance to consider it, Cary was back on the line, virtually begging me to join him at the house.

There was no way I was going to agree. Whatever our problems, the sexual charge between us had always remained strong and overpowering. It was the most consistent thing about our sometimes inconsistent relationship. The last thing I wanted to do was return to his territory and fall into bed with him, which could only obscure the real issue.

I finally said I'd meet him at a restaurant. It was a Chinese place on Pico Boulevard called Lotus West. It not only had great food but, more important for this occasion, also had large booths which would allow us to have a private conversation.

I got there first and had already ordered wine when Cary arrived. The summer sun had enhanced his year-round tan so much that he seemed to be glowing. Nothing appeared to diminish his physical appeal as the years went by. As the advertising slogan promised, he wasn't getting older, he was getting better.

I decided to offset this tactical advantage by getting right to the point after we'd said hello.

'Cary, I just don't know how in the world you can justify doing that to Jennifer,' I began, taking the offensive. 'A child's privacy is so precious. How could you tape her like that?'

'Because I love her and I want what's best for her,' he replied. 'You know how little control I have over her life. I do it in order to see what she's saying or thinking about Dyan. I can't ask her directly because she would just protect her mother.'

'So you tape her conversations with *me* so you can find out what's really going on in *her* head about Dyan?'

'Yes,' he said. 'It's just that simple.'

A chill ran through me. This explanation was totally unacceptable, at least to me. It was almost a year after the Watergate scandal which had forced Nixon's resignation, and the whole idea of secretly taped conversations horrified me.

'You never even thought to ask my permission?' I said, peering directly into his eyes.

'Of course I did. But I knew if I told you it would inhibit you when you chatted with her. You have a very special rapport with her and I didn't want to do anything to disturb that.'

'You didn't?' I said, laughing. 'What do you think you did with *this*? Besides, she knows what you're doing, Cary. She's the one who brought it to my attention.'

'Oh, no!' he said sadly. 'How can I make her understand?'

A part of me still wanted to reach over and comfort him because, even though his devotion to his young daughter had caused him to overreach terribly, I knew how deeply he loved her.

'What will I do?' Cary said. 'I didn't —'

'Your only chance is to tell her the truth,' I offered. 'And you have a chance if you promise never to do it again.'

'Do you really think so?' he said, anguish covering his

face. The radiant man who'd walked into the restaurant just minutes before now looked colorless and blank.

'Yes,' I said, beginning to console him. 'She's a very bright and very loving little girl, Cary. If you tell her simply and it comes from your heart, then you won't have a problem.'

'Good God!' he said, looking up at me. 'What would I do without you?'

'You'll do fine,' I said, making my best effort to sound neutral. 'Jennifer is unique. You're lucky.'

Slowly he took my hand in his and looked into my eyes. 'I'm not talking about Jennifer now and you know it.'

I smiled but slipped my hand out of his.

'I love you, Cary, but I can't live with you,' I sighed. 'I could go on, but there's no point. You're a very smart man and you know exactly what I mean. I think we've had something very special and I will always remember it with love, but if I stayed, all we'd be left with is bitterness.'

'Look,' he said, taking my hand in his again. 'I know the past few weeks have been potty. Absolutely potty. You think I don't trust you. That's what your real message to me has been over and over, hasn't it?'

'I'm sorry, Cary, but there are times when you treat me like an enemy, not your friend, much less your lover.'

'I know,' he said. The words came faster and faster. 'And I've tried to tell you why. You're bright. So I don't have to draw a map for you where these things are concerned, now do I?'

'No,' I said, 'but it's like you cut off my arm while I'm trying to get a grip on the bloody thing, if you know what I mean.'

'I do,' he whispered. 'And I do trust you. You're right about not wasting time. If trust is the issue here, then there's only one way I can show you I trust you completely. I would like you to become my wife.

'Cary ... ' I protested. 'That's not what —'

'What other way can I show you? I've shown you my world. I've invited you to share my home. My friends are now your friends.'

I would never cease to be amazed at what he would pull out of his bag of tricks.

Well, this is it, I told myself. It sure didn't come the way you expected or even hoped for, but here it is. He's asking you to marry him.

Do you know how many other women have dreamed of this man asking them to marry him? Yes, my internal voice told me, but they didn't hear him on that phone when I was in London. And they didn't hear him when he talked about his mother. And they didn't hear him when he attacked me after I dropped by the O'Malley box.

These incidents were flashing through my mind like scenes from a movie. Then I saw other scenes from our relationship — his kindness to my parents ... his incredible love for Jennifer ... his rescuing that poor old mutt from that drunk outside the Tonga Lei ... the sight of Cary square-dancing on the terrace with a bewildered Willie.

I was tearing myself in two directions. Why did this proposal make me feel so schizophrenic? Shouldn't I be overjoyed at such a moment?

'No,' I finally heard myself saying. 'We have a problem and this is not a solution.'

But Cary was not about to be dissuaded.

'I understand how you feel now,' he said. 'You're still upset after all this turmoil. Don't give me your answer now, but give me a chance to put it behind us forever.'

'How?' I said, part of me deeply curious.

'Well,' he continued, 'you know I have Jennifer for a month this summer and we're planning to go up to Alaska.'

It had become an annual rite: Cary, Willie and Jennifer would take a cruise up to the frozen wonderland while I tended to my career.

'I'm not scheduled to leave for Alaska,' he went on, 'until three weeks from now. So why don't you and I go off to Greenhorn for a night or two by ourselves?'

It sounded tempting. Greenhorn was a dude ranch up in northern California near San Francisco. Guests were left to themselves to ride, hike, or eat whenever their fancy struck them. With my love for horses, the idea of being able to grab the reins and ride to my heart's content sounded splendid. Cary had described the place countless times and it had always intrigued me.

'We'll just rest and get up when we want to. We can really sort it all out because we'll have so much time together. Now you can't say no to that, can you?'

I couldn't, but it would take some persuasion at work to get more time off after my recent 'vacation' in London. If I could manage that, we'd take off in a couple of days.

'Good stuff!' Cary declared. 'Let's have a drink on it!'

We did but I didn't go home with him that night. I was still feeling cautious and tense.

By the time we flew up to Greenhorn, my defenses were significantly reduced. They vanished completely when I caught sight of the stable of horses and the quaint rustic cabins. I was in a different world. Everything was so green and serene as we lazily soaked up the sun and took to the horses. And that's when I fell in love with Dandy, a majestic stallion at the ranch. Sometimes an animal and a human connect on such a profound yet simple level that words cannot describe the bond.

While he was no big animal lover, Cary did love to ride and he quickly picked up on the amazing link between Dandy and me. Even the ranch hands and other guests couldn't help commenting on how much the horse had taken to me. The camp held mock elections in which guests voted among themselves to pick the best rider. I could see the pride in Cary's face as I was selected the winner.

Cary said it would be a shame to separate Dandy and me once the trip was over. I found it hard not to agree when I thought of the horse's combination of strength and gentleness. With Dandy under me, I rode as I'd never ridden in my life. It would be very hard to say good-bye to him, but this was his home.

'Nonsense!' Cary said. 'You two should not be parted. I'm going to talk to the owner about buying that horse for you. We'll stable him in Malibu next to Jennifer's horse. That way he'll never be lonely.'

'Do you really think you could?' I said, seriously considering the idea.

'I don't see why not,' Cary replied. 'Besides, your birthday's coming up in September, isn't it? Dandy would make the perfect gift.'

I hugged Cary and hoped for the best. But the ranch owner refused to sell Dandy and I could understand why. Dandy had been at Greenhorn for years and had become a favorite of many regular guests, not just Cary Grant's girlfriend. Cary did not like taking no for an answer from anyone, but I persuaded him that leaving Dandy where he was most needed made the most sense.

Knowing I had only a limited time with this magical animal, I began to photograph him constantly. And when I wasn't snapping away, Cary was shooting me atop Dandy. Cary later kept one of the photos he'd shot of Dandy and me in a gold frame in his bathroom.

Dandy wasn't the only one with whom I forged an unbelievable link that August. Cary and I picked up our unraveling relationship and wove something new and special together. It was not destined to last long, but it was unforgettable in its intensity. Cary was so caught up in me we made love each day, even if it was still in the shadows of the later afternoon or very early morning.

And I was so enthralled I decided I wanted to have his child. I still wasn't sure about marriage, but I was certain I wanted to give him a child. And perhaps with another child in his life, he'd loosen the reins on Jennifer some more. At least that's what I was thinking as the mountain air, the long summer nights and Cary's tender attention toward me formed an intoxicatingly seductive combination.

Late one afternoon Cary went into the bathroom after we'd explored our passion for each other. As he came back into our little cabin bedroom, I'm embarrassed to admit he saw something he'd never forget — I was standing on my head on the bed. Cary wasn't the only one who believed in old wives' tales. I had heard the one that assuming such a position after making love helped a girl get pregnant.

'What on earth are you doing?' he said, laughing.

When I told him about this radical technique, his face lit up and he gathered me in his arms.

'What a lovely thought!' he said enthusiastically. 'But for a moment there, I thought you were auditioning for Bob Pender's Knock-About Comedians!'

Our stay at Greenhorn couldn't have been more idyllic. And the trip back down to Los Angeles was equally memorable because we decided to rent a car. We didn't rush and we spent a couple of days sightseeing, eating at truckstops and stopping at some of the little fruit stands and souvenir shops along the way. Cary acted as if he'd spotted the Taj Mahal every time we pulled up to a gas station with a gift stand or shop nearby.

We were taking the inland route, so we could hit more than a few places off the main freeway. Soon the backseat was full of assorted junk Cary had purchased at these dusty shops. It was all worthless, but Cary loved playing tourist. And no one recognized him 'off the road,' so his enjoyment was enhanced even further. As he sifted through racks and bins of knickknacks and even tried to get the clerks to lower prices a bit, I couldn't help thinking of the story he'd told me about his mother in her later years as she hunted for bargains among the shops in Clifton.

But Cary was looking for much more than souvenirs on our trip back. He really wanted me to marry him. He had only alluded to the subject of marriage while we were at Greenhorn. But now as we leisurely made our way down to Los Angeles, he began to press me.

For all the beauty of our time at Greenhorn, I couldn't say yes. I wasn't thinking just of our recent series of explosions before the peace we found together at Greenhorn. I was also thinking that since I'd left home at the age of eighteen, I'd made my own living for some ten years now. I had even managed to help support my first husband and some of his family when the Donaldsons were leaving performing behind them and establishing their own studio.

Now I was perched on the edge of a whole new career as a photographer. Did it make sense to make another leap on top of that one by marrying Cary, especially when I considered his negative opinion of working wives?

And I couldn't stop thinking of Dyan's words about her marriage to Cary. 'I lost my individuality after I married Cary,' she said once. 'I was so in love, so eager to please, I allowed it to happen, but it wasn't at all helped by Cary.'

Dyan's words about individuality haunted me. Mine was so precious to me. Would I lose it if I married Cary? Or was I already in the process of losing it? He was such a strong, stubborn man.

'I have to think about it,' I told Cary as we drove on and he pressed on. 'And I think you have to decide what you really want and expect in a wife. I'm going to have to devote a lot of time to getting a new career off the ground.'

'And I'll be there to help you do just that,' he said. 'Don't forget I'm the one who told you it was a gift you had to pursue.'

Yes, but was photography something he expected me to follow on his terms and on his exclusive timetable?

My doubts simply would not go away, no matter how persuasive Cary was. And there were more questions.

Why was I so scared?

Perhaps it was Cary's marital track record. He admitted it wasn't a good one. Four wives. Four divorces.

'But think about it,' Cary said as we neared Los Angeles. 'You know, some women would still find the idea of marrying me rather attractive.'

I had to laugh.

But I also had to think about those four women he had already married — and what he really felt about them.

22

EVERY GIRL SHOULD BE MARRIED

'I NEVER left any of my wives,' Cary often told me, 'they all left me.'

I could understand that.

He also regularly insisted that he never cheated on his wives, with the exception of Betsy Drake.

That I found much more difficult to believe.

It didn't matter. What *did* was the kind of perverse pride Cary took in maintaining his wives had left him. The implication was that there wasn't very much he could do. Just as when Elsie, the first woman in his life, 'left' him.

From the way Cary talked to the press about his ex-wives, he sounded like a gallant, somewhat befuddled gentleman. He just couldn't stop them from going. There was even the suggestion the women found him boring. Then there would be a shrug of his shoulders and a grin as if to say, '*C'est la vie.*'

But from the way Cary talked to me about these women, I came to realize that none of them really left him — he subconsciously pushed them into leaving or 'abandoning' him. Of course, he never admitted that to me — and I sincerely doubt to himself either.

Yet there was no mistaking the process, not only from his behavior with me earlier that summer but also from the way he discussed these women.

'My first wife accused me of being a homosexual,' Cary said of Virginia Cherrill, the pretty blonde actress he married in 1934. 'All the women except Betsy have accused me of being a homosexual. She was just the first.'

Given the circumstances of their wedding, it's little wonder the marriage did not even survive a year. It came at the tail end of Cary's disastrous return to England and his ill-fated reunion with his father.

'I thought I'd put all that behind me,' Cary said. 'I'd start a whole new life with Virginia. She was a beautiful girl and she really wanted to get married. But we were never one. We were always competing, as I was with most of my wives.'

Virginia's career was in decline when she married Cary, while his was shooting skyward. Though she'd been personally discovered by Charlie Chaplin and played opposite him in *City Lights*, her career never really took off because of her nasal voice and Chicago accent which clashed with her angelic beauty.

'Perhaps she thought being married to me would help her career, but it only increased her resentment. She was a cold woman.'

Cary and Virginia separated eight months after their marriage. She accused him of excessive drinking and threatening to beat her. A divorce was granted in March 1935, only thirteen months after they married.

The thing that upset Cary most about this alliance was the allegation that he'd tried to commit suicide after Virginia left him. Papers at the time printed the story that he'd been discovered unconscious in his bedroom, with tablets from a bottle marked 'Poison' beside his bed.

'I just got drunk and passed out,' Cary maintained to me. 'Dead drunk. That's all there was to it. The papers had a field day with the story. But it didn't hurt me. Not one little bit,' he said defiantly.

If Ronald Reagan was America's first Teflon president, Cary was its first Teflon actor. No matter how sensational the story — a suicide attempt, the rumors of his homosexuality, Dyan's charges about his use of LSD decades later — it just bounced right off him and did nothing to damage his popularity with the public.

Three years after her divorce from Cary, Virginia Cherrill married into nobility, becoming the Countess of Jersey. In her later years, Virginia would call Cary from time to time from her home in Santa Barbara. He was always unfailingly polite, but it wouldn't be long before he'd signal me or his secretary to call him so he could make his excuses and cut the conversation short. Perhaps she remained too painful a memory for him, particularly if what Cary told me about her role in his second marriage was true.

Cary told the press that he'd met Woolworth heiress Barbara Hutton through an introduction by a mutual friend, the Countess Dorothy di Frasso. But on more than one occasion, Cary insisted to me the real connection was Virginia.

'I married Barbara as a form of revenge against Virginia. They were friends, and I would've done anything to upset Virginia at the time because our marriage had ended so badly. But the whole thing backfired on me. Barbara was more screwed up than I was.'

The way Cary described her, Barbara had to have suffered from anorexia nervosa long before the illness was commonly known. 'All she would eat is RyKrisp,' Cary recalled. 'She was stick thin. She stayed in bed all day with two female companions holding court beside her. I felt as if I had to ask their permission to talk to my own wife.

'The other problem was her jealousy. She demanded constant attention and reassurance. She accused me of having an affair with Ginger Rogers when we were making *Once Upon a Honeymoon*. Then she got the notion *she* would become an actress and be my leading lady in *Mr. Lucky*. Believe it or not, the studio probably would've gone along with the idea — just think of the publicity! — but I would have none of it. I told her the whole idea was insane.'

What drew Cary closest to Barbara was her young son from a previous marriage, Lance Reventlow. 'He was a marvelous kid and he helped me realize what I was missing by not having children. The boy loved me so much he sometimes called himself Lance Grant, which enraged his father, who was always battling with Barbara about the boy.'

I asked him if he'd tried to have children with Barbara.

'There was no way she could,' he revealed. 'She was all torn up, very heavily scarred. She'd already lost one ovary during a caesarean section for Lance's birth. And she wouldn't hear of adopting children. That was that.'

Cary spoke about Barbara with much more fondness and tenderness than he ever did about Virginia, but I also got the impression that there'd been long periods during their marriage when they lived all but separate lives. Still, she must've remembered him fondly — Barbara repeatedly told the press he was the only one of her husbands who had refused to take a dime from her. (Cary had signed a premarital agreement before they wed in 1942.)

The frail heiress touched a chord deep within him too. When she was dying, Cary could not bear to come to the phone to talk to her. And he still cherished some of the gifts she'd given him during their marriage.

I was helping him sort out some things one day when I noticed a box with a ribbon tied around it.

'What's that?' I wondered aloud.

'Oh, I'll show you,' he said as he took the box and began to untie the ribbon. He resembled a small boy sharing his most precious treasure.

It was a pair of rather worn woolen socks. Barbara had personally knitted them for him and, though the marriage had come to an end in 1945, he still kept those socks in a special place. I had trouble imagining this immensely wealthy woman sitting by the fire knitting some warm woolies for Cary, but Cary could inspire women to do the most amazing things, as I well knew.

It was Cary's third wife, Betsy Drake, whom he spoke of with the most kindness and affection.

'I gave her Hollywood on a platter,' he liked to say to me, 'but she gave me something much more valuable — my peace of mind.'

They met each other in the summer of 1947 on the

Queen Mary, which was sailing from London to New York. Betsy, whose father's family had built the Drake Hotel in Chicago, had just finished appearing in a play in London. Cary immediately recognized her from the play, which he happened to have seen, so he prevailed on his friend Merle Oberon to arrange an introduction.

'She fascinated me,' Cary remembered, 'because she wasn't like most actresses. She was really a bookworm. She studied everything from astronomy to hypnotism. I guess you could say she hypnotized me!'

Cary was so enchanted he persuaded Betsy to move to Hollywood, where he got her the role opposite him in *Every Girl Should Be Married*. He also got RKO and his friend, producer David Selznick, to offer her contracts and made 20th Century-Fox an offer it couldn't refuse: He would star in *I Was a Male War Bride* if they would give Betsy the lead in *Dancing in the Dark*.

But Betsy's career wasn't remotely as important to her as Cary was. They were married on Christmas Day, 1949. She decided she would do everything to help him — she helped him quit smoking with hypnosis. She introduced him to the wonders of vitamins. And she was the one who set him on the path to psychotherapy and then LSD.

For this Cary was eternally grateful.

'Most actresses are interested in only one thing — the mirror,' Cary said. 'But Betsy was interested in the world. She was one of the most determined people I've ever met.'

Cary had one regret about Betsy and that was that he didn't have children with her. 'She wanted them so. If only I had started a family with *her*!'

His guilt was compounded by what happened to Betsy after she discovered Cary's affair with Sophia Loren. Betsy had been on location with Cary in Ávila, Spain, in July 1956 when the romance became an open secret on the set of *The Pride and the Passion*. She decided to sail for the United States from Gibraltar, where the Italian luxury liner the *Andrea Doria* was stopping.

Betsy was sleeping when the ship collided with another about sixty miles from Nantucket Island off the coast of

Massachusetts. Over fifty people died in the tragedy, but Betsy was among those rescued. She lost not only a lot of the jewelry Cary had given her, but also a book she'd been writing for over a year.

When Cary finally got through to her on the phone, she wanted to put up a brave front.

'She tried to make a joke of it,' Cary said. 'She told me, "Well, I guess I lost *everything* to the Italians this year!" But I could tell she'd been shaken up very badly. It affected her for years.'

They separated in 1959, as Cary attempted to persuade Sophia to marry him while they were making a second movie together, *Houseboat.* But there was no bitterness between Betsy and Cary. It wasn't until 1962 that they finally divorced. Cary talked to Betsy only a few times on the phone during the years I was with him, but she never lost his esteem. He said he didn't even mind that she got a percentage of some of his films as part of their divorce settlement.

'She earned it,' he said simply.

As for Betsy, she went on to become a psychodrama therapist and teacher. She rarely talked to the media, but I found something she once said about Cary especially revealing.

'Cary wanted to be free,' Betsy told the reporter, 'yet he wanted me [to be] always on tap.'

Dyan Cannon, the woman who I know got under Cary's skin more than any other, also talked about freedom — or the lack of it — in her petition for divorce from Cary in 1968.

They met in 1962, married in 1965 and separated for the first time in 1966. Throughout the relationship they frequently broke off and started all over again, Dyan said. I certainly knew the feeling.

I found a few other things familiar in the allegations Dyan made in divorce court.

Cary humiliated her in public.

He was completely irrational at times.

And he threw constant accusations of infidelities at her,

even pointing the finger at the doctor who treated her during her pregnancy.

Cary had a lot to say about Dyan too, though he didn't testify in that divorce hearing.

He saved some of his most damaging testimony for my ears a few years later. You've heard most of it already.

What you haven't heard thus far is the one thing he said that finally convinced me not to marry him.

He said it over and over.

He liked saying it so much he even said it a few times to the press.

'Once the female has used the male for procreation,' Cary declared, 'she turns on him and literally devours him.'

23

MERRILY WE GO TO HELL

ACTIONS speak louder than words. And Cary's actions after I told him I didn't think we should get married convinced me I'd made the right decision.

Cary went off on the cruise to Alaska with Jennifer and Willie in high spirits, despite my decision. He was sure I would reconsider. 'Think about it while I'm away,' he said before they set sail. 'That's all I ask.'

The campaign continued in earnest when the happy trio returned.

Cary and I went to a wild party Peter Sellers gave for Keith Moon, the drummer of the rock group the Who. Peter and Cary had healed their earlier rift. At one point, they formed an unlikely duo at the piano. They pounded the keys mercilessly while Keith kept time on the top of the piano. But I got Cary's message when he played a few bars of 'Going to the Chapel.'

At such times all I could do was manage a weak smile to hide my uneasiness. I stopped smiling on the night of September 27. It was my twenty-ninth birthday and it was on that occasion I realized Cary had decided that if I wouldn't marry him, the reason had to be that I was in love with another man.

The evening started off jolly and light as we saluted each other at one of my favorite restaurants, La Scala in Beverly Hills. Cary and I had shared many a quiet dinner at this intimate Italian retreat. My spirits were raised not only by the wine but also by the presence of Dee, whom

Cary had invited along. I had my man and my best friend at my side and I was feeling no pain.

Cary also was drinking, but he felt something else. I began to detect a change in his spirits when he started talking about the booth we were sitting in. It was his favorite, located far in the recesses of the restaurant, where no one could see him, yet he could view other people from this vantage point.

'This is a great spot!' Cary declared. 'You can see all the women who come in here to cheat on their husbands, having dinner with the men they really love.'

What an unpleasant thought, however accurate. I shot Dee a look. I could tell by her response I wasn't imagining this shift in the prevailing wind. 'How dumb those women must be,' Cary continued as his voice took on an edge, 'if they think they're fooling anyone, least of all their husbands.'

I knew not to agree or to argue with him. It was best just to let him run out of steam. But he wouldn't stop.

'It takes a certain kind of arrogance to think you're smarter and better than the man you supposedly love.'

I stopped drinking and just stared at Cary. I gave him a look that I hoped would signal him to stop this train. We had a guest with us. Why ruin it for Dee?

But Cary ignored my ocular plea. He did, however, change direction. Now his attention had turned to the waiter, an exceptionally good-looking man. He was a swarthy Italian with carefully coiffed hair, the follicular magnificence of which would've made Sylvester Stallone green with envy. But he did nothing for me — his appearance suggested a degree of self-absorption I find unappealing.

'I bet he has no trouble with women,' Cary said as he pointed with his drink in the waiter's direction. 'A very good-looking man, isn't he? And he must think *you're* good-looking from the way he stared at you on the way in.'

I looked at Cary, confused. The man had looked me over carefully as we came into the restaurant, but I thought he just wanted to see what Cary Grant's girlfriend looked like.

'Oh, Cary,' I said, 'stop it. That man's too interested in himself to be really interested in me.'

'No, no, no,' Cary insisted. 'He was giving you the eye. I'm not saying I blame him, mind you. And I wouldn't blame you for finding him attractive. I'm not stupid, you know.'

How was I going to get Cary off this track?

I turned to Dee, my eyes begging for help.

'Why don't we order now?' she suggested.

Cary chugged along pleasantly through dinner without any more references to the waiter. And I was positive the waiter had completely slipped Cary's mind as a birthday cake, complete with candles, arrived at the table.

'Make a wish!' Cary and Dee cried in unison. It wouldn't take much for Dee to guess what I was wishing for: a *happy* birthday. Cary then presented me with an expensive lens to go with the Nikon he'd already given me. I thanked him profusely. It certainly would get a lot of use — I had officially launched my career in photography and quit the magazine.

I reached over to kiss him but he pulled away slightly. He must have remembered Dee was with us, because he then accepted it benignly. And soon he was running on and on about the waiter again.

'Please, Cary,' I said with an edge to *my* voice. 'There's a million like him in this town. Why are you making a fuss? Who *cares* about him?

'You don't fool me,' he said sharply.

'What?' I said, both disturbed by the statement and embarrassed my best friend had heard it. Dee had heard enough about my skirmishes with Cary. The last thing she needed was to *see* one.

'*That's* the kind of man you want,' Cary snapped. 'I'm sure that is no news to Dee.'

'This conversation is over. This so-called celebration is over!' I declared as I got up, grabbing my purse.

'You are being irrational, Cary, and I won't have it. I

think you should go home and get some sleep. And the only way you're going to get home is if Dee or I drive, or you take a taxi. Am I making myself clear?'

He stared at me for several moments with a curious, wide smile on his face, as if he were assessing an unfathomable work of modern sculpture.

'Isn't she something, Dee? A real fighter!' he said.

Now I didn't know whether to laugh or to leave. I also didn't know who was really doing the talking — Cary or the wine he'd consumed all evening. 'C'mon, Cary, let's go,' I said, softening. 'Time to go home.'

'I will do anything Madame suggests,' he said as he unsteadily began to rise from the booth. Dee and I surrounded him as we made our way out the back exit.

My birthday was over, but Cary was not remotely finished with his obsession that I was in love with someone else. It would flare up at the most unexpected times after long intervals of hiding in the back of his mind.

More than two months of relative calm had passed when Cary and I went to Frank Sinatra's sixtieth birthday party, on December 12. The volatile singer was one of Cary's closest friends from the entertainment world. Cary admired not only Sinatra's talent but also his constant scuffling with the press. 'Give 'em hell!' I'd hear Cary yell as he read about Frank's latest run-in with a reporter or photographer. (Not incidentally, Frank and Cary had first met at a boxing match in the forties.)

Sinatra's party was thrown by his youngest daughter Tina. It was a small, intimate evening and my pleasure was doubled when Jimmy Stewart arrived. It had been almost three years since I'd first met him at the Henry Hathaway tribute in Beverly Hills where I also first saw Cary. He and his wife, Gloria, couldn't have been more gracious to me. That occasion also marked my introduction to future president Ronald Reagan and his wife, Nancy. Ronnie, as Cary called him, had an affable quality that put me very much at ease.

As for the guest of honor, Mr. Sinatra surprised me with his warmth as well. In the company of his family and close friends, he was a very different man from the high-strung hothead the newspapers made him out to be. Like everyone else at the party, he went out of his way to make me feel an indispensable part of the celebration.

It was on the way home that this perfect evening was permanently blemished.

We were in the car and I was still basking in the party's afterglow. It was always nice to feel I'd been accepted in such a home as an individual on my own terms, not just as Cary's girlfriend or armpiece. But my ego received a rude shock as Cary maneuvered the wheel.

'Do you know what it looks like when you behave like that?' he said.

My internal warning system began ringing loudly.

'Behave like what, Cary?' I said.

'You made a spectacle of yourself, staring at Frank all evening long,' he said. 'It reflects worse on you than it does on me, I hope you know. Everyone had the good taste to pretend they didn't see it.'

'They didn't have to pretend because I wasn't staring at anyone, Cary. *Really*. Now what's this about?'

'It's about what you did tonight,' he said coldly. 'It's about what you do when you think I'm not looking.'

I wasn't going to cap this magnificent evening with a huge row about my imaginary transgression.

'Do me a favor,' I said, trying to contain my anger. 'Take me to my apartment. I think it's best I sleep there tonight if this is really how you feel.'

Without a word, Cary turned the car around and deposited me in front of my apartment building on Oakhurst. He did not get out to open the door as he usually did.

'Thank you for a *wonderful* evening,' I said as I struggled with the door handle. 'I'm just going to forget the part about my making goo-goo eyes at Mr. Sinatra, if you don't mind.'

'You do that,' he said as he reached over and pushed the door open. 'But I assure you I won't.'

I ran into my apartment crying. I called Dee and told

her the whole story. Then the discussion fell to what happened on *my* birthday.

'I don't like saying this,' Dee said, sighing, as we wound up our call. 'But it's like he wants you to cheat on him.... It's like he's doing his best to push you into someone else's arms so he can say he was right about you all along.'

That only made me cry more because I knew it rang true.

And I had to tell Cary the truth. Was he aware of what he was doing? I doubted it, but I owed him the truth. He was not only my lover but also my friend. And if a friend was doing this to himself and someone he loved, I'd warn him.

So when Cary called two days later and, predictably enough, pretended nothing had happened, I told him we had to talk. He agreed and I went up to Beverly Grove.

I should have been able to predict his response as well — I was totally crazy. I was exaggerating. It was the wine, not him.

Besides, he maintained, he had *already* detected and stopped the destructive patterns of his life many years ago with LSD.

I wanted to believe that so badly, but my heart and mind couldn't anymore. And I didn't know how to help this man grasp the truth.

Cary had an idea.

'The holidays are no time to hash out something like this,' he said.

'The minute we can get free after Christmas and Boxing Day, we'll go to Serge Semenenko's place in Acapulco. It's beautiful down there and we'll be off by ourselves. We'll work it out there for once and for all, I promise.'

This proposition also had a familiar ring, but it was worth a try. I cared about him too much not to give it a shot, but I think I knew the way it would come out the second I said yes. In the meantime I did my best to make our third Christmas together a happy one.

With Cary in a truly idyllic
setting.
*(Courtesy of
Suzanne McDonnell Long)*

I was privileged to share
Christmas with Cary and
Jennifer, and I loved cooking
Christmas dinner for them.

Top (from left to right):
Cary's cousin Eric Leach,
my mother Elsie, my father
James, Eric's wife Maggie,
and Cary outside a pub in
Bristol in the summer of
1977.
(Maureeen Donaldson)

This is one of the first shots I
ever took of Cary. It was he
who suggested I switch
careers from entertainment
writer to photographer.
(Maureen Donaldson)

There was another side to Cary – the pensive, lonely man in this shot taken along Malibu beach.
(Maureen Donaldson)

Bottom: One of my favorite shots of the man I loved. His vaudeville humor surfaces in this photo, taken on a speedboat in Westhampton, New York.
(Maureen Donaldson)

Top left: At seventy-two, Cary was actually shy about posing in his swimsuit. 'I'm too old!' he protested. But after seeing the shot he admitted: 'I guess I don't look so bad for an old man, do I?'
(Maureen Donaldson)

Top right: This is the only time I ever saw Cary doing push-up, because I insisted so vehemently that it would make a great shot. But he thought the whole idea was ridiculous. In fact, it struck him as so funny he couldn't complete even one push-up.
(Maureen Donaldson)

Bottom left: Cary suggested this shot – his love of physical humor dated back to his days with a boys' acrobatic troupe in England and then vaudeville in the United States.
(Maureen Donaldson)

Bottom right: Cary doing what he loved most – reading so he could clip and store anything that struck his fancy. Astaire may have been born to dance, but Cary was born to clip. He even had a paper cutting machine in the bedroom!
(Maureen Donaldson)

Like a little boy, Cary loved sweets. He fondly remembered the tuckshops, or sweetshops, in Bristol and almost always had ice cream with a wafer for his nightly dessert.
(Maureen Donaldson)

Bottom left: This was one of the photos of himself that Cary really liked. I will always remember him this way because he looks so happy.
(Maureen Donaldson)

Right: But I will also remember the other side to Cary – the man his public rarely saw. A man troubled by his childhood and his realtionships with women; a man who desperately wanted always to think 'happy thoughts' but sometimes found it impossible.
(Maureen Donaldson)

Cary on the steps of the Fabergé jet. Close to a million dollars had been lavished on the interior, and being served caviar and champagne made this girl – born in a fireman's cottage in Muswell Hill – feel like royalty.
(Maureen Donaldson)

My life has taken me from fire engines to private jets, from a fire house to the White House ... but once a fireman's daughter, always a fireman's daughter. This snap of me was taken in October 1988.
(Roger Smith)

On Christmas Eve we took Jennifer to a party at the home of Bob Arthur. He had produced some of Cary's hits at Universal including *Operation Petticoat*. The sight of children caroling and opening presents put Cary and me in the proper Christmas spirit, especially as Jennifer scampered around with all the other kids.

Christmas at Beverly Grove was equally enjoyable. Dee came up to help me cook the holiday dinner for Cary in the kitchen, which was still peeling, still cluttered and still being remodeled. How Willie managed to function smoothly within it was between her and God. Among my presents, Cary gave me new stationery for my new career, while I gave Cary more of the cashmere socks he loved, as well as a scarf.

I thought all the gift giving was through when Cary went into the bedroom and came out with one more box. It was wrapped exquisitely in silver paper.

'I want you to have this,' he said almost shyly.

I opened the box and inside was the pair of woolen socks Barbara Hutton had herself knitted for Cary so many years before.

'Oh, Cary,' I said, touched. 'I can't take these. They mean too much to you.'

'But I want you to have them,' he told me. 'They were given to me with love and now I give them to you with love.'

'Thank you,' I said, doing my best not to look him in the eye. I knew I would cry if I did.

Two days after Christmas I did cry.

It was the night before we flew down to Acapulco. We went to a dinner party at the home of Norton Simon and his wife, actress Jennifer Jones. They had an elegant Malibu beach house that had just been remodeled. After years of unhappiness in the arms of others, the billionaire and the star of *The Song of Bernadette* had finally found a lasting love with each other.

And they wanted us to find a similar happiness.

They took us on a tour of their impressive showplace carved out of wood and stone, and we eventually entered a guest bedroom. It was located on one side of the house, which was divided into two massive wings.

'Wouldn't our home be a lovely place for a wedding?' Jennifer said softly. 'It's brought us so much happiness, I'm sure it would be the perfect place to begin a marriage.'

Fortunately, Jennifer was beaming at Norton as she spoke. I could not speak and I could not look at Cary. I can only imagine the look on my face.

'Well,' Jennifer resumed, 'what do you two say? Wouldn't this be a wonderful place for a wedding?'

Cary looked at me for an answer.

I started to cry.

'For the right couple,' I said under my breath before I turned and walked out of the room.

On the long drive back to Beverly Hills, I asked Cary if he really thought we should still go to Acapulco.

'Of course,' he said matter-of-factly.

But Acapulco was pointless. Beautiful, radiant, luxurious, but pointless. We talked about everything but what we were supposed to. When I thought I'd found an opening, Cary shut me off. Elegantly. Gracefully. Smoothly. But completely.

As my tan deepened, so did my resentment. If we were to have any kind of a life together, our problems had to be discussed calmly in the light of day.

They never were. Cary got a phone call from his attorney. His daughter was unexpectedly available for a day if he didn't mind flying back to Los Angeles.

He asked me if I'd like to go back with him to stay until he returned in a couple of days. I'd already played this scene in London six months before. Would he do the same thing to me if I stayed?

I knew the answer but I had to be sure. I couldn't end this relationship without being absolutely certain.

I got the answer the night Cary arrived in Los Angeles.

He phoned me to say he'd gotten reports that I had something going on with somebody in Acapulco.

The second time I played this scene with Cary, I was not furious. I was not coming apart at the seams. I was not trying to escape.

And I was not about to play it ever again.

The London *Daily Mail* ran the first report on our breakup. It ended with this paragraph:

'[Cary's] affection for Miss Donaldson was evident right up to the point that she walked out — and close friends are confident that his charms will eventually woo her back.'

24

THE GRASS IS GREENER

SOMETIMES close friends know us better than we know ourselves.

Cary and I didn't speak for two months. I called Willie a few times and even managed to chat with Jennifer a bit, but it was awkward for all concerned. Jennifer seemed confused by the situation; I didn't know what Cary had told her. Willie, of course, knew the truth and sympathized with me: 'I love Mr. Grant,' she'd say, 'but he can be impossible.'

Something else was true — I missed both Cary and Jennifer. At first I was so busy with my photography I really didn't have time to wallow in the loss. There were shooting assignments, more contacts to make, and more and more equipment and supplies to acquire. And as the time passed, the jealous and irrational scenes with Cary began to take a backseat to the much more pleasant ones in my mind. Absence not only makes the heart grow fonder but can turn your memory into mush. At least it did mine.

Especially when you get sick and are at your most vulnerable. In March 1976 I learned from my doctor that the sharp pain that had been bothering me on and off for the past several months was the result of an ovarian cyst. Surgery was scheduled immediately and I told only Dee about my fears. The pain was not a good sign, but I hoped this usually minor operation would not turn into something major.

Willie happened to call the night before I was scheduled to go into the hospital and I couldn't help mentioning my uneasiness. Over the years we'd become friends apart from our relationship with Cary. And next to Dee she was my real confidante as far as Cary was concerned. Since she worked for him and lived at his house most of the week, she certainly knew him better than most people.

'You're going to be all right,' Willie reassured me. 'I know it sounds strange, but I always get a feeling about these things. It probably wouldn't have been fine if you'd let this thing go, but you're taking care of it in plenty of time.'

Willie's prognosis did a lot to alleviate my fears. I was scurrying around my apartment taking care of last-minute details when the phone rang.

'I know you hate me,' I heard the familiar clipped tones say, 'but I just want to make sure you've got everything you need.'

It was Cary and his concern was heartfelt. I could feel it in his voice. Willie must have told him about the operation.

'Cary, I don't hate you,' I said. 'I'll never hate you. We just can't help driving each other crazy.'

He laughed. Then he wanted to know all the particulars. Was I sure my doctor was the best in his field? He could get someone for me if I wasn't. Had I gotten a second opinion? What hospital was I staying in? Did I have a private room? With such delicate surgery I had to have complete rest. What did I need? What was going to happen to my fledgling business while I was in the hospital?

I assured him everything had been taken care of properly. He was so solicitous it couldn't help but move me.

'Are you alone tonight?' he asked.

Yes, I explained, but it was my choice. But his indirect offer to be at my side to lend support was deeply appreciated.

'Cary,' I said as we finished our conversation, 'I want to thank you for calling and making me feel so much better.'

'Oh, don't mention it,' he pooh-poohed. 'It's the least I could do.'

Actually he did much more. He made sure his influence was felt by the staff of the hospital where I stayed, and had an extra nurse hired to watch over me. And when I woke up from the operation, the room was full of flowers.

More important, Cary was sitting in a chair reading a book.

'How are you, dear?' he said as he saw me coming awake.

'Oh, fine,' I said, still somewhat groggy.

'You've got the right word,' Cary assured me as he took my hand. 'The operation was a complete success. You are fine and you'll be fine if you take it easy for the next couple of weeks, the doctor says. And he's good. I checked up on him.'

Always the perfectionist. I had to smile to myself.

I felt completely safe under his watchful eye. It wasn't a feeling I wanted to let go of now. I accepted his offer to stay up at Beverly Grove for my recuperation and as long as I'd like him to after that.

'There'll be no talk of marriage or other men,' he promised me. 'You'll have Willie and me to take care of you the way you should be taken care of. And Jennifer wants to see you so much. You know how good that'll make you feel.'

It didn't take much persuasion. I wanted to be back there, especially if Cary would keep his promise. I didn't doubt for a second his sincerity, though a part of me questioned his ability to keep it. We'd see. If it got too crazy, I could leave. I already knew how to do that.

Not surprisingly, the house was still being remodeled and still in a state of transition and disrepair. Two months had made not one bit of difference. It was almost as if Cary was scared to finish it. But soon I was in great shape, thanks to the attention Cary and Willie lavished on me.

And my reunion with Jennifer was equally restorative. But at first she was understandably nervous and cautious. She'd been hurt when I left so abruptly. She didn't want to get close again and then be left in the lurch a second time.

I promised her that if it ever became necessary for me to leave again, I would tell her myself. There would be no secondhand notice or partial explanations.

'It's a deal!' she said, sounding like her father as her small hand locked into mine. We were sitting on the terrace in the early-afternoon sun.

We quickly caught up with each other. I told her all about my photography career. She told me all about her life — by now, she was going to a Montessori school Dyan had picked out. Cary had not approved of the decision because Jennifer would be allowed to study what she chose instead of following a prescribed program as most children her age did. But since he didn't have the final say, he decided that if it made Jennifer happy, then he was happy.

I was still doing my best to get Cary to release his grip on Jennifer. It had already been considerably loosened. Now when I took her into Beverly Hills to shop for clothes, he didn't insist we take back *all* the jeans and sweatshirts she adored. Now we could easily talk him into letting her keep a few along with the dresses he preferred. He even permitted us to play rock music infrequently, but it wasn't enough — Jennifer and I would occasionally escape to my apartment to dance and turn the stereo up. Once at an Elton John concert held at Dodger Stadium, Jennifer and I even got Cary to bump along with the music. The presence of Jennifer's friend Lisa, a black girl from Jamaica, particularly spurred him along. She kept encouraging him in her distinctive accent to '*Leev* it up, Mr Cary! *Leev* it up!' Cary resembled an electric eel out of water as he tried to get with it for our sake.

The only discouraging thing I saw amid all the good times with Jennifer was the way Cary let her know she had done something wrong or had displeased him. He would silently withdraw from her to the point she'd get upset and ask, 'What's wrong, Daddy?'

Perhaps it was the former nanny in me, but I felt compelled to tell Cary he was short-changing himself and the child by such tactics. Wouldn't it just be best to tell her what was on his mind?

'She's too young to understand that,' he told me. 'She won't pay attention if I do that. But if I act as if I'm not interested or I'm ignoring her, you'd be amazed how attentive she becomes.'

He sounded proud as he described this process.

'She's a very intelligent child,' I said, not wanting to start a fight yet concerned about the implications of this silent treatment. 'I think she can understand almost anything you tell her. What she can't understand are games. I mean, would you want it done to *you*?'

There also was an edge to the way he'd sometimes look at Jennifer when she was off playing by herself. It wasn't like the many times I'd observed Cary looking at her before, when he would well up with tears of happiness at just the sight of her. He would stare at her with an almost frightening intensity. Then he'd turn to me and announce: 'She's perfect!'

'That she is,' I said absentmindedly in agreement the first few times I heard him say it. 'A beautiful child ...'

'She's *perfect*!' he'd repeat as if 'beautiful' were not good enough or the wrong word. He was so insistent it became disquieting.

It reminded me of a scene from *Funny Girl*, Barbra Streisand's first movie, in which she played the homely but brilliant entertainer Fanny Brice. After giving birth to her young daughter, Fanny is working out in a rehearsal hall with an old friend named Eddie.

'The way that baby slowed me down, I oughta sue her!' she sighs in exhaustion. 'But she's so pretty, isn't she, Eddie?'

'Frances?' he says. 'Cutest thing I ever saw. Alive. Alert —'

'But she's *pretty*!' the woman insists.

'Yes, Fan!' her friend says, exasperated. 'She's pretty. *Very* pretty.'

I began to sound like Eddie in real life as Cary would proclaim, 'She's *perfect*' and I'd say, 'Couldn't be more if she tried!' It seemed to reassure him and it wasn't far from the truth. She was special and such a loving child. I couldn't have loved her more if she were my own daughter.

But now I wasn't thinking of having a child. I was thinking of my health and my career. So was Cary, especially my career. I think he was pulled in two directions about it. On one hand he was very proud of my work and the fact that he'd guided me in this direction. He was constantly praising the photographs I took of him for the selected interviews he gave. Cary told one British publication, *TV Times*, that some shots I'd taken of him one weekend in Palm Springs were 'the best ones I've had taken in years. Maureen's very good at her work and she shoots in no time. I can't stand it when photographers fiddle about.'

Cary was so impatient I'd better be good and quick. We were once at the beach in Malibu as the sun was going down and I was rushing to get a shot. I fell flat on my face and scraped my leg on a rock, but I didn't dare stop. I'd never catch the light — or Cary — again that day. The picture was worth the scraped leg. It's a very contemplative shot, taken from a side angle. My efforts were not in vain. In 1977 he told another British publication that another shot of mine was 'the best anyone's managed to get throughout my whole career.'

Cary was not lavish with his praise, so I knew it was sincere. But I also knew he was becoming threatened by my career. Cary liked the fact my hours were now my own. I wasn't tied down to one job. But he didn't like it when I went off to photograph other people. He'd offered to use his connections and influence to get other stars to pose for me, but I didn't want that. I had enough contacts from my days with the magazine; I just needed to build them up. Besides, I didn't want to depend on him that way. It was enough that I was the only photographer he'd sit still for when he consented to do an interview. If he'd done more, my competition would have said the only reason I was getting jobs was my relationship with Cary.

I detected Cary's vacillation where my career was concerned when he started saying that the only reason male photographers got into the profession was to find women they could seduce. I didn't have to ask what the female corollary to this proposition was. About the third time Cary said it, I told him I got the implication.

'You're just distorting what I said,' he proclaimed.

'Then there's no point in your bringing it up again, is there?' I volunteered, hoping to retire the remark permanently.

'You got it,' he said evenly.

By this point, Cary was as careful as I not to ignite an argument. We'd both gotten badly burned by our past fireworks and the scars were still fresh.

When I wasn't busy tending to my photography, I found a new part-time occupation: assistant gardener. Cary had a very capable Japanese gardener who took care of the grounds, but one afternoon after Cary again mentioned the vegetable garden his father had planted back in Bristol, I suggested we plant our own veggies, Beverly Hills style.

'Marvelous!' Cary said enthusiastically.

The idea of harvesting some low-cost food had to have a certain appeal to him. So the next day Cary, Willie and I trudged down to a nursery where a large assortment of seeds were available. We rushed back to the house and I began tilling the soil on a patch of ground near the kitchen. We planted carrots, broccoli, beans and some herbs.

The next day, unbeknownst to Cary, I planted a special herb of my own — a marijuana plant — right smack dab in the middle of our vegetable garden. Soon the marijuana was shooting skyward, far ahead of the vegetables.

'What's that one?' Cary asked. 'It's really going to town, isn't it?'

'An herb I found,' I replied.

'Well, at this rate we're going to have to beat it down with a stick!'

Of course, Willie and Cary's gardener knew what it was, but they never let on to Cary. But later I got busted.

One Sunday, Cary's attorney, Stanley Fox, and his son came up for a visit. Cary was proudly showing them the vegetable patch when Stanley's son caught sight of the weedlike plant which was outgrowing all the others. It reached my waist while the carrots and other vegetables were at the most only a foot high.

'What's that?' Fox Junior asked.

'Tarragon?' I said as innocently as I could manage.

'Doesn't look like tarragon,' he said.

A few minutes later Fox Senior pulled me aside.

'My son tells me you have a marijuana plant growing in your vegetable garden,' he said.

I said nothing.

'Does Cary know about this?' he continued.

'No,' I finally laughed. 'He thinks it's one of my herbs.'

'Well,' the older gentleman said sharply, 'I hate to spoil your fun, Maureen, but the next time I come up to the house, I'm going to have to tell Cary what it is if it's still in the garden. After the LSD thing, you know what the press would do if they found grass in his garden!'

Of course Stanley was right, so I pulled up the plant and threw it in the trash that night. Then we lost another part of our garden.

I went into the garden one morning to discover all the broccoli had been chewed up. 'It must've been those deer!' Willie said as she joined me. There were a few deer that sometimes ventured down the hill to look for food. They were the culprits!

'After all the work I put into those plants!' I shouted, almost in tears. 'What a waste!'

I ran into the house and bumped right into Cary. He could tell by the look on my face that something was wrong.

'What's the matter, dear?' he asked, his face the picture of concern.

'The deer ate our broccoli!' I cried.

'I'm so sorry, darling,' he said as he broke into laughter, 'but I thought something was really wrong....'

'Oh, I know,' I said. 'It's just that we spent so much time on those silly plants....'

'You're right,' he said, consoling me. 'You have every right to be upset. But I tell you what. We'll plant something now the deer won't touch.'

'What's that?' I said.

'Prayer flags,' he replied as he grabbed my hand and took me out to a spot near the side of the house with a breathtaking view.

Prayer flags, he explained, were a tradition in some countries by which people could send beautiful thoughts about loved ones on the wind. They took a stick, attached material to make a flag, and planted it in a special place of honor. The name of the person being honored was inscribed on the material.

Cary decided an old shirt of his, one of his favorites, should be cut up to make the flags. Then we found three bamboo sticks. All we had to do now was select our three names.

'One must be for Jennifer,' Cary said as he scrawled her name across one piece of material.

'And one for Mummy and Daddy,' I said as I took another piece and wrote their names.

'Who should get the last flag?' Cary wondered.

I searched my mind for a few moments, then I saw Cary's face light up.

'I got it!' he exclaimed.

'Who?' I said.

'Bobby Birkenfeld.'

25

THE PRIDE AND THE PASSION

WHILE I was now making my living behind a camera, Cary was approached once again to consider seriously going before the cameras.

Warren Beatty was mounting a remake of *Here Comes Mr. Jordan* called *Heaven Can Wait* and he was moving heaven and earth to persuade Cary to play the role Claude Rains had played in the original. Ironically, Dyan had already been convinced to end a hiatus she'd taken from films in the mid-seventies, and to play a scheming adulteress in the Beatty effort, which Warren was also producing and codirecting. Cary wanted nothing to do with the project and his refusal had nothing to do with Dyan's participation. It had everything to do with Jennifer.

When Beatty first approached Cary, it was 1976, ten years since Cary had been on screen. (His last movie was *Walk, Don't Run*.) His hair was now a stunning silver that made him look different from how he did in most of his movies. And he liked that difference because he wanted Jennifer to know him as her father not as an actor. There simply was no way she — or he — was going to see him on the screen with silver hair.

Aside from Jennifer — who was the main consideration — Cary told me that no one was going to accuse him of not knowing when to quit. He repeatedly brought up the example of Jean Arthur, his costar in *The Talk of the Town*, who also scored in such films as *Mr. Smith Goes to Washington* and *Shane*. In the sixties she attempted a comeback in a lame comedy series on CBS. 'Her time had passed,' Cary told me, 'but she couldn't see that. No one will say I didn't know when to get off the Hollywood trolley.' According to Cary, Hollywood was a Streetcar Named Aspire where there were always scores of people waiting in the wings to take your seat. If you were good, either you kept your seat for a long time or, after those times you got bumped off, you discovered another way to get back on and retake your rightful seat. But there would come a day when you should graciously give up your place so some new blood with new aspirations could help keep the trolley going.

In this regard he wanted to be like Garbo, the woman he admired so much when he was starting out as an actor. After the lukewarm response to her 1941 comedy *Two-Faced Woman*, Garbo announced her retirement from films and never went back on that decision. 'If she came back now, it just wouldn't be the same,' Cary would tell me. 'And the public wouldn't like it if she tried, believe me.' Not coincidentally, Cary's own *Walk, Don't Run* had been accorded a lukewarm response at the box office and he subsequently announced his retirement from films. 'Jennifer's the only production I'm interested in now,' he proclaimed — and he meant every word of it.

That doesn't mean offers stopped coming in at regular intervals. During the time I lived with Cary, he was approached to star in everything from a projected remake of *Grand Hotel* ('A Garbo movie? Fat chance!') to a remake of *Harvey* in which he'd take over the role Jimmy Stewart played in the original movie and Elton John would play the imaginary, oversized rabbit. Cary was tickled by the *Harvey* offer because he thought Jennifer might like to see such a movie, but he didn't give it one moment's serious consideration. The only thing that would have tempted him would have been the opportunity to narrate a documentary for children. He wouldn't need to appear before the camera, yet he could make his presence felt. But Cary was never asked to become involved with such a project.

Cary was always gracious in declining whatever comeback offers came his way. There was no point in being rude, and he thought it was lovely to be remembered by the industry. So when the *Heaven Can Wait* offer appeared, Cary thought the least he could do was let Warren make his pitch in person before giving him the inevitable turndown. So he invited Warren for breakfast. Warren prevailed on me to do what I could with Cary.

'He's his own man,' I told Warren, 'and you should know what that's like. If anyone could persuade him, it would be you, but I can't lie to you. I just don't think he'll do it. But give it your best shot ... It's certainly worth a try.'

Warren was at his most charming and persuasive, but Cary could not be budged. Warren did get a lovely breakfast out of it, though. Afterward Cary and I were talking on the terrace where we had just sat with Warren. Cary made a prediction I'm still waiting to see come true.

'You know,' Cary sighed, 'Warren reminds me a bit of myself when I was his age. I think he's afraid of commitment. He should have a child as I did. And he will, late in his life just as I did. And it'll change his life. He will find more happiness that way than he could with any woman.'

I then brought the subject back to Warren's offer. I said he really should think it over twice. With Dyan in the same film, the publicity would be phenomenal. Besides, Cary didn't have to carry the film — it was a supporting role with many of the best lines (James Mason eventually took the role). Even if the movie somehow flopped, he wouldn't be blamed. It was Warren's movie as actor, producer and codirector.

But Cary was not having any of it.

'My decision is final,' he said with unmistakable conviction, 'and you should know why better than anyone else. I don't need to act. Can't you see I'm acting every time I let Jennifer go back to her mother, knowing it'll be days and sometimes weeks before I see her? That's the best performance I've ever given!'

As for the performances Cary had already given on the

screen, he professed to have little or next to no interest in them. That always was his posture with the press. It was a *different* matter in the privacy of his own home. At the beginning of our relationship, it would take some persuasion to get him to sit and watch one of his own films. But since watching television was one of his favorite activities, it became increasingly easier to rope him into watching. Since video recorders were not yet widely available, what we watched was dictated by which of his movies was available on local television. Some of his films — especially *Father Goose* and *His Girl Friday* — were shown regularly, while others were not shown at all.

It was fascinating to sit there and watch him on film and then turn to him and compare his on-screen image to the man I'd come to know and love. The contrast could be surprising. For example, one of Cary's favorite gestures in movies is putting his hands in his pockets. In a shipboard scene for *An Affair to Remember,* he made it look so smooth and so impossibly elegant. But in real life, he thought people who put their hands in their pockets were just being rude. (He had a similar aversion to performers who spelled their names in unusual ways. He thought Barbra Streisand, who had dropped an *a* from her first name, did so only out of insecurity. He also didn't like to watch male performers who were bearded. 'Those men are trying to hide something about themselves,' he'd say.)

Cary hid nothing from me as we sat next to each other watching his movies over the years. He rarely censored the observations he made about his costars or the memorable times he had while making his films. I'd like to share some of those with you now.

SHE DONE HIM WRONG

This was the first film I watched with Cary and it happened to be the first film he made with Mae West. (The other was *I'm No Angel.*) According to Cary, West did him wrong by propagating the legend that she discovered him as an extra on the Paramount lot. (He also hated the erroneous impression he ever said, 'Judy! Judy! Judy!' on the screen.)

'I was *never* an extra!' Cary said. By the time he made this 1933 film, he'd already costarred or been featured in seven Paramount films. When Cary met his buxom costar for the first time, he told me, he'd been scared of her. When I asked why, he said: 'Wouldn't you be?' I had to agree, because her larger than life persona reminded me of a drag queen.

'Funny you should say that,' Cary observed. He went on to outline a theory to explain West's sometimes mannish air. I, of course, had heard the outlandish speculation that West was really a man, but I'd never heard anything remotely like Cary's explanation. He said the information dated from his days back in vaudeville in New York. West also appeared on Broadway at this time.

Cary said West suffered from a genetic disorder called testicular feminization, or Tfm. Victims usually have female secondary sexual characteristics and a feminine appearance, but they also have internal testes. They never can have children and often feel fate has suspended them between the two sexes. The person affected by this disorder is genetically a male who appears in female form.

'Poor thing,' Cary said about Mae West, 'I don't think she ever really knew who she was.'

In the mid-seventies, Cary was approached to make a cameo in Mae's final film. It was a sex comedy called *Sextette* in which Timothy Dalton played her husband! Cary absolutely refused to do the film — 'Doesn't she know when to quit?' he said, obviously thinking of Jean Arthur — but he did pass along *my* suggestion that Mae get Alice Cooper to do a cameo to enhance the film's appeal with younger audiences. Unfortunately, no one could help the creaky farce. It flopped quickly when it was released in 1978.

GUNGA DIN

Douglas Fairbanks, Jr., Victor McLaglen and Cary played

three British soldiers in India putting down a native uprising with the help of the title hero. Cary said he couldn't wait to make this 1939 film because Rudyard Kipling's poem, upon which the film was based, had been his favorite to recite as a schoolboy back in Bristol.

Cary also remembered the movie as a constant source of off-screen fun. The movie was filmed in California's bleak Death Valley and director George Stevens was such a perfectionist the filming went on and on and on. To relieve themselves of the monotony one afternoon, Cary and Fairbanks decided to pull a trick on their much older costar McLaglen.

'He and George Stevens were droning on and on about some scene while Doug and I just wanted to get the silly thing over with,' Gary recalled. 'So at a moment when Victor was immersed in what George was saying, we both very quietly unzipped our trousers and began to relieve ourselves down Victor's leg. He was so engrossed it took him at least a minute before he caught on to what we were doing. Then he chased us around the set!'

During another lackluster afternoon Cary decided to have fun with a portable radio, one of the first available. It was late in the day and most of the crew was sitting or standing near a tent, going over the next day's schedule. 'I excused myself for a minute and went to get the radio,' Cary recalled. 'I crept around the back of the tent where all the crew was and turned it on to the highest volume. You never saw so many grown men run so fast or so scared!'

THE PHILADELPHIA STORY

This was one of the four films Cary made with Katharine Hepburn, one of his favorite leading ladies along with Deborah Kerr, Audrey Hepburn and Ingrid Bergman.

He was particularly proud of the movie's opening scene, in which his character, who's walking out on his marriage, shoves Kate to the ground.

'I thought it would be a funny idea if I got even with

her,' Cary reminisced. 'I had made *Sylvia Scarlett* with Kate four years before and she really got to give me a good sock in that one. So I went to the producer and he loved the idea. What really surprised me was how hard I pushed her. I didn't expect to and she didn't expect it either. I practically lifted her off the ground. When she went sprawling down and started laughing, I told her she had had it coming for four years!'

I once told Cary how beautiful I thought Hepburn looked in this movie as well as some of her other ones from the thirties and forties. He laughed at me. 'She looks like a horse!' he guffawed.

'If she's a horse,' I replied, 'then she's a true thoroughbred!'

PENNY SERENADE

Though he was rightfully proud of his performance, which earned him his first Academy Award nomination, Cary found the plot (about a poor couple trying to keep the daughter they've adopted) much too close for comfort. 'Please, Judge . . .' his character cries as he begs a judge to let him and his wife keep the baby, promising to find work so he can give the child the home it deserves.

It was one of the few times I saw Cary cry, apart from the moments when he was overcome with emotion watching Jennifer at play.

SUSPICION

Cary had one word for his costar Joan Fontaine in this Hitchcock movie in which it's impossible to tell until the very end whether or not he really wants to kill his wife.

The word was 'bitch.'

'She was no fun on the set of *Gunga Din*, in which she also appeared with me, and she was no fun during this. She had one big fat head about herself. It wasn't hard to play someone who looked as if he wanted to kill her!'

Cary's harsh opinion of Joan may have been influenced by the fact that she won an Oscar for her acting in this film

— and Cary did not. And thought he should have.

'All she had to do was look frightened all the way through the movie,' he told me. 'What's so hard about that? But with my character, you never know whether he's a killer or not for almost the entire film. Try conveying *that* for an hour and a half!'

ARSENIC AND OLD LACE

This was one of Cary's least favorite films and not just because of his hysterial overacting. The comedy about a young man whose two maiden aunts have been knocking off gentlemen boarders calls for his character to be openly worried about the possibility that insanity runs in his family.

'Look, darling, you wouldn't want to have children with three heads, would you?' he says to his bewildered fiancée. 'I mean, you wouldn't want to set up house-keeping in a padded cell? ... Look, I probably should have told you this before, but you see — insanity runs in my family. It practically gallops!'

The parallels to his own unspoken fears in this domain had to be on his mind when we saw the movie. Though Cary had resisted my suggestion we see this movie when it was broadcast, he relented and sat through all of it — until this scene came on.

Then he shut the TV off.

NONE BUT THE LONELY HEART

Here was another movie, with even more echoes of his own family, that he found painful to watch. Cary plays a wanderer named Ernie Mott, while Ethel Barrymore costars as his mother.

Mrs Mott is a strong, powerful woman who desperately yearns for her son to settle down before she dies, but they know only how to bicker with each other. Once they finally soften toward each other, the mother buys her son a pin-striped suit because he's gotten so industrious around her little shop. The elderly woman encourages her son to go down to the local fish-and-chips place, so the girls there can get a good look at him in his new suit, and show off 'just like your father did.'

'Did you love my old man?' Cary's character asks.

'Love's not for the poor, son,' she replies. 'No time for it.'

Another scene that had to stir memories inside Cary occurs near the end. Ernie's mum has landed in the prison hospital after having been pinched for possession of stolen property.

'Love me, son?' she begins to cry, ashamed. '[I] disgraced you!'

'Disgrace me, Ma?' Ernie replies emotionally, 'No, Ma, *no*! No, you didn't disgrace me, Ma. This is your son, Ernie Mott. The boy who needs you, loves you, wants you!'

Then he grabs her and buries himself, weeping, in her arms.

His powerful performance earned him a second Academy Award nomination.

THE BISHOP'S WIFE

Cary plays an angel who comes down to earth to help a bishop (David Niven) raise money for a cathedral. Cary was very proud of the scenes in which his character had to glide about on ice skates, something he'd done as a child in Bristol but had to relearn for this role.

When Cary learned I had never ice-skated, he was bound and determined to get me on ice. Jennifer joined in the conspiracy. They would take me to an ice rink in Santa Monica for lessons. Jennifer had already learned and would be my teacher.

Because it had taken Cary quite a few days to reacquire his skills on the ice, he was sure I'd end up on my behind the minute I got on the rink. I was pretty sure of that myself, so when we got there I began to pull back, saying I'd just watch Jennifer and the other kids. But he wouldn't hear of it.

'If these kids can do it, Maureen, so can you!' he challenged me.

I put on my skates and got on the ice. Before I took a step, I was already embarrassed because I was the only grown-up out there. Then I positioned myself on a ledge, with Cary lending me support, and started to move my feet hesitantly. Suddenly I just took off. It reminded me of roller-skating, which I'd loved as a kid. I was really flying! The only problem was that I didn't know how to slow down. So I had to grab a couple of tykes' heads in order to stop.

On the way home Cary had a kind of paternal pride as he spoke of my skill on the ice.

'You were really wonderful,' he laughed, 'but I have to admit I wanted to see you fall on your bum at least once!'

PEOPLE WILL TALK

This is a strange little comedy with Cary playing a doctor who decides to wed a girl pregnant by another man. At the end of the movie, Cary's character triumphantly leads an orchestra after all the vicious gossipers in town have been put in their place.

As we were watching the final scene, Cary informed me that if he hadn't been an actor, that's precisely what he would've liked to be — a conductor.

'Why?' I asked.

'Most conductors live to be very old,' he said quickly. 'It's all that exercise with their arms, flailing about. It must be good for their hearts.'

I'm sure this is the reason Cary loved to watch Leonard Bernstein conduct on television. Neither Jennifer nor I could say a word while the maestro was wielding his baton on TV.

MONKEY BUSINESS

Cary was not at all taken by Marilyn Monroe, his costar in this dizzy comedy. (However, he did like and at one time dated Ginger Rogers, who also costarred.)

'Marilyn was a very calculating girl,' Cary said. 'She was never late on *our* set, I'll tell you that. She was trying to get me to go to bed with her while she was trying to get Howard [Hawks, the director] to do the same thing! We both knew it and — I can speak only for myself — it just turned me off. Completely.

'Plus, I never believed all those stories she told about her childhood and being a poor orphan and her mother being cuckoo. She'd tell them to *strangers* at the drop of a hat. The girl had no subtlety, no discretion. She was much too blatant for me.'

The mental problems of Marilyn's mother were quite real. It's a shame Cary and Marilyn couldn't have become friends, because they had a lot in common.

TO CATCH A THIEF

Grace Kelly was the woman who brought Cary out of a brief semi-retirement in the mid-fifties. The girl from Philadelphia who later became the First Lady of Monaco was his favorite leading lady and he constantly talked about her. She was incredibly beautiful. She was the epitome of class. She worked with you, not against you, unlike a Joan Fontaine. If she hadn't married Prince Rainier, she and Cary would have done more pictures together. She was just so relaxed on and off screen.

Cary was so effusive about Grace I was convinced they must've had an affair, but he always denied it vehemently. Besides, he said, she was going with Oleg Cassini when she made this movie. But Cary knew it was over for Oleg when Grace met Rainier.

'After all,' he laughed, 'she did have good taste — and he had a cleft too!'

There was one other thing Cary mentioned about her — he hated to go driving with her. Her erratic driving in the hills overlooking the Mediterranean while they were on location on the French Riviera convinced him never to let her take the wheel while she was with him.

THE PRIDE AND THE PASSION

Cary did fall in love with Sophia Loren, his leading lady in this turgid spectacle set during the Spanish revolution against Napoleon.

Cary told me he first resisted the idea of starring in this big-budget drama with Loren, who was then unknown to American audiences. But when he met her, that all changed.

'I fell in love with her and I like to think she fell in love with me, at least for a time. I know she did while we were in Ávila and we were going to out-of-the-way restaurants in the hills. It was terribly romantic. She wasn't terribly fluent in English, but she understood me.

'Soon I was telling the press she was the new Garbo and I had to tell Betsy the truth. I was a goner.'

Cary said he was drawn to Sophia not only because of her staggering beauty but also because of the deprived childhood she'd suffered through.

'I could identify a lot with her. She didn't really have a father most of the time. She didn't meet him until she was five — and he did that only because Sophia's mother tricked him, saying Sophia was very ill and he better hurry and see her while he could.

'I knew, from what I gathered from her English, she felt a lot of bitterness about her father. So I suggested she undergo psychotherapy. I had several good doctors to recommend, but she wouldn't hear of it.

'Carlo [Ponti], who eventually became her husband, really became her father as much as he did her husband. I mean, they met when she was sixteen, started living together when she was nineteen, and got married when she did *Houseboat*, her second movie with me.'

Cary said that he proposed to Sophia during the making of *The Pride and the Passion*, but she finally and tearfully told him no after thinking it over for several days. Since they both came from such insecure backgrounds, she was sure there was no way they could make a secure marriage.

'She broke my heart,' he said simply.

HOUSEBOAT

This movie was made about a year after *The Pride and the Passion*.

Cary played a recently widowed diplomat who barely knows his three children. It's only when Sophia comes into their lives as their housekeeper that they really become a family.

Ironically, the screenplay had been suggested by an idea of Betsy's, who was originally supposed to costar. But after Cary met Sophia, he got Paramount to sign her for the role. When it later came time to do *Houseboat* — after Sophia had turned down his proposal — Cary tried to get out of doing the film altogether. Only when Paramount threatened to sue Cary did he agree to go ahead and make the movie.

Not surprisingly, it was very painful for him.

'Sophia had made her decision and there was nothing I could do to change her mind. I just didn't want to be around her. Then we started making the film and I fell in love with her all over again! There was one scene I'll never forget, where I had to kiss her in my arms while we were in a red rowboat. A man would have to be inhuman not to respond in such circumstances.

'I proposed again. But before she could give me an answer, I opened a newspaper to read that she and Carlo had gotten married by proxy in Mexico! Then, a few days later, we had to go through the scene in the movie where our characters get married.

'I did not enjoy it.'

For Cary there was another scene that seemed to sum up their relationship.

'It was a lovely interlude,' Sophia's character tells Cary after they've had a big disagreement. 'I enjoyed every minute of it — until we both had too much champagne and spoiled it all.'

'It was just an interlude, was it?' Cary's character says skeptically.

'Yes,' Sophia says with chilling finality, 'an interlude.'

Cary never held a grudge against Sophia. In fact, he

was the first to phone her in Italy after she won the Oscar for Best Actress for 1961.

AN AFFAIR TO REMEMBER

Cary had great regard for Deborah Kerr, with whom he also costarred in *The Grass Is Greener* and *Dream Wife*. He always referred to her as 'a first-class lady who made work a lot less like work with her professionalism.' It was one of his supreme compliments.

For me one of the most interesting things about this tearjerker was learning how much of its dialogue Cary had personally tailored. Some of the rapid interplay between Cary and Deborah was suggested by him, making the characters much more down-to-earth.

One scene he influenced illustrates this technique perfectly.

Deborah and Cary are in a carriage on the way to see his grandmother in her French villa. As they ride along, the Mediterranean weaves its watery spell in the background.

'Isn't it beautiful down there?' Cary asks Deborah.

'Huh?' she says.

'I say, isn't it beautiful down there?' Cary repeats.

'Yes, but do you want to hear an old joke?' she asks him.

'What?' he says.

'If it's so beautiful down there —' she starts, but he joins her for the punchline, 'what are we doing up *here*?'

'It's an old joke, all right!' Cary laughs.

The scene was a playful reminder to me of Cary's constant 'It's lovely out, then I better leave it out!' routine.

INDISCREET

Cary loved Ingrid Bergman, who also starred in *Notorious* with him.

'She was a lady who was treated like a whore,' he said, referring to the way the American press almost pilloried her in the late forties. She reaped headlines when she had a child by Italian director Roberto Rossellini while still married to her first husband.

Almost ten years later Cary set the stage for her triumphant return to the United States when he accepted the Best Actress Oscar she won for the 1956 film *Anastasia*.

'Dear Ingrid,' he announced as he grabbed the statuette, 'if you can hear me or see this, I want you to know we all send our love and admiration.' She did hear it — she was sitting in her bathtub at her Paris apartment.

Two years later, Ingrid finally stepped back on American soil. At the Oscars ceremony held in 1959, she was nervous about presenting an award. But Cary set the tone when he introduced her as 'a great actress and a great lady. Welcome back, Ingrid Bergman!' The audience roared its overwhelming approval.

But *Indiscreet* reminds me of more than Cary's gallantry. There's an extended sequence at a dinner dance that became one of my favorite scenes from all his movies. Ingrid is peeved at him and is trying to pretend to have a grand time. But her heart isn't in it.

So Cary dances a wild jig to get into the spirit of things. He's doing anything to show Ingrid what a swell time *he's*'s having. He whistles, he skips, he slides, he whoops. He even does a mean backstep along with an Irish jig. He whips himself into such a frenzy he seems to defy the laws of gravity. The scene ends with Cary madly clapping, his hands high above his head, while he gleefully cries, 'Wheee!'

Since the rest of the film is nothing more than a dry drawing room comedy, I was totally unprepared for this madness when it popped up in the movie. Cary was so delighted by my laughing that he promptly got up and began to dance a jig for me in the bedroom! But just for me, he managed to throw in a couple of jetés.

I exploded into laughter once again. From that point on, if I ever needed to be cheered up, Cary would promptly 'get down' for me. As with everything else he did, he threw himself into it completely.

NORTH BY NORTHWEST

We saw this Hitchcock thriller several times and each time Cary never failed to mention that the famous scene in which a crop-dusting plane tries to mow him down in an open field 'came too close for comfort. It was the closest I ever came to an accident while making a film.'

I also remember what Cary said about Eva Marie Saint, cast as the cool blonde who seduces him on a train. 'Not a bad substitute for Grace Kelly, wouldn't you say?' Hitchcock and Cary begged Kelly to come out of retirement to reteam with Cary for the movie, but Cary said she couldn't. 'The prince wouldn't have it. It was either making a life with him or her career, but not both. We had to respect her choice.'

THAT TOUCH OF MINK

Cary spoke of Doris Day affectionately, but he had nothing good to say about Martin Melcher, her husband at the time this 1962 movie was made. Melcher was also the film's coproducer but in name only, said Cary. 'He was in on a pass, as they say in society. He meddled in everything. I hate to speak ill of the dead, but the best thing that ever happened to that poor woman was when he died.' Doris herself later accused Melcher of mismanaging her fortune and making bad investments on her behalf.

The most surprising thing Cary ever said about Doris was that he would have liked to have been her costar in the musical *Love Me or Leave Me*.

In that movie James Cagney starred as a gangster totally devoted to the young Ruth Etting, whom Doris plays. He does anything and everything to make her a star, but in the process loses her with his jealousy and overzealousness. Doris later admitted she was thinking of Melcher's own influence upon her and their relationship when she played the role.

'God, I would've loved to have played that role,' Cary said one night as we watched the movie for the umpteenth time. 'I could've played the stuffing out of that role.'

'So why didn't you?' I asked, assuming Cary Grant could get any role he really wanted.

'They didn't ask me,' he said.

CHARADE

This comedy-mystery contains another of my favorite scenes.

Audrey Hepburn drinks Cary in with her eyes and then says, 'Do you know what's wrong with you?' When he asks her what, she hastily replies: 'Absolutely nothing!'

The chemistry between Cary and Audrey was terrific. He gave her a custom-made chrome-plate phonograph, which he bestowed on only a privileged few of his fifty-three leading ladies.

A few years after *Charade* was released, MGM made an offer to Cary to costar with Audrey again in a musical remake of *Goodbye, Mr. Chips* (which eventually starred Peter O'Toole and Petula Clark). But Cary had already retired by then and there was no going back.

Charade was actually the third script Cary was asked to do with Audrey. Before this 1963 movie, he was offered the Humphrey Bogart role in *Sabrina* and Rex Harrison's Professor Higgins in *My Fair Lady*.

'Not only will I not play the role,' Cary said at the time he turned down *My Fair Lady*, 'but if you don't hire Rex, I won't even go see it!'

FATHER GOOSE

This was Cary's favorite film. I think he loved it because he got to go around unshaven throughout the entire movie as a cantankerous hermit saddled with a French school-teacher and the children in her charge in the middle of World War II. More important, the chance to work with all those kids also left him with many happy memories.

Cary also remembered how madly in love with Dyan he was when he made the movie — and how deeply in love Warren Beatty was with his costar, Leslie Caron. 'I don't care what people say about Warren and Julie Christie,' Cary repeatedly claimed, 'it's Leslie who was the love of Warren's life. I saw them together on the set and they were bonkers for each other. Just bonkers!'

In 1970 Cary was given a special Oscar saluting the entire body of his career, seventy-two films in all.

Cary was very proud of that honor. His Oscar occupied a special place on a bookshelf beside his bed. He often said he was much more pleased getting an honorary Oscar than a so-called regular Oscar because he'd been hailed not just for one performance but for his whole career.

It was one hell of a career.

26

ENTER MADAME

'**D**EAR,' my mother was saying on the phone, 'you may have a problem with this Barbara.'

It was June 1976 and my parents had dined with Cary in his suite at the Royal Lancaster in London. I had some complications from my earlier surgery, so it was impossible for me to get away to England. Besides, as Cary pointed out, he'd be gone only a few days. He'd make his appearance at the annual Fabergé trade fair and then drop over to Bristol to see Eric and Maggie Leach for the afternoon. He'd be back before I knew it.

But my mother saw something at the Lancaster that disturbed her. It was Barbara Harris, the hotel's public relations person assigned to look after Cary during his stay there. She was four years younger than I and, at the time, had blonde hair to complement her pert, pleasant looks. Ironically, today I have blonde hair and Barbara has brown.

'There was just something about the way she was around him,' Mummy was saying on the phone the day after she and Daddy had dined with Cary. 'She had more than a professional interest in him, if you ask me. I think you've got some competition there, Maureen.'

I reassured Mummy the best I could. She was generally aware of the storms and squalls that had become part of my relationship with Cary. If Cary's suspicions about my falling in love with another man were directly responsible for much of that rough weather, it didn't seem likely he'd casually turn around and do what he accused me of.

And as I told Mummy, if a man's really interested in another woman, I don't believe there's one thing on earth you can do stop him from scratching that itch, short of a loaded gun. 'If Cary's really interested in this Barbara and vice versa,' I said as we finished our conversation, 'it's only a matter of time, isn't it?'

Actually, I was not as concerned about this woman as I was about a man I'll call Jason. He was the latest in the long line of Cary's male secretaries. He bore a more than passing resemblance to a weasel; in human terms the kindest comparison I could make would be to the odious characters Richard Benjamin played in *Diary of a Mad Housewife* and *Goodbye Columbus*. I detested Jason on sight.

And the feeling was mutual. He had the ability to make me feel like an intruder in his employer's home. I immediately alerted Cary to my uneasy feelings about this man. Jason was sending me a very negative signal on purpose. In everything he did around the house, his message was clear: 'Cary is *my* territory. Hands off.' He did the same thing to Willie and even the workmen toiling around the house. He was a master manipulator, always doing his best to interfere and complicate things yet appear, to Cary at least, to be doing his gosh-darnedest to help in any way he could. On more than one occasion I called the house and asked Jason to let Cary know I was going to be late for dinner. But each time Cary did *not* get the message — and Jason swore he couldn't remember my calling.

But Cary wouldn't hear of removing this man from our otherwise relatively happy household. 'Oh, he's *indispensable*!' Cary would insist when any of us made known our objections to Jason's overall creepiness and working procedures. I tried to ignore Jason and his influence over Cary, but he was the type who *liked* making his presence felt. It got so oppressive that if I'd been out for the day on a photo shoot, I would park my car at the bottom of the hill and wait for Jason to leave before I'd come back into the house at night.

Then one day Jason did his best — make that his *worst* — to imply in so many words that Cary was interested in him, but he did it by choosing words that, upon reexamination, could pass inspection as perfectly innocent. It would seem as if he were describing a paternal interest, not a gay one, on Cary's part, if I brought it up with Cary or anyone else. I was convinced that if a moral CAT scan had been performed on this character, Jason could be proved to be the illegitimate offspring of Eve Harrington.

So now Cary's secretaries had graduated from making their accusations to my friends to making them to my face, but in the most underhanded way possible. I had to press Cary further on the issue.

'Jason is doing everything to let me know without coming out and saying it that he and you are lovers,' I told Cary one night after dinner.

'There you go again, Maureen, exaggerating out of your insecurity,' Cary said. 'Jason is really a very nice boy and if you'd only try to get along with him, you'd see that.'

'But Cary,' I protested, 'that's exactly what I've tried to do from day one, but he's done everything to make me feel uncomfortable around him. He's a manipulator and a schemer. I don't know why you won't believe me. Everybody else is saying the same thing.'

'But Maureen,' he shot back, 'you're the one who's told me from day one of *our* relationship that I shouldn't give a damn about what everybody else thinks. Just try to get along with him. He makes my life up here so much easier when he's around. He really does. And you should appreciate that fact.'

'What *you* should appreciate, Cary,' I replied, 'is that this man makes me feel uncomfortable, uneasy and unwelcome in *your* home. If that's how I really feel — and let's forget, like you say, what everybody else feels — then why don't you get rid of him? You've had so many secretaries. What's one more or less?'

'Because, my dear young lady,' Cary said, getting haughty, which I knew was a sign of extreme anger, 'if you really knew anything about business or at least my business, you'd know how invaluable the right secretary is. I'm going to sit you two down together tomorrow morning and work this out.'

'Don't bother, Cary,' I said, defeated. 'He'll just sit

there with this wounded-puppy look on his face, trying not to cry to show you how hurt he is. He'll pretend he doesn't know what I'm talking about. Frankly, if I want to see acting — good acting, that is — I'll go to the movies.'

That was it for a while about Jason. I pushed Cary as far as I could. Unfortunately, Jason would grow from a small wedge to a significant one. He was always there, an unpleasant and malignant force growing between us.

Happily, however, our sex life was as strong and powerful as ever. It got an added kick when I organized an exercise class with some of the women who lived in the building where I kept my apartment and office. This was long before Jane Fonda was working out with millions on videotape. I was rapidly approaching my thirtieth birthday and, more than ever, I was determined to keep in shape. At first Cary took a casual, positive interest in this group effort.

'Good stuff!' he'd encourage me. 'Healthy stuff!'

But then one day I came to Beverly Grove still wearing my long-sleeved black leotard, with a skirt wrapped around the bottom. That's when Cary's interest in exercise became much more personal.

I came bounding into the house and Cary took a sideways glance at me.

'What's that you're wearing? I mean the top,' he said.

'It's my leotard. I didn't have time to change if I was going to make it up here in time for dinner.'

I was halfway apologizing because I knew he sometimes didn't like too casual clothes on me or Jennifer.

'Oh,' he said simply.

But I could tell from the way he looked at me as I peeled off the leotard later in the bedroom that something about it turned him on. So I began wearing it more and more often. And I started making a fairly elaborate routine out of removing the leotard.

First I would slowly unzip it and then slowly wiggle out of one sleeve. Next I would slither out of the other sleeve. Then I would start peeling the rest of it off, rolling it effortlessly below my buttocks and on down my legs. I could tell by the way Cary stared at me that he was utterly fascinated.

This routine became known as my striptease as we two joked about it. Late one afternoon I was starting to remove the garment when Cary said, 'Let me do that for you, darling.'

Now it was his fingers guiding the zipper downward. Soon they were delicately, gently removing the leotard section by section off my body. I felt as if I were a butterfly and the leotard was my cocoon which Cary was personally casting to the wind as I emerged more sensual and more beautiful than ever before. Under Cary's spell and in his hands, I felt magical.

And I felt that way every time we repeated the process.

Then one day I told Cary I was going to get him in shape.

'I'm pretty limber, you know,' he said idly, not yet quite catching my intention.

'You'll be in the best shape of your life if you let me be your personal trainer,' I whispered.

He enrolled for classes *immediately*. Now he sat before me, nude and somewhat shy as always.

'I can see we have our work cut out for us,' I said in my most professional manner. 'We have to get you in shape quickly. I think we'll start with your legs. We'll do some leg lifts but first you better let me take a look at your legs. Stretch out, please.'

He loved every second of it, though he was in better shape than most men of any age. I took one of his legs in my hands and began to massage it firmly. Then my hands began to travel all the way up his thighs, as I kneaded, pressed and moved his flesh.

'You'll kill me if you keep this up,' he sighed.

'Yes,' I said, laughing softly, 'but it'll be worth dying for, won't it?'

The way he laughed told me we were moving in the right direction.

One day in that summer of 1976, I donned another

garment that affected Cary, but it was hardly in the heat of passion.

It was just a few days before the Republican National Convention in Kansas City. Cary had agreed to introduce the First Lady, Betty Ford, at the event, and he'd promised to take me with him. And I really wanted to go. I loved Betty Ford, plus I wanted to witness close-up the unique American political process in full operation.

I walked into the house and I heard Cary on the phone in the bedroom.

'Don't worry,' he was assuring the person he was speaking to, 'I'm sure Miss Donaldson will have an evening dress you can borrow, and since she can't go now, I'm sure she won't mind.'

As Cary put down the phone, I walked into the room and turned to him.

'I can't go *where* now?' I said, both curious and apprehensive.

'To the convention,' Cary said. 'As you know, I'm taking Jennifer, but Dyan says the only way I can take her is if I have a nanny with her. The girl doesn't have any proper evening clothes, so I told her she could borrow one of your dresses.'

'What does that have to do with my not going?' I said, starting to see red.

'Well, you know perfectly well there are accommodations for only four people — myself, Jennifer, her nanny and Jason. I'm sorry, dear, but there's just no room for you. I'll make it up to you, I promise.'

'I'm sure it'll be as good as your original promise to take me to Kansas City, Cary,' I said coolly. I had uprooted my whole schedule to make sure I'd be free to go to the convention with Cary. Since I'd missed London with him, I especially wanted to make this date.

'Don't be nasty,' he said, his voice assuming the condescending tone it took on when he was annoyed.

'I *feel* nasty and I have every right to be and you know it, Cary,' I snapped back. 'I understand the thing about the nanny. What I don't understand is how I got aced out of this happy foursome. You always planned to take three people with you — me, Jennifer and Jason. Why don't you keep Jason here to look after things? You know I can type and take notes, so on the off chance you needed anything secretarial done while we're in Kansas City, I could handle it very easily.'

'Maureen,' he insisted, 'you're just not thinking clearly. You can't do half the things he can. You can't look after and carry the luggage as he will, for example. It's just not practical, dear. I'm sorry.'

I turned on my heel and went into the kitchen. Of course, Willie had heard the whole thing. She reached for my hand to give me a sympathetic squeeze, but she missed me as I reached for a bottle of white wine on the counter. I took several healthy swigs. I was so angry I was reeling. How could he treat me like this? Then to top it off, he was so insensitive about my disappointment, he thought I wouldn't mind lending the nanny a dress for an event I so dearly wanted to attend.

Suddenly I had a brainstorm. If he was going to treat me so shabbily, I might as well dress the part. 'Come with me,' I said to Willie as I led her to her small quarters near the kitchen.

Two minutes later I walked into the kitchen and then into the bedroom wearing one of Willie's old white maid's uniforms. It was ripped and soiled and ready for the rag pile. I was carrying the bottle of white wine.

'Excuse me, Mr. Grant,' I said in the most sarcastic tones I could summon. 'Since I can't go to the convention in one of my own dresses, I thought you'd like to see what I'll be wearing back here at home while you're living it up in Kansas City with your friends.'

Cary's mouth dropped open and he angrily slammed his glasses down on his night table.

'I suppose you think you're hysterical,' he said angrily.

'Why, yes,' I said woozily as the wine began to hit me. 'Yes, I do, as a matter of fact. Don't *you*?'

'Well, you are hysterical,' he continued 'but you're not hysterically funny. You're just hysterical. And I think you should know that by putting on that uniform, you're not hurting me, you're just insulting Willie.'

'*Really*?' I said. 'Then why is she laughing in the other room? She started laughing the moment I put it on, Cary. Somehow I don't feel like laughing myself, though I think this whole thing is very funny. Very, very funny. It's so bloody funny, in fact, I think I'll scream. But if you don't like what I'm wearing, I'll take it off!'

I took off one of my shoes and flung it at him. I clipped him on the hand.

'Willie!' Cary yelled. 'Come in here this instant! Maureen is hysterical!'

I began to fall back but Willie caught me.

'What's going on in here?' she said, pretending to be confused.

'Miss Donaldson is totally hysterical,' Cary repeated, 'and I want you to put her to bed immediately to Jennifer's room. I can't handle her tonight!'

Cary said he would make it all up to me, and he did on my thirtieth birthday. It was September 27, but I was prepared to be disappointed once again. Cary had said we'd spend the whole evening together with Dee up at the house. Willie would make a special dinner for the three of us. Then Cary was asked to go on stage and introduce Frank Sinatra, who was beginning an engagement at the Universal Amphitheatre on the night of my birthday.

'I've got to do it,' Cary explained. 'Frank's too good a friend. He asked me personally to do this and I can't let him down. But I will rush back here and spend the rest of the night with you. I'll be back at the house no later than eight or eight-thirty. How does that sound?'

It sounded okay. Frankly, the idea of a thirtieth birthday didn't strike me as something I should go out of my way to celebrate anyway. I told Cary not to worry about it.

When the evening arrived, I kissed Cary good-bye as Dee and I went to meet some friends at a Polynesian restaurant. We had a few drinks and everyone was kidding me about hitting the big Three-Oh.

Dee and I started to head back for the house about

eight and I told Dee, who was driving, not to hurry. There was no way Cary would be back before nine or nine-thirty. But when we pulled into the driveway, there was his Cadillac. I exchanged a glance with Dee. How in the world could he have gotten back here so quickly? It was exactly eight-twenty.

I put my key in the front door but Willie was already on the other side, opening it. As the door swung open, Dee and I could see straight through the living room to the piano, where Cary was sitting in top hat and tails. Behind him the lights of Los Angeles twinkled below like a backdrop from one of his movies.

There were no lights on in the house, but I could see Cary's face beaming as Willie held up a birthday cake with candles and brought it toward Cary and the Steinway. Dee and I followed, too stunned to speak.

As Dee and I arrived at Cary's side near the piano, Cary took my hand and put it in his.

'Happy birthday, darling!' he said.

Then he got up and kissed me. I started to cry as he sat down and began banging out 'Happy Birthday' on the piano.

'Make a wish!' Dee and Willie said, so I blew out the candles, not making a wish. I'd already gotten mine — Cary had made me just as important as his commitment to Frank, rushing home to make sure this night was truly special for me. He had to have broken speed records to get to the house before Dee and I did.

We opened some champagne. Now I really felt like celebrating. Cary had given me a night I shall never, ever forget.

He also gave me a beautiful gold chain with a large gold cross.

'God bless you,' he whispered as he put it around my neck.

Of course I thanked him when he presented it to me as Willie and Dee watched. But later that night when we were alone, I thanked him again in a way I knew he'd never forget.

* * *

That birthday made us quite close again. For a couple of months we shared a lovely plateau amid the ups and downs of our relationship. We even planned to go on a Caribbean cruise together. But given our past pattern — something wonderful followed by something hideous — somewhere in the back of my mind I was waiting for that unpleasant something to appear.

On November 30 the London *Daily Mail* ran an item about my relationship with Cary. It read in part:

'The fluctuating relationship between Cary Grant, 72, and Maureen Donaldson, daughter of a retired fireman from London's Muswell Hill, is back on as they celebrated Thanksgiving Day together....

'Part of their problems have been over Maureen pursuing her career and Cary, international ambassador for Fabergé, has agreed [she should pursue it].'

In mid-December, as we planned to celebrate our fourth Christmas together, I was looking for a pen on Cary's desk when I found a note from Barbara Harris to Cary. She said that she'd read the item about us in the *Daily Mail* and, judging from that, she guessed she wouldn't be welcome now at Beverly Grove despite his earlier invitation. She ended the letter with her best wishes.

I knew Cary well enough to know that his leaving this note out where I could find it so easily was not an accident or a coincidence.

But I had an odd reaction. I wasn't angry at Cary or frightened about Barbara. What I felt — and I had a hard time saying the word even to myself — was relief.

I was relieved that the man I loved appeared to be on the brink of launching a relationship with another woman.

Now who was being irrational?

Cary and I would have to have a serious talk after the holidays.

27

MONKEY BUSINESS

WE never really had that talk.

This time Cary got sick and it was my turn to show my support and love. His ailment sounded like a simple one — a groin hernia. It required a relatively painless, uncomplicated operation. But Cary told me he'd been putting it off for months and months. It was now February 1977.

'Why don't you just get this over with?' I asked him.

'You're going to think I'm stupid,' he said in that way of his which made him sound like a shy and frightened little boy.

'Don't be silly,' I said. 'Of course I won't.'

'I'm afraid if I go under the knife I'll never wake up and see Jennifer or you again,' he said, glad to get it out. 'I know it sounds silly, but I can't tell you how many friends I've had who've gone in for supposedly minor things and they never made it out of surgery. I've got clippings about all kinds of cases like that too. I've got scads and scads of them, I really do.'

So many of his friends had passed away in recent years. The previous November Rosalind Russell had finally succumbed in her long, gallant fight against cancer. Cary had introduced her decades ago to her husband, producer Frederick Brisson, and served as Freddie's best man at their wedding. Cary had refused to go see Roz while she was dying, at least that Willie and I knew about. (But he did talk to her on the phone.)

'I just can't bear it,' he told me. 'To see such a wonderful woman go so slowly and so painfully. I hope I never go that way. I want to remember Roz the way she was, not the way she is now.'

Another reason Cary was so afraid of surgery had to do with his long-standing fear of knives. For many years, whenever Cary happened to be in the kitchen and caught me holding a knife so it was pointing toward me, he would rush over and snatch it out of my hands.

'Never hold a knife that way!' he'd scold me. 'You really could hurt yourself. Always carry it so it's pointing away from you. Promise me you'll do that.'

Of course, I'd promise him I'd do just that but sometimes I'd forget in my rush to help Willie or to fix a little something for us. He was so insistent I became very curious about his fear. One afternoon he finally told me what it stemmed from. It went back to his childhood in Bristol when he was seven or eight years old.

'I had a crush on a girl whose father was a butcher,' he said. 'She was a pretty little thing and I used to follow her home or sometimes to her father's shop, where she'd do little things to help out. For some reason her father just hated me. Most people would've found this kind of puppy love innocent, but he was disturbed by it.

'One day I was hanging around outside the butcher's shop when the father came out and headed straight for me. He was holding a huge knife and it was pointed right at me. "If I ever catch you around my daughter again, Archie Leach, I'll use this on you!" And I could tell he meant what he was saying too.'

Knowing these fears, I reassured Cary every step of the way before he was due to go under the knife. I promise I'd be right there beside him. I also emphasized over and over what magnificent health he was blessed with. During our years together the only regular thing I'd seen him go to a doctor for were brown liver spots on his hands, which he had his doctor in Beverly Hills burn off. A scab would form over the area where the dreaded spot had been; then when the scab fell off, the spot was virtually gone. (It was one of only two concessions Cary ever made to his vanity — the other was having his eyebrows regularly dyed black. He didn't mind his hair turning silver, but he wanted his eyebrows dark.)

Then, after all these reassurances, I'd tell Cary he was too mean to die. I'd been saying it cheekily for years now. He loved the joke because he loved the idea of living forever. 'Just think, I could see Jennifer with her own children, happily married.' That was his fondest wish. Cary was terrified Jennifer would forget him if he died before she was grown. The public could permanently retire him in its mind, but he would die an unhappy man if Jennifer had only childhood impressions of him to remember the rest of her life.

Cary was scheduled to go into St. John's Hospital in Santa Monica on a Tuesday in early March and be out by Friday. Jennifer came the weekend before the surgery and Cary was so fearful that he wanted to tell her good-bye in case he never saw her again. Cary asked me to be with him so I could explain to Jennifer anything she didn't understand. But Cary didn't need my help. He had just the right touch with her. On a Sunday afternoon on the terrace, he sat down with his daughter, who had just turned eleven.

'Jennifer,' he said slowly, 'you know Daddy is going into the hospital soon.'

'Yes,' she said, 'Maureen said you've got a bump near your tummy.'

'That's right, dear,' he said, smiling. 'This is a very simple operation and I'll be out of the hospital in two or three days.'

'Can I come see you there?' she asked.

'Oh no, dear, you wouldn't want to miss school, would you? But I'll give you my number and perhaps you can give me a call.'

'Don't forget!' she admonished him.

'Don't worry, I won't,' he continued. 'But just in case something happens, I want you to know something, darling. And that is how much Daddy loves you, and even if something happens to me, I will always love you. It doesn't matter where I'll be — you might not be able to see me like you can right now — but you must know that I love you and I'm with you and that love can never go away, even if I do. Do you understand?'

She reached up and put her arms around his neck and kissed him.

Then he changed the subject.

When Tuesday arrived, Cary was determined no one from the tabloids was going to snap a photograph of him entering the hospital. He'd seen shots of celebrities entering or exiting hospitals, and the naked vulnerability in such shots upset him greatly.

We pulled up to the back entrance of St. John's and I looked around for photographers. I gave him the all-clear signal and he raced in. He went directly to a private room. He'd already given the hospital all the information they'd need. The last thing he wanted was to be standing around filling out forms while nurses buzzed among themselves, 'There's Cary Grant!' And because of the rather delicate nature of his surgery, he insisted only male nurses and aides attend to him.

By the time I'd parked the car and taken the elevator up to his floor, Cary was already safely ensconced in his room. I was about to enter when an extremely robust female nurse, who must've trained under Nurse Ratched, stuck out a stubby finger and began poking me in the chest.

'You can't go in there! It's strictly private!' she warned as she poked and pushed me.

'I'm afraid you're mistaken,' I said calmly. 'I'm expected in there. If you'll check with Mr. Robbins's doctor, you'll see I am the *only* person allowed to visit him, aside from staff.'

Robbins was the pseudonym Cary had adopted for this visit.

Nurse Ratched was not about to let me in the room *or* check to see if I was permitted in.

'Look, young lady,' she said with a contemptuous flourish, 'my orders are not to let anyone in there. You're going to have to leave.' Then she began poking me again.

'If you poke me with that stubby little finger of yours one more time,' I snapped, 'you're going to find it in a part of your body it's never been in before!'

With that I heard an eruption of laughter coming from Cary's suite.

'Nurse, you can let Miss Donaldson in. She does have my permission,' he said, still laughing.

I walked into the room. Cary was putting some of his things away. He reached over and hugged me.

'Good stuff!' he practically bellowed. 'No one's going to keep you out of here!'

'Damn right,' I said, beginning to laugh myself. 'Over-zealous cow!'

'Rather a large one, isn't she?' Cary giggled.

'I've seen African nations that were smaller,' I said. 'But I should be cross with you. You heard the whole thing right from the beginning, didn't you?'

He smiled guiltily.

'Yes,' I continued. 'But you just wanted to hear me give that cow a bad time, didn't you? You're a very naughty boy.'

'Let's play Spite and Malice!' he said, admitting nothing.

I'd brought a couple of packs of cards with me. Playing the game always put him in a good mood.

He wasn't doing too badly and I thought I might even let him win a game. I knew it would lift his spirits immeasurably. But half-way through the game he gave me that look only a woman who knows her man well recognizes as his and his alone.

In several hours he'd be operated on for a groin hernia, but right now he wanted to make love.

'God,' I said, sighing, 'you really are naughty.'

He laughed again, but his look was just as intense.

'Do you really think it's safe?' I asked. 'I mean, considering the nature of the operation, Cary ...'

'Perfectly all right,' he assured me. He was such a perfectionist, he certainly would've checked out that particular detail.

'Nurse Ratched?' I said, glancing at the door.

'We'll close it and leave word not to be disturbed.

They're already terrified of me anyway.'

We put down the cards and walked over to the hospital bed.

'Well,' I said, chuckling as I took off my jacket, 'it'll be a first — at least for me.'

'Me too!' Cary said eagerly.

So I personally prepped Cary for his operation, but there was nothing clinical about it.

Afterward I could tell Cary wanted to be alone. He wanted to face this by himself. He'd brought several papers and magazines and was going to clip the night away. On the way out I told him I'd see him the next morning before the operation — *if* they let me in his room again.

'Don't worry,' he said as I kissed him good-bye, 'I'll take care of that.'

'You do that,' I said, 'and you take care of yourself. No clipping past midnight. Doctor's orders, understand?'

He nodded his head bashfully, not remotely looking like a seventy-three-year-old man. He reminded me of a small boy bravely going off to camp for the first time, determined to keep his fears to himself.

'Nice dreams,' I said.

'Happy dreams!' he replied.

The next morning he was nervous and irritable before the operation. But after I arrived to calm him down, he got much better. As they rolled him away to the operating room, I squeezed his hand.

'I'll be right here,' I said, 'and so will you, in about forty-five minutes. You'll see.'

Fortunately nothing went wrong. He was still groggy when they wheeled him back into his suite.

'Maureen?' he said, not quite sure where he was.

'I'm here, Cary,' I said, 'I'm here.'

'Good!' he managed before losing consciousness again. I stayed in the room with him until he woke up several hours later. I held his hand and started to stroke his hair. He didn't move his head or try to brush me away as he might a lot of the time.

'You're a hundred percent,' I assured him. 'No complications whatsoever.'

'Did Jennifer call yet?' he asked, still somewhat weak.

'Yes,' I said. 'She left a number where she'll be if you want to call her before she calls you tonight.'

'Thank God,' he said, almost inaudibly.

A month later, Jennifer was also in Cary's thoughts when we flew to Lake Tahoe with Jean and Kirk Kerkorian. Kirk had taken over the operation of the Cal-Neva, a nightclub straddling the California and Nevada border, and he'd invited us up with him and his daughters to celebrate the grand reopening.

After the ribbon-cutting and other hoopla for the assembled press, we all retired to the lounge of the hotel for a quiet drink together. Tracy, Kirk's oldest daughter, who was then sixteen, sat between Kirk and me. Kirk was so proud of Tracy because she was blossoming into a stunning young lady. Then a young man who'd been eyeing her from across the room came over and asked Tracy to dance.

Kirk didn't know how to handle it. This was obviously the first time a man, other than her daddy, had asked his daughter to dance. His baby girl was now a woman in the eyes of other men. Tracy looked to her father for permission to dance with the young man.

'Of course,' Kirk said, 'have a good time, darling.' But his voice told the rest of us he felt this special moment in his daughter's life had come too soon.

'Don't worry, Kirk,' Cary consoled him as Kirk watched Tracy walk away, 'she'll be all right. But I know it's tough. I know I'm going to have to go through this myself someday with Jennifer.'

'I really want to get up and tap that guy on the shoulder,' Kirk sighed. 'I want to tell him, "That's *my* girl you're dancing with there."'

'It's tough to let her go, isn't it?' Cary offered sympathetically. 'But you've got to, my friend. Every day that she gets older, you're losing her in some way. That's why we cherish every day we can spend with our children.'

I didn't know it then, but my days with Cary were already numbered. The countdown began the day that spring when I met a young musician named Bryce. I'd gone to a party thrown by a girlfriend who had an apartment in my building.

When I first spotted Bryce, I couldn't stop looking into his eyes. They were so blue and so soulful. I was convinced he knew exactly what I was thinking. He was young — five years younger than I — with sandy brown hair, and he projected a vulnerability that reminded me of Steve Winwood.

'I don't mean to be rude,' I said when we were introduced. 'But I can't help looking into your eyes.'

'Thank you,' he said in a gentle, low voice. 'I know the feeling. I've been looking at you and I hoped you wouldn't think I was being rude myself.'

I'd felt drawn to a man like this only two times before in my life. Once with Dee, my first husband, and then with Cary. I knew there was no point in ignoring such an attraction. It was like a surge of electricity shooting through me. And just as I instantly knew I'd go on to have relationships with Dee and Cary, I knew Bryce was going to be an important part of my life.

It was confirmed when Bryce and I talked most of the night away, mostly about our likes and dislikes in music. Then he asked me about Cary; someone must have told him I was Cary's lady. But that fact did nothing to deter him. I think he was as positive as I was about where we were both headed.

As I said good-bye to him that night. Bryce's hand brushed my shoulder. I felt something I hadn't felt in a long time with Cary. Hope. When I got downstairs to my apartment-office, I phoned Cary and told him I was going to sleep there for the night.

'Are you all right?' he asked.

'I need to be by myself,' I said, trying to sound casual.

'I understand,' he declared.

God, I said to myself, *I hope he will.*

28

CHARADE

I CALLED Dee and told her what happened.

Now I had to tell Cary what I felt or I wouldn't be able to forgive myself for being so dishonest with him. Besides, hiding things was Cary's speciality, not mine. I could not lie to him.

'I respect that,' Dee told me, 'but you've just met Bryce once, Maureen. Why set off this explosion with Cary until you're absolutely sure about your feelings for Bryce? Are you absolutely sure Bryce feels the same way about you?

'See Bryce a couple more times, then do what your heart tells you to do. You have so much invested in this relationship. Be very, very careful before you start drawing the curtains on it.'

As always Dee made a lot of sense. I waited until Bryce called me and we made arrangements to have lunch at a small Chinese restaurant a few days later. It was clear the spark that ignited between us at the party had not been extinguished. I talked nervously about everything and everyone under the sun, including Cary. Naturally, Bryce wanted to know how I'd met Cary and what he was really like.

As I started telling Bryce about Cary, I started feeling guilty. There were so many wonderful things we'd done together. There was his extraordinary tenderness and devotion to Jennifer. There was his encouraging me to start a new career I really loved. After a half-hour I felt so guilty I thought I was going to choke.

Bryce and I made a date to go to a rock concert later in the week, but I was positive I wouldn't keep it. 'I'm one confused mess,' I wept as I talked to Dee later. 'I love Cary, but I feel something so special with Bryce. I don't know what to do.'

Dee suggested seeing Bryce one more time to lay all my cards on the table. Find out where *he* wanted us to go, if anywhere. What was *he* feeling?

Bryce met me at my apartment a couple of hours before the concert. He was so gentle and so easy to talk to. I didn't feel as if I were on pins and needles as I had more and more with Cary. I didn't feel like the disobedient schoolgirl with Bryce. I felt I was in charge of my life. And I felt everything was possible.

I looked at my watch and it had been three hours. We were never going to make it to that concert. We sat in my apartment, drinking cranberry juice and listening to music on my stereo. Later I was amazed at the fact I hadn't consumed one drop of liquor all night. With Cary, white wine had become a frequent escape.

Something was happening, and everything Bryce said reinforced that feeling. He told me about his family and how he'd fallen in love with music. He also told me he thought he was falling in love with me.

'You know I'm involved with Cary,' I said tentatively. 'I can't become further involved with you until I clear things up with him. We've been through too much together for me to just walk away without a word of explanation.

'You've got to give me time to do this the right way, at the right time. It may take me just a few weeks. It may take me a few months. I don't know exactly. Will you wait?'

'However long it takes,' Bryce said. The determination in his voice helped give me the strength I knew I'd need.

It was now May 1977 and Cary had already begun to mention his annual trip to London for Fabergé, with a swing-over to Bristol to visit Eric and Maggie. We were scheduled to leave on June 17.

Cary was busying himself with travel arrangements and other details one morning at his desk. He was in a good mood, whistling to himself.

'Darling, when we're in London,' he began, 'would you—' I started crying.

'What's wrong, dear?' he said, turning to see me.

'I'm not going to London with you,' I started sobbing.

'Why?' he said. He put down his pen and sat still, almost as still as a statue.

'You were right,' I sobbed, trying to stop myself, but it was impossible.

'About what?' he said, coming over to the bed, where I'd been having my morning coffee. He put his arm around my shoulder. He was being so considerate it only made me cry more.

'A younger man,' I finally blurted. 'You were right about my falling in love with a younger man. It's happened. I didn't plan it, Cary. I swear to you. It just happened. He was there and I was there and we both knew.'

I had feared he would fly into anger, whipping himself into a fury. But he was calm and cogent. He was making more sense than I was.

'Let's start at the beginning,' he said, patting my hand. 'Who are you talking about?'

'His name is Bryce and he plays guitar,' I said. 'I met him at a girlfriend's apartment a few weeks ago.'

'How well do you know him?' he asked, but I knew what he was really asking.

'I've been with him three times, but nothing's happened yet. But I know it's going to and I just hate sitting here pretending it's not. I can't do that anymore. I didn't want to tell you because I didn't want to hurt you. I wanted to be sure.'

'You've met this chap three times and you're *sure*?' he said skeptically.

'I knew about you the minute I met you,' I replied.

At that moment, Jason came into the room with a handful of papers for Cary to sign.

'Later!' Cary snapped harshly at him. It was so rare I ever saw Cary take command of Jason that way, I secretly cherished the moment in the midst of all this agony. Jason slipped away so quickly it was as if a vacuum cleaner had sucked him out of the room.

'What am I ever going to do?' Cary said, suddenly sounding more lost and forlorn than I'd ever heard him.

'I'm too old to begin another relationship. It's all I can do some days just to get out of bed. . . .'

I started sobbing again. 'I'm sorry. I'm so sorry. But I can't lie to you and I can't lie to myself anymore. I know how I feel.'

'I appreciate your honesty,' Cary said. 'I really do. I don't want you to lie to me. But I think you may be doing you and me a dis-service.'

'What do you mean?'

'We've been together almost four years now and you've met this chap a grand total of three times. How do you know you love him? It doesn't make sense.'

'It may not make sense to you,' I said, trying not to sound harsh, 'but I know what I feel. And so does he.'

'Well,' he continued, 'if you're so sure about your feelings for this man, then I have a proposal for you. We're scheduled to go to London in a few weeks. Promise me you won't see him and you'll go with me to London.'

'What would that prove?' I said.

'Whether you feel what you think you feel, for one thing. If after this trip we get back and you still want to see him, I won't stand in your way and I'll wish you well.'

'I don't understand, Cary,' I said. 'We've been to London before. What would be different about this trip?'

'I'm not talking about London, dear,' he said, gently. 'I'm talking about getting some distance between you two. And some time. If your feelings are as deep as you say they are, then this time and distance shouldn't matter. I'm just asking you to be sure — for your sake as well as mine. There's too much at stake to be premature.'

I talked it over with Dee. She also thought London was worth a try. If I still felt the same way about Bryce when I got back, then I'd be free to go forward without feeling any guilt. At least I would know I'd given Cary the benefit of the doubt.

It may have made sense to Dee and me, but Bryce initially was confused and a bit angry. But he said he'd wait for me, regardless of how cockeyed he thought the whole idea was.

'I have to do this,' I told him, 'or I run the risk of feeling guilty — and I don't want that.'

'Then go, with my love,' Bryce said. 'I'll be here waiting for you when you get back.'

He was an extraordinary man.

The trip to London was pretty extraordinary too.

I had assumed we'd be going on the Fabergé jet we usually took, but on the drive to the airport Cary told me we'd be 'hitching a ride' with Kirk Kerkorian on his private plane, an L-1011.

I entered the aircraft and found Priscilla Presley sitting very prettily in a chair. Kirk greeted me and introduced me to Priscilla.

The plane itself was like a very elegant motel with two bedrooms, a kitchen, a living room and a dining area.

As the plane took off for London and an eight-course meal was served, Priscilla and I began to talk. This was her first trip to London. When she learned I'd been brought up in England, she just had to know where the best shops and so on were. She had a particular passion for shoes, she confided.

Cary and Kirk soon got bored with our end of the conversation and promptly went to bed. Priscilla and I couldn't get to sleep so we stayed up most of the night, drinking Château Lafite and comparing stories on, as she put, 'what it's like to live with a legend.'

She was very curious about my relationship with Cary and I filled her in on some of the highlights. Then she wanted to know what I considered the most difficult thing about loving Cary.

'There are two Carys,' I said cautiously, fearful that anything I said about him might get back to Kirk. 'One is a wonderful man who's changed my life forever. The other is ... less wonderful.'

Priscilla knew what I meant. She talked at length about the dual nature of the man who'd changed her life.

'So what was the most difficult thing about loving Elvis?' I finally asked.

'We were never alone,' she said. 'We rarely had any time to ourselves. And of course the drugs. I miss him and I still love him, but I can't be with him.'

I knew what she meant.

I hated to say good-bye to Priscilla. There was a core of steel beneath that soft exterior. I wanted to see her again, but our paths never crossed.

When we got to London, Cary was so attentive and so much fun it reminded me of our first trip to London together, when he gave me a royal tour. I was so captivated I managed to put our horrible experience the year after that out of my mind, as well as the fact that Barbara Harris worked right in the Royal Lancaster, where we were staying.

What I couldn't get out of my head was Bryce. I wanted to call him, but I didn't. There was no way I'd break my word to Cary.

Pleasant as our stay in London was, it was destined to come to an end much sooner than either of us had planned. The beginning of the end occurred in a pub in central London. It was nothing special, just a place to grab a quick bite to eat. We'd spent most of the day shopping and Cary suggested finding a place on the way back to the Royal Lancaster. The driver recommended the place and Cary liked it the minute we walked in because there were booths near the back where he could sit and watch the action without having anyone scrutinize him.

As we were being escorted to the booth, I could see a waitress watching Cary with a special gleam in her eye. *Must love his movies*, I thought to myself as we took our seats. She came over and asked us if we'd like anything to drink.

'Vodka and tonic for me,' Cary said, 'and the house white wine for the lady.'

'Thank you,' the waitress said.

She was plump with a rosy red face. When she returned a couple of minutes later with our drinks, she couldn't help but stare at Cary again.

'Excuse me, sir,' she said as she started to walk away,

then stopped in her tracks. 'Aren't you Mr. Leach?'

'Well, if you mean Archie Leach,' Cary said genially, 'that was my name a long time ago. Most people call me Cary Grant these days. Actually, it's been many, many days.'

'Oh, yes,' she said, 'I've seen your movies. I hope you don't mind my asking, but how is your brother's family?'

I didn't know what to make of what she'd said. Cary's brother had died in infancy. Cary sat there, not saying a word.

'You must mean Mr. Grant's *cousin*, Eric,' I said after a few moments. 'As a matter of fact, we're going to see him and his wife in Bristol next week. How long have you known them?'

Cary still said nothing.

'I'm sorry,' the waitress said, 'I don't mean Mr. Grant's cousin. I mean his *brother*, Eric. He passed away not long ago and I just wondered how his family was making out.'

I looked at Cary for some kind of explanation, but he offered none. The waitress tried to fill the awkward silence coming from Cary's direction.

'My husband knew Eric,' she said, 'They both worked at the electric meter company.'

I turned to Cary again, demanding with my eyes that he say something to the woman.

At last he smiled a wide grin and turned to her.

'Actually, we hadn't seen each other in years, but I heard from his son not too long ago and he sounded fine.'

What on earth was going on? I put down my wine very carefully as the waitress left. She asked Cary to give Eric's son her regards.

'Would you like to tell me what's going on, Cary?' I said angrily. 'I'd like to know, considering how you've told me all these years that your brother was dead and that your only living relative was your cousin, Eric. Who in the hell is this *brother* Eric?'

'Don't get your knickers all twisted in a knot,' he said, trying to make light of the whole thing. 'The waitress was talking about my half-brother, Eric. He was born a year after I left Bristol. Once my mother was at Fishponds, my father fell in love with another woman and had a son by her.'

'That's interesting,' I said, trying to contain myself. 'So why have you lied to me all these years?'

'It didn't matter to me and so none of this should matter to you.'

'It matters to me a great deal when you lie to me,' I said. 'I'd like to know what else you haven't told me about your family.'

There was much more. His late half-brother had three children now living in Bristol — two girls and a boy. And his cousin Eric was hardly his only cousin. There were many cousins on both his father's side of the family and his mother's, also living in Bristol.

'But Eric's the one I like,' he said simply.

'You like him so much,' I scoffed, 'you complain behind his back about how lazy he is.'

'You don't know what you're talking about,' he said with a sneer.

'I know the difference between truth and untruth.'

This man who'd wept because he'd had only one child during his lifetime actually had nieces and a nephew to whom he could also have given his love. There was no way they could have been a substitute for his own children, but they would have allowed him to express more fully and more frequently his deep love for children.

Cary was not remotely contrite or ashamed about his deception. In fact, he seemed rather proud of it. It made me sick to my stomach. If he had lied about this, what else had he lied about? I shuddered to think about it.

'Take me home,' I said finally.

'I'll get the driver,' he said, starting to rise.

'No, you don't understand, Cary. I want to go back to Los Angeles.'

'You can't!' he almost yelled. 'All the plans have been made. And I can't leave England without saying hello to Maggie and Eric.'

'What about your other cousins, not to mention your nieces and your nephew?' I said, more in sadness than anger.

'Why are you going on so, Maureen?' he said, impatient and hostile. 'Why do you care about them? All my relatives are crazy, anyway. So what's the point?'

'Cary, if you don't understand, then I certainly can't tell you.'

We drove back to the Royal Lancaster in silence. If I had any doubts remaining whether I should leave Cary, they were gone now. He had become as much an expert in the art of concealment as he had in the art of acting.

I simply saw no point in continuing this trip. But Cary knew my weak spot — my parents. We'd planned to take them down to Bristol to meet Maggie and Eric.

'How can you disappoint them this way?' Cary said. We were in our suite and I was packing. 'Forget about yourself and think about how much they've been looking forward to this. Now you're just going to snatch that away from them?'

One part of me said my parents would understand. They'd understood everything else I had done. Another part of me said Cary was right — they deserved a good time.

'Okay, we'll go to Bristol,' I said after thinking it over. 'But not in a few days. I'll call Mummy and Daddy and see if they can move it up. Let's leave tomorrow for Bristol if they can manage it. I'm sorry, Cary, but that's the only way I'll stay.'

'Fine,' he said. He'd wrap up whatever business he had the following morning and we'd drive down to Bristol in the afternoon if Mummy and Daddy were free. Fortunately they were.

For the life of me I couldn't figure out why Cary was so determined to go on to Bristol. After what had happened in the pub, one would think that would have been the last place he'd want to go. Or could it be as simple as the fact he wanted to hold onto me as long as he could? I didn't know what to think anymore.

Cary and I did our best on the way to Bristol to pretend everything was, to use one his favourite words, 'copacetic.' Daddy bought the act for a while, but Mummy knew something was wrong. I'd explain it to her once we checked into the Grand Spa Hotel, the same place where Cary and I had stayed three years before. The place where he'd told me about his mother treating him so cruelly in the penny bazaar. Or had he made that up, too? How could I ever be sure of what he told me?

I phoned Mummy later that night and asked her to come down to my room. I told her everything ... from Bryce all the way to the discovery about Cary's group of relatives living now in Bristol.

'We should pick up the phone and invite them over,' I said half seriously. 'I'd like to see what he says about that.'

'Oh dear, I'm so sorry,' Mummy said, 'He's such a lovely man, it's hard to believe the way he acts sometimes.'

That was it in a nutshell.

We had two days scheduled for our stay in Bristol with Mummy and Daddy. And I must say Cary did his best to show them a marvelous time. First he introduced them to Maggie and Eric. Then the six of us went down to a local pub for Cary's beloved pint of wallop. I have some pictures taken during that visit and we look like a jolly group.

Our jolliness was abbreviated when Cary called the hotel in the afternoon for messages. Once again it was his lawyer and once again Jennifer was unexpectedly free. Did he want to fly back? Cary called me over to the booth from which he'd phoned. He was leaving it up to me. We could stay for the rest of the trip or go back now.

'We're not really fooling Mummy or Daddy,' I said. 'Why prolong this? Let's go back as soon as possible.'

Cary got on the phone to make the arrangements. Mummy and Daddy were naturally disappointed, but they were even more worried. It had been raining almost all day and a big storm was on its way in. It might not be safe to drive all the way back to London.

'We're not driving,' Cary informed them as we started to leave the pub. 'We're flying back.'

'From *here*?' Daddy and Eric said in unison.

'Why, you can't!' Mummy broke in. 'I heard a man in the pub say that the Bristol airport is already closed.'

'We've worked our way around that,' Cary explained.'

Peter Cadbury, the candy tycoon, had offered to send his small private plane with its pilot to Bristol. If Cary could convince the authorities to let it take off, then Cadbury's plane could take us to Shannon, where Kirk Kerkorian was waiting with the L-1011 to fly us back to Los Angeles.

'It's insane,' Daddy announced. 'I will not let my daughter go up in a plane in a raging storm.'

'Daddy,' I protested. 'I want to get back as badly as Cary. We'll be all right. I know we will. When it stops raining, the driver can take you back to London today or tomorrow. But we must leave *now*.'

Cary had to get back to see Jennifer. Someone important was also waiting for me.

We dropped Maggie and Eric off at their home and then returned to the Grand Spa. We packed as quickly as possible. When we all met at the front of the hotel, it was raining even harder than before. Daddy was paralyzed with fear, but I kissed him and tried to reassure him.

'We *will* make it,' I said.

'I know,' he said, not really convinced.

We rushed to the Bristol airport, where Cary had somehow managed to get us cleared for takeoff. But we had to leave immediately or wait for another break in the weather.

'This is suicide,' Daddy said, not letting go of my hand as we raced to the plane. Mummy tried to appear less frightened but she wasn't very successful.

'Call us when you get to Shannon if you can,' she said.

'Don't worry,' Cary said as he bade my parents goodbye. 'I'll make sure nothing happens to her.'

We got inside the tiny plane and buckled up. Before it took off, we opened a magnum of champagne. We weren't celebrating anything. We needed the courage in a bottle that it provided.

'Here goes nothing,' Cary said as the plane flew into the storm. He actually sounded almost cheerful.

Then I managed a little smile of my own.

After all, this was the last storm I'd ever have to brave with Cary.

29

TO CATCH A THIEF

WE slept most of the way to Los Angeles, but once we got back to the house we had to face each other.

'I hoped you were going to be the one to finish out this life with me,' he said as I was packing some of my things. 'But apparently you're not the one.'

'You will find the right person,' I said as gently as possible. 'Someone who wants to live here on *your* terms, Cary. You'll find her, I know.'

'I told you I'm too old and too tired to start all that up again,' he sighed.

'As you always say, "fat chance." And when you do find the right woman, you will be much happier. What about Barbara? She seems pleasant enough....'

'What would be the point?' he said, sitting on the bed and picking at an imaginary piece of lint. 'All the women leave me. I told you that too.'

'I know,' I said, closing a closet door. What he couldn't tell me, or anyone else for that matter, was why. But I could. There was no point in getting into all that now, however. We were long past the point where it would matter.

'Would you do me a favor?' I said, changing the subject.

'Of course.'

'I promised Jennifer the last time you and I split up that I'd never leave her hanging without a word of explanation. When it's okay with you, I would like to talk to her.'

'I understand,' he sighed, 'but you're going to hurt her terribly, you know.'

'I know,' I said. 'I love her and it hurts me to tell her,

but I must.' Now I was sitting on the bed with him.

'Well,' he offered, 'I suppose you feel the sooner the better?'

'Yes, I think so. But if you'd prefer I wait, I can.'

'No,' Cary said. 'I'll let you handle it as you want. I know you'll do the right thing.'

'Thank you,' I said, trying to sound calm. 'If you don't mind, I think I'd like to take her down the hill, maybe to the Magic Pan. It's very quiet there. I'd prefer not to do it here.'

'I hate endings,' he said, the words rushing out of him suddenly. 'I've always hated them. You know that. Doesn't matter if they're happy or sad, I just hate them.'

'You'll see me again,' I volunteered, trying to sound positive. 'I will need to come up here to get the rest of my things. And why do you have to think of us as ending? Think of us as changing. We won't be as close as we were, but we will go on loving each other.'

'But you know what I mean ...' he said, distracted.

'I do, but —'

'You don't hate me?' he asked.

I took his hand. It sat lifeless in mine.

'I don't like the word "good-bye" either,' he said as he got up, his eyes starting to fill with tears.

I had to look away or I would never find the courage to go out the door.

'Then we won't say it.'

And then I left with Jennifer.

It was early evening in the restaurant, before the dinner crowd. If nothing else, we would have privacy. But how do you tell an eleven-year-old girl that you love her but you can't live with her father, whom you also love?

We'd been able to communicate with so few words so often or even without them entirely. This time I couldn't count on that. It was far too complicated. But I still had to try to make her understand.

I told her I was starting a new life and that she would always have a place in that new life as well as in my heart, but her daddy and I would no longer be together. We would still love each other, but not in the way we had before.

That's what it came down to. I looked to see if she understood any of it. Those big brown eyes of hers so wise beyond their years did most of her talking. And I could see most of the message had gotten through.

'I love you, Maureen,' she told me. 'You're my friend.'

'I hope I will be your friend for a long, long time,' I said when I could find the words.

Leaving Cary was inevitable. But I felt I'd left a part of me with Jennifer that afternoon.

I went home and slept for over twelve hours.

Two days later I went up to Beverly Grove to get the last of my things. I had tried repeatedly to arrange it so Cary and I would miss each other. What more could we say to each other?

But when it became clear that Cary was going to be there no matter how long I waited, I came up late one morning after I'd checked with him.

Since the last time we'd spoken in his bedroom had been peaceful if not painless, I hardly expected a scene of any kind. These great expectations were shot down almost immediately after I walked in the door.

I was in the bathroom going through the medicine chest, looking for a prescription I'd forgotten, when Cary cornered me.

'You're a thief,' he said, standing before me. 'A common thief.'

'What's this?' I said.

'You've been taking toilet tissue and light bulbs from this house from the moment you moved in.' I could tell by the expression on his face he was perfectly serious.

I was determined not to get into an argument with him. This was painful enough for both of us.

'Cary,' I said, 'you must be mistaken. I haven't taken anything of yours.'

'Oh yes, you have,' he insisted. 'I keep an inventory here and you've been taking toilet tissue and light bulbs for years, haven't you?'

'No, Cary. *Please* don't do this.'

'The figures don't lie, Maureen,' he said, starting to sound oddly excited. 'They just don't lie.'

'I'm glad you mentioned numbers, Cary,' I replied. 'Because if you added up all the times I've put in an extra few dollars when Willie was out shopping for groceries, you'd be the one who owes *me*.'

'I don't believe you,' he sniped back. 'Besides, you're not the type to do anybody any favors. And I certainly don't need your charity.'

'Ask Willie,' I said, starting to go through some drawers. 'Besides, have you ever added up all the times I picked up dinner for you on the way home from work? You paid me sometimes, but not all the time by a long shot.'

I hated this. We had gone from arguing over toilet tissue to dollars and cents. It may have given Cary some thrill, but it was making me ill. If he couldn't stop this, I had to. I wanted to leave right then and there but that would mean coming back again later and facing the possibility of another irrational attack like this.

'Okay,' Cary said, now really warmed up. 'Forget the toilet tissue and the light bulbs. I'll call us even. What about my sheets?'

'What about them?' I said, mystified. 'They're white and they're very clean. Is there something else?'

'You know perfectly well what I mean. They have my monogram on them and you've been selling them all over town.'

'Do you really believe that?'

'Of course I do!' he huffed.

'So you lived with a thief all these years? Do you really believe that, Cary?'

'I told you I do!' he repeated, now next to shouting.

'Then I don't know who the hell I lived with all those years either.'

I couldn't take any more of this. I had to leave *now*. Whatever I left behind could be replaced. My self-respect couldn't.

'*Good-bye*!' I said, not bothering to turn around to see Cary as I ran to the door.

'I think you should know you're out of my will!!' Cary yelled as I reached the door. 'Do you understand?'

I turned around and walked slowly back to where he was standing.

'No, Cary,' I said. '*You* don't understand. I'm out of your life.'

A week later Cary called.

The last thing he wanted, he said, was bitterness between us. All he wished for was my happiness.

'I wish the same for you, Cary,' I said simply. 'We'll pretend it never happened. It was two different people.'

'Thank you,' he said warmly. 'You are a dear girl.'

'I'm going to be thirty-one in two months,' I told him. 'Make that a dear *woman*.'

'Agreed,' he laughed. 'Will you let me buy you a birthday drink?'

'Sure,' I said. 'Call me when it gets closer and we'll set something up. Give my love to Jennifer.'

Bryce and I started living together within a matter of months. I gave it much thought, especially since I'd just won my freedom from Cary. But the closer I became to Bryce, the freer I felt.

And Bryce was so free in expressing his affection with me. He was constantly touching and holding me. In some ways I'd come to feel emotionally starved. Perhaps it was my insecurity, but I needed such affection and re-assurance now. Cary probably was more physically demonstrative with me than he'd been with most of the women in his life, but it wasn't enough. I wanted back what I was giving out. Cary simply could not have given any more if he tried — and I know he really did try, but it still wasn't enough.

It was also liberating to be in a relationship where my every action wasn't being questioned or placed under suspicion. Bryce loved and trusted me completely. He was not perfect, but neither was he moody or withdrawn as

Cary could be so often. Bryce was consistent and it was amazing how consistently happy I was.

As my birthday approached, I began dreading that promised birthday drink with Cary. I was afraid seeing him would jinx this new-found harmony in my life. Maybe he wouldn't even call. Then on September 22, five days before my birthday, Hank Grant ran an item in his *Hollywood Reporter* column about my 'playing tennis regularly' with Warren Beatty. 'Warren insists it's not a romance,' it concluded, 'but it's still a net gain.'

The item bothered me because there was no romance except with Bryce.

That night Cary called me. The item hadn't escaped the clipper's eyes.

'If you're playing with Warren,' he laughed, 'I hope you're beating him.'

I told him how ridiculous the item was.

'Maybe you should give Hank a call,' he suggested.

'Maybe I will,' I said. (I did later, but for now I'd had my fill of the press, at least where my personal relationships were concerned. I decided to let it go, especially since Bryce thought it was hilarious. But after the tabloids later picked up the item and reported the story, I asked Hank to set the record straight.)

'Am I going to see you on your birthday?' Cary asked as we wound up our call.

'If you still feel like it,' I said, hesitating for a moment. 'Are you going to be in town?'

'Absolutely!' he declared. 'Would you like to come up for a drink and have lunch? You tell me....'

'Some friends are taking me out to lunch, so if you don't mind, why don't we make it a drink? Let's say five or six....'

'Six is best for me,' he said.

'Six it is,' I agreed.

I hoped for the best.

Cary couldn't have been sweeter when I went up to Beverly Grove that day.

We had a drink and then started playing Spite and Malice. He really was addicted to the game. He was so pleasant I decided to let him win.

My apprehension about the meeting was now a thing of the past. He was wearing gray slacks with a turtleneck sweater, looking elegant and handsome as always. Nothing could diminish that.

'I know you said not to have Willie make a cake or anything,' he said as we had another drink. 'But I did find this in a shop and thought you'd like it.'

It was marzipan shaped like a candle.

'You've gotten me so much marzipan, I thought it was time to return the favor. Would you like a piece?' he said as he sliced off a sliver.

'Sure,' I said, touched and pleased.

Then he sliced off a piece for himself. As he popped it into his mouth, he leaned back in his chair.

'You look happy, Maureen. Are you happy?'

'Yes,' I said.

'How are you?' I asked.

'I'm fine,' he said, sounding almost as if he meant it. 'But this place just isn't as much fun as when you were here.'

'Thank you,' I said softly. 'Well, I like to think I brought you two things, Cary — lust and laughter. I hope I don't sound too egotistical.'

'Why? It's the truth, isn't it?' he said, laughing.

'I thank you for that too,' I said.

'We didn't do too bad then, did we?' he said, pleased at the thought.

Then we stopped talking about the past and talked about the future. For Cary that was Jennifer. For me it was Bryce. Cary wanted to know all about him, especially his ambitions.

'He sounds like a good person,' Cary said after I'd talked about Bryce for a while.

'He is,' I said.

'Then I wish you well. And I hope you'll accept my birthday present.'

He handed me an envelope. I opened it and there was a check for five hundred dollars.

'Use it to build your future,' he said sincerely. 'It will make me happy.'

I hugged him. It was a lovely, gracious gesture. Soon it was time to go.

I started to get up, when he surprised me again.

'I have something else for you,' he said as he reached into his pocket.

'Oh, Cary,' I said, embarrassed, 'I didn't expect anything. You've been too kind already. Let's —'

'I want you to have this,' he said as he opened a tiny box, revealing an antique ring. It was gold with clusters of diamonds.

'I was going to give you this some time ago,' he said as he slipped it onto my finger. 'But I never got the chance.'

'Cary, this is so sweet,' I protested, 'but I can't. Not now. I'm sure you understand.'

'You would make me happy especially now if you accepted it,' he insisted. 'It was my mother's.'

His eyes locked into mine. I said nothing for more than a few moments.

'Please keep it,' he said finally.

'I think Jennifer should have this, don't you?' I said when I could find the words.

'It's *yours*,' he insisted again.

'Thank you,' I said.

Several minutes later we said good-bye at the door.

'Happy dreams,' I murmured. He'd wished it for me so many times.

Cary smiled. It was a generous smile, one I'd seen so many times before at that door as I walked into the house. But now I was walking away for good.

'Take care,' he said. 'God bless, and all the other kind noises.'

He kissed me on the cheek, squeezed my hand and then let me go.

30

NONE BUT THE LONELY HEART

IN early December, Cary called me on the pretext of trying to find something in the kitchen since it was Willie's day off. The place was *still* being remodeled and he didn't know where anything was.

'Cary,' I chided him gently, 'you don't need an excuse to call me. We're friends.'

From that moment we embarked on a very different relationship. The passion had gone out of it, but not the love. Cary was constantly calling to share new things and discoveries. He had discovered Phil Donahue's show, and if the day's topic was something Cary thought was important, he'd call me at the beginning of the broadcast.

'Turn on your set to *Donahue*!' he'd say breathlessly before saying hello.

Of course, I always knew who it was. Who could forget that voice?

Cary was also immensely pleased about video recorders, which had become widely available. He was thrilled with the prospect that now he could tape his movies from television broadcasts for Jennifer, instead of having to drag the projector out every time he wanted to show her one of his films. Later, when his movies started coming out on videocassettes, he was even more delighted. He'd always harbored a fear that he would be forgotten by America's younger generations. Just as important to him was the fact that his films were now available uncut, rather than chopped up as they frequently were for commercial television.

Cary also took a deep interest in my career. He still suggested people I should photograph and sent me clippings about new publications I should contact to see if they'd be interested in my work. He was also diligent about remembering not only my birthday as the years went by, but also those of Dee Joseph and Bobby Birkenfeld. Bobby had been involved in a serious car accident since his operation. Again, he was profoundly moved by Cary's attention and care. Cary kept in touch with Bobby regularly, continuing to encourage him to look to the future instead of the past, which had been blemished with misfortune.

When I asked Cary what was new in his life, he talked about Jennifer, of course. But after about six months he began mentioning Barbara regularly. In 1978 she came to California to live with him. She worked for a local publicity firm for a while but then devoted herself exclusively to him. I was truly happy for him, as I knew Cary was for Bryce and me.

At first Bryce was a little intimidated when Cary would call. That was understandable, but eventually his uneasiness faded. Our relationship was strong and solid. My friendship with Cary was completely separate. I think once Bryce realized Cary's interest in me really had evolved into a paternal rather than a residually romantic one, he relaxed completely. And that was fortunate because Cary was always going to be a part of my life on some level.

Sometimes Cary and I would talk once or twice a week. Other times it would be just once a month. It was erratic but we always seemed to pick up where we left off. Very occasionally I got to speak with Jennifer, but after Barbara entered Cary's life, the last thing I wanted to do was place Jennifer in another tug-of-war. I missed her, but just as Cary had to let me go to follow a new life, I had to let her follow hers. But she remained close by, in my thoughts.

In early 1981 Cary asked me what I thought about his getting married again. So I asked him the question he'd always asked me: 'Are you happy?'

'Yes,' he said. 'Very. She makes my life complete.'

Jennifer approved, he said. She was now fifteen years old and enrolled in a boarding school in Monterey.

'She's grown into such a lovely young lady,' Cary said proudly. 'And she has a mind of her own, I'll tell you.'

'Just like her father and mother,' I teased.

'That's right!' He laughed.

I was most encouraged by the fact that Cary was now speaking kindly of Dyan. There was no doubt in his mind how much Dyan loved Jennifer and wanted, as he did, only to see her fulfilled and happy in the life she chose.

'Then this marriage couldn't come at a better time for you,' I said. 'I wish you both well.'

And I meant it. This man who had known so little happiness in his personal life deserved all the happiness he could find in the time left to him.

But I couldn't help feeling a pang. As Cary was preparing to bind himself even closer to Barbara, Bryce and I were untying the bonds of our relationship. It had become too intense and I needed my freedom. This time I would not rush into another relationship as I was finishing the other. I was thirty-four years old and needed time to myself. There would be plenty of time for other relationships. And they did come when I was ready.

As for Cary, he had finally found the woman who would share the rest of his life with him.

Cary married Barbara on April 15, 1981. The ceremony took place in the living room of Cary's home. He said he'd finally finished remodelling Beverly Grove. That was another good sign, I said to myself.

Since I didn't really know Barbara, I now usually left it up to Cary to call me. It would be much less awkward that way. Now I knew how Bryce must have felt when Cary called.

In May 1981, Cary gave an interview to the London

Times in which he said that 'nobody is ever truthful about his own life.' Then, as if to underline that point, a friend in England sent me a couple of clippings from the *Bristol Evening Post*. The headline read: 'Film Star Cary's Family Surprise!'

The articles read that 'past reports about Mr. Eric Leach being the only living relative of Cary Grant in the Bristol area' were completely untrue. There were cousins, 'too numerous to mention,' on both his father's and his mother's sides of the family. Ernest Kingdon, then seventy-one, told the paper he felt as if he were coming back from the grave. Other cousins stated they'd never bothered to contradict what Cary had told the press because they figured if that's the way he wanted it, then that's the way they'd leave it. Until now.

I didn't discuss these revelations about his family with Cary because there was no point. We'd already had that discussion in London in 1977. But I did ask him in the fall of 1981 about reports circulating around Hollywood that he was seriously considering returning to acting in the film version of the best-selling book *Gorky Park*.

'Rubbish!' he proclaimed. 'I'll tell you how that started. We were out at the racetrack and Howard Koch gave me a copy of the book. Because his son had bought the rights to do the movie, people leaped to the conclusion I was making a comeback. Never!'

If Cary was still turning down film offers, he was finally beginning to accept more tributes in his honor. He still hated to dress up, but he seemed to enjoy the attention.

'It makes people feel good to do this,' he told me, 'and that makes me feel good.'

In December 1981 he agreed to accept one of the Kennedy Center awards for achievement in the performing arts. It was the first major award he'd accepted since the special Oscar he'd taken home in 1970. Then, in May 1982, the New York City Friars Club held a Man of the Year dinner for him at the Waldorf-Astoria. Everyone from Peggy Lee to Frank Sinatra was there to see this friend accept a gold watch, a trophy and a lifetime membership. The Friars, who traditionally roast the celebrities they honor with raunchy, ego-deflating 'tributes,' said they couldn't find anyone who had a bad word to say about Cary Grant.

But 1982 brought Cary as much sorrow as it did joy. In August, Ingrid Bergman succumbed to cancer, and in September, Princess Grace died as a result of a car accident. Her daughter Stephanie was also in the vehicle but suffered minor injuries.

Princess Grace's death made Cary particularly anxious as far as Jennifer was concerned because he'd just bought her a car for her sixteenth birthday in February.

'I've forbidden her to drive it,' Cary told me one day shortly after Princess Grace's death. 'It's just not safe out there. And she's so inexperienced — she just started to drive, you know.'

I also knew Cary was equally concerned Jennifer would face other dangers — especially drugs.

'Dyan and I have had to take her out of several schools because they couldn't control the drug problem there. I know she has too much common sense and self-respect to abuse herself that way, but we just don't want her around that kind of environment. Believe it or not, the private schools are just as bad as the public ones!'

Cary's fears were allayed two years later, when Jennifer started attending Stanford University. That year, 1984, also was the year Cary turned eighty. He called shortly before this milestone. He insisted he wasn't going to go out of his way to celebrate it, much as he'd tried to ignore his seventieth when I was with him.

'I think you should be proud,' I lightly admonished him. 'I know I would be. Especially if I looked as good as you do!'

He laughed amiably.

'That certainly makes me feel like celebrating,' he acknowledged. 'I did get good genes that way, didn't I?'

'No question about that,' I added.

Then I started talking about the gift he'd given me so many years before.

'What do you mean?' he said, a bit confused.

'You opened a whole new life to me, Cary,' I said. 'And I don't mean just my career and the fact I wouldn't be a photographer today if it weren't for you. I mean the way you tried to teach me about the world and about people. I know I fought you sometimes, but I'm so grateful for it all now. And I know I never really properly thanked you. I just felt I should do that now.'

I couldn't see him, but I could tell he was crying.

So was I.

That had been his gift to me and now my gratitude was my gift to him. With such a special birthday fast approaching, it seemed like the right moment — especially since it had been over six years since we broke up.

'But there's one thing I didn't give you,' he said a few moments later.

'What's that?' I asked.

'The interview,' he replied. 'I never did give you that interview, remember?'

'I know,' I said. 'I got something so much better.

About a week later I received a clipping from him. He underscored a line from Robert Browning:

'That what began best can't end worst.'

In October 1984, Cary suffered a mild stroke.

After experiencing dizzy spells and headaches, he'd checked into Cedars-Sinai Hospital in West Hollywood, where doctors put him through extensive tests and gave him their verdict. They warned him to slow down. But he wouldn't hear of it.

Two years before, he'd begun touring the country with a ninety-minute one-man show called *A Conversation with Cary Grant*. Film clips from his favorite movies were shown and then he'd answer questions from the audience. He rarely appeared in larger cities because he didn't want the show to become a big thing. It was his little way of bringing pleasure to himself and to the people who loved his movies.

But after this stroke I begged him to cut back on his schedule of personal appearances. He wouldn't hear of it.

'I need to keep active,' he said. 'And it's fun. It really is. It keeps me on my toes. I'm not going to sit at home like an old man, especially with such a young woman in my house.'

But I think Cary knew his years were limited, especially after Charlie Rich died in April 1986. That same month Cary renewed his wedding vows to Barbara.

I heard from Cary in June. He sounded tired and it worried me. His customary curiosity and enthusiasm were muted. He was reflective, almost sad.

'Are you happy?' he asked me.

I told him I was. There had been a couple of relationships after Bryce. Now I was between relationships again. But my happiness did not depend on one specific man or relationship. It now came from within, from me.

'You know what?' he said, brightening suddenly. 'I was looking around the house for something last night and you know what I found? That little red double-decker bus you got me in London. Do you remember it?'

'Of course,' I said, but I couldn't believe he'd hung onto it after all these years.

'Seeing it brought back some happy memories,' he offered. 'We had fun in London that time, didn't we? We had lots of fun. You brought a lot of laughter into my life, Maureen.'

'Thank you,' I said.

'And a lot of love,' he added.

'I'm afraid I also gave you my share of trouble.' I laughed. He'd touched me so, I didn't know what to say.

'Well, I made a definite contribution to you in that department myself,' he said, chuckling. 'But I'll tell you, dear. As I've always said, I'd be a nut to go through all that again, but I wouldn't have missed it for anything.'

I knew what he was saying and I knew how hard it had been for him to say it.

I accepted it with love because I knew he offered it with love, just as I had given him my gratitude when we talked shortly before his eightieth birthday.

It was the last thing I ever heard him say.

31

WALK, DON'T RUN

ON November 19, 1986, Cary died in Davenport, Iowa. It seemed somehow fitting for an ex-vaudevillian to be still 'out on the road' on the last day of his life.

He'd been scheduled that night to present his *Conversation with Cary Grant* at the Adler Theatre. But during an afternoon rehearsal, while he was double-checking everything from the position of his chair to the placement of microphones in the audience, Cary complained he wasn't feeling well.

He stayed in a dressing room for an hour. Then he and Barbara retired to the hotel where they were staying in Davenport. The man who accompanied Cary and Barbara back to the hotel said Cary refused medical treatment, but the aide grew so concerned he called his own doctor to treat Cary. When the doctor arrived, Cary again insisted everything was fine. He just needed to take a little rest and again refused to go to a hospital. He wouldn't budge for hours.

Finally Cary was taken to the hospital over his objections. He died there of a stroke over two hours later. It was 11:22 P.M. At three in the morning, Barbara accompanied his body back to California. Kirk Kerkorian had sent his jet for Cary's final journey back to Los Angeles.

It was late morning when I heard the news. I was staying up in San Francisco with my friends Roger and Jennifer Smith, at his parents'. It was a beautiful Sunday and I was in the bathroom brushing my teeth before going out for a walk with Jennifer.

There was a knock on the door.

'Who is it?' I said.

'It's Jennifer. Can I come in?'

'Sure,' I said, opening the door.

She came in and just looked at me. Then she took my hand.

'I'm sorry, Maureen, but I just heard on the radio. Cary died yesterday. It was a stroke.'

I burst into tears. Cary was not supposed to die. In a rare editorial about a star's death, *The New York Times* said what I felt at that moment. 'Sure, we all knew he was getting on,' the paper said. 'But die? *Never.*'

Jennifer closed the door and let me cry in her arms for a few minutes. Then I didn't know what to do. Part of me wanted to be alone and part of me couldn't be alone. Cary would have understood.

'I've got to use your phone,' I said.

I called Willie in Los Angeles. She had retired, but we had stayed in contact through the years.

When she picked up the phone, Willie was crying too. She'd obviously heard the news.

'I thought he was too mean to die,' I sobbed. 'At least that's what I always told him.'

'He lived a long life,' she said, trying to console me. 'And he did get to see Jennifer all grown.'

'That's true,' I said, trying to make myself feel better. 'He always talked about that.'

Then I started crying again.

'Maureen,' Willie scolded me in her loving way. 'You know he'd hate this. The thing he always said about you is that you brought love and laughter into his life when he really needed it.'

'Thank you,' I said.

I hung up, promising to see her when I got back to L.A. the next day. When Jennifer asked me what I wanted to do, I said I'd like to walk up the hill near the back of her parents' house and just sit at the top for a while. Staring at the azure sky, I felt a little better.

But I didn't feel really at peace with myself until the next day when I walked into my house. I was now living in Hancock Park, a neighborhood of beautifully landscaped gardens and neat, carefully tended homes. Just being back in this ordered environment made me feel calmer.

I began to unpack when I noticed my *Daily Word* booklet. Though it had been nine years since I'd left Cary, I still subscribed to it and greeted each day with its inspirational message, as Cary and I used to do together. The page was open to Saturday, November 29.

The key word for that day was 'peace.'

Now I could feel some too.

I couldn't bear to look at any of Cary's movies for a month or so. Then one day *Houseboat* came on TV and I thought I'd give it a try. Cary would always be around me on film. I had to face him this way sooner or later. A comedy like *Houseboat* would be the perfect way to get reacquainted.

About halfway through the movie I saw something that told me I'd made the right choice.

Paul Petersen portrays Cary's son, one of his three children who recently lost their mother. The boy is fishing off the houseboat when he catches a perch, but it dies almost instantly once it's out of the water.

'Why does everything have to die?' the boy says mournfully, still thinking of his mother.

Cary sees his son's pain and confusion.

'I prefer to think no one ever really leaves,' he tells the boy.

Paul doesn't understand, so Cary picks up a pitcher of water. The pitcher is his life force and the water is him, he explains.

'Try to lose that,' he says to Paul as he instructs him to pour the water into the river. The boy is still confused and looks up questioningly at his father.

'The only thing is,' Cary continues, 'it isn't lost. It's still part of the whole river. It's still in the universe. You haven't lost it.'

But the boy isn't convinced. He now takes the pitcher and pours some water right on the deck of the houseboat instead of into the river. Then he slowly realizes that the water will evaporate, become a cloud and return to the earth and the river someday.

'You can't lose anything,' he finally agrees with his father.

'Probably not even life itself,' Cary elaborates. 'It's just that everything is constantly changing. So perhaps when our life force, our souls leave our bodies, we go back to God's universe and the security of being part of all life again and all nature. So for all we know, that sort of life after death may be very beautiful.'

It was a beautiful thought, and a fairly radical one for a movie made in the late fifties. Knowing that the movie had been originally suggested by an idea of Betsy Drake's and also knowing how deeply Cary immersed himself in every aspect of his films, I knew the presence of such a thought in the movie could not be a coincidence.

As I watched the scene, I felt as if Cary were personally reassuring me he was now part of the beautiful process he outlined so eloquently and so convincingly in the movie.

Now I knew there was no way I could ever lose him.

When I used to go to the movies with my great-aunt in the fifties and sixties, souvenir programs were sold in the lobby for big-budget epics such as *Ben-Hur* and *Mutiny on the Bounty*. I especially loved the program my aunt got me from *Lawrence of Arabia* because a few of the photos inside, capturing the film's spectacular panoramas, were projected by a delicate covering of tissue. Every time I lifted one of those tissues, the scene from the movie filled my mind again with all its power and majesty. But as the years went by, it was like lifting a veil and seeing not what I saw the first time — nothing could repeat that experience — but something new. The tissue remained the same, protecting the past, but *I* had changed.

For many years I put a similar tissue or veil over my life with Cary. That way it would remain protected and unchanged. But when I agreed to do this book, I knew I'd have to lift the veil and I was afraid to disturb it. After I'd left Cary in 1977, it was easy to forget most of the turbulent times and remember only the many wonderful experiences. After all, I was no longer in the eye of the storm. Now I didn't want to change that peaceful patina that had settled over our time together. If I plunged myself back into our sometimes stormy life together, what would I see this time?

It has been painful and embarrassing because I saw how imperfect and naive I was. There is no manual on how to fall in love with a movie star like Cary Grant and, more important, how to maintain a relationship with someone like him. I was still a girl in many ways when I came running into Cary's life. But when I walked away four years later, I was my own woman. I had to learn, as they say, on the job. I gave Cary my love and he gave me as much love as he could give back. Ultimately it wasn't enough and I left.

Sometimes I'll meet someone who doesn't really know much about my years with Cary. And that person will say to me:

'Just to think of it, Maureen. If you had agreed to marry him, you never would have another financial worry in your life. You screwed up!'

I'm sure I did screw up, but not that way. I have always followed what my emotions told me to do, not my pocket-book. Maybe I could have been more forgiving or less volatile. But eventually I learned to forgive not only myself but Cary as well. I did the best I could at the time and so did he.

Cary's life began in the shadow of his brother's death and it was played out in the shadows. He would make love only in the shadows. And he became a legend in the shadows of theaters all over the world. Film critic David Thomson once said something about Cary's cache of movies that I think applies also to his personal life:

'There is a light side and a dark side to him,' Thomson wrote, 'but whichever is dominant, the other creeps into view.'

The dark and light did live side by side within Cary. He meant it every time he said 'Happy thoughts!' and 'Nice dreams!' to me and everyone else, even if his own thoughts and dreams often turned much darker. He was, as he once wrote about himself, 'a series of contradictions too evident to be coincidental.'

For me the most challenging contradiction was that he was both self-revealing and self-disguising. When he told me the traumatic memories he had of his mother, it was both a form of confession and a form of self-mutilation. And when he lied to me later about his family, it was another kind of mutilation — of the trust I had in him. At the time it was so painful I could not bear being around him anymore.

But as the years passed by and I got older, I realized the facts were not most important. It was what Cary *felt* that really mattered. He felt his mother deserted him, even though she had been involuntarily confined. He felt his wives had hated and abandoned him, though I suspect they all loved him but were forced to leave him in much the same way I was.

This much I do know is true: What happened to Archie Leach changed Cary Grant forever. That boy from Bristol went on to create a new name, a new identity and a new life for himself in America. But in the end he could not change what happened to him so many years before in England.

And if Cary invented everything from the way he talked to the number of his living relatives, I know now that he couldn't invent the way he felt about me.

Sometimes I'll be in the kitchen cooking with the TV on in the next room. And I will hear Cary's voice and forget that he's gone and it's just one of his movies playing on TV. I think he's still here and in the next room ... Jennifer's playing on the terrace ... and Willie's in the kitchen with me, helping to make the turkey sandwiches he loved so much.

I feel more needed and more desired that I ever have in my whole life. And then I realize I'm alone and he's not with me, but just a voice from the past on a box in the next room.

But I'm not sad, at least not for very long. I smile. I had something only a few women in the world had — a romance with Cary Grant. It was not as idyllic or as care-free as many of his movies, but it was real.

And it was unforgettable.